A

Z

A

Volume
Five

Journal of Korean Literature
& Culture

L

E

A

Korea Institute Harvard University

2012

AZALEA
Journal of Korean Literature & Culture

Number Five ⁓ 2012
Publisher: Korea Institute, Harvard University
Editor: David R. McCann
Editor-in-Chief: Young-Jun Lee
Editorial Board: Bruce Fulton, Hwang Jong-yŏn,
Kwon Youngmin, Heinz Insu Fenkl
Copy Editor: K.E. Duffin
Design: Wayne de Fremery, Ryu Byung-wook
Proofreader: Beyond Words Proofreading

AZALEA is published yearly by the Korea Institute, Harvard University,
with generous funding by the International Communication Foundation,
Seoul. Translations from the Korean original were supported by the
Korean Literature Translation Institute.

Subscriptions: $30 (one year); $55 (two years); $80 (three years).
Overseas subscriptions: $45 (one year, air mail only).

Inquiries to: *AZALEA*, Korea Institute, Harvard University, Center for
Government and International Studies, South Building Room S228, 1730
Cambridge Street, Cambridge, MA 02138
Phone: (617) 496-2141, Fax: (617) 496-1144, Email: korea@fas.harvard.edu
Submissions are welcome. Submitted manuscripts and books sent for
review become the property of *AZALEA*.

Printed on acid-free paper, in Seoul, Korea, by Haingraph Co., Ltd.

ISSN: 1939-6120
ISBN-13: 978-0-9795800-8-6
ISBN-10: 0-9795800-8-0

CONTENTS

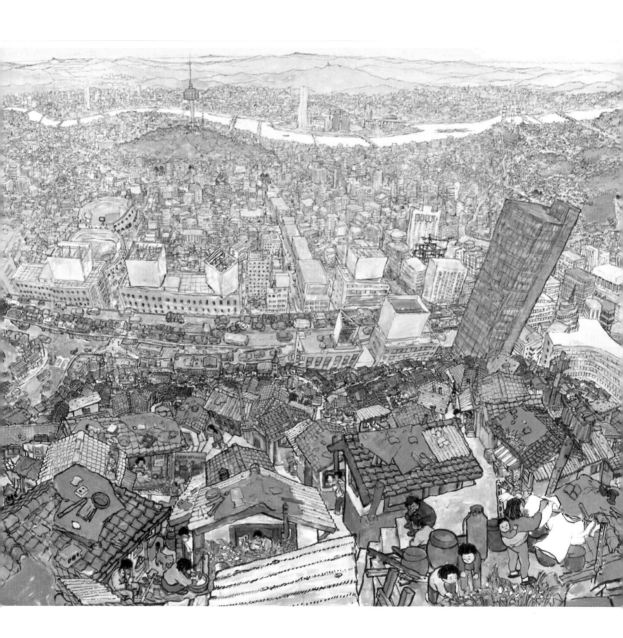

Editor's Note

As becomes more and more apparent, Korea and Korean cultural and literary practices have been open and engaged for centuries. Korea was part of the complicated, dangerous, and demanding world during the Koryŏ dynasty when Mongol conquest or the threat of it had unfurled from Korea to Vienna. (And as they say still in Vienna, *Wien bleibt Wien*; Vienna stays *Vienna*.) Peter Lee in this issue presents an extraordinarily full account of the cultural context of the Koryŏ songs that have come down to us, through a variety of travelways, to register their voices from a time when even in Korea there was not a cell phone to be found anywhere.

What was Korea, Japan, or life like in the twentieth century under Japanese colonial rule? John Frankl has been pursuing that and other questions in his studies and translations of the proto-modernist writer/artist/flâneur Yi Sang. There is something poignantly as well as literally expressive to be found in the scene when Yi Sang the essayist discounts all famous sites in the Japanese capital city as he stands taking a satisfying break at a public toilet. In an old story, a policeman whacks a fellow on the shoulder who was urinating against an alley wall, and points at the sign. "*See that? Sobyŏn kŭmji! Urination forbidden!*" The old fellow laughs and points, reading the sign in the opposite order: "*Chigŏm pyŏnso: Right now, a toilet.*" In the same earthy and direct manner, Yi Sang the writer, artist, and individual reversed the cultural readings of Korea's colonized state.

7

The present gathering also includes examples of contemporary Korean fiction and poetry, and the reincarnation of Kubo the Novelist from the widely known 1934 fictional work "A Day in the Life of Kubo the Novelist," but in a new form and magazine medium as Kubo the Film Critic, a witty out-take on Korea's current-day film culture.

To be able to tell the story, and sing or say the poem, are signs of a culture's freedom, even within the close confines of political or cultural norms imposed from outside. For all its didactic purposes, the example of "The Sky," the 1937 children's story by Hyŏn Tŏk, still gives us voices and events that in turn afford a palpable sense of the life of that time. Just as Peter Lee has done with the details of Koryŏ life and culture that frame the Koryŏ songs, this issue's other stories and poems likewise give the reader a lively sense of Korea's 20th and 21st century literature and culture.

The astonishingly vivid images in Choi Ho-Cheol's cartoons deserve their own eloquent praise. One might note the vivid detail, the extraordinary depth, the range and active participation in life by all the figures in the pictures, the sweep of the landscape, from house porch to landmark skyscraper, and suggest that the same range, the same array of vivid details, the same sense of an exuberantly vital cultural community are to be found in all the work of our current issue. We owe thanks to the managing editor for once again assembling such a repast, as well as to the writers, translators, artists, and other participants in this lively issue.

David R. McCann
January, 2012

A

Z

A

Volume
Five

L

E

A

Writer in Focus:

Kim Aeran

Flugdatenschreiber

by Kim Aeran

Translated by Jamie Chang

Somewhere on this sun-parched island, on patches of green, amidst pedestrian and time-honored labors, mysterious rumors and tedium, and sometimes a wind so cool it makes you want to shout out someone's name, people live who keep on producing children, year after year. Flugdatenschreiber is its name. It used to be part of the peninsula, but the sea level rose at the end of the last Ice Age and made it an island. At the time, there was nothing surrounding this island but ocean. Time was its sole gift from the universe.

Time passed. After tens of thousands of seasons and yet another, a group of people arrived on the island. The first thing they did was name it. They searched the map for the highest point and found a large peak above the clouds. Laden with their possessions, they climbed hills, crossed plains, and trekked up the mountain. The ocean around the island had turned crimson, rising and falling like amniotic fluid. At last, they made it to the top. They saw what unfolded before their eyes and were awestruck. The pits, gorges, and fields they had crossed were all parts of lines that formed a shape. It was an expansive drawing made of ancient hieroglyphs, beautiful simply because it had a pattern. They knew they could sound it out even though they would never decipher its meaning. The leader of the group looked down at the hieroglyphs with anxiety and wonder. His lips parted at last and sounded the word "Flugdatenschreiber." All quietly echoed, "Flugdatenschreiber." That's how this island got its name. It's been thousands of years. Toothless old men still talk about the ancestors. There are varying opinions on how the hieroglyphs got there and who wrote them, but the island formed a single village. The hieroglyphs have long since disappeared.

Mainland folk rarely visit Flugdatenschreiber. The island is not a resort, and is one of the islands farthest from the peninsula. Its population is neither large nor small. Their routine resembles the common notion of 'everyday life.' In the spring, the men sail out to sea to catch glassfish, and shine as they draw up nets full of light. The island has most things one would expect to find there. Unnecessary things also coexist in a hushed and harmonious way. There's a school, televisions, and a tea house. There was once a population of eagle owls, a Natural Treasure. When the island was revealed to be an important habitat for the owls, Flugdatenschreiber became of interest—to mainland folk and the Cultural Properties Committee—for the first time since the end of the late Ice Age. The attention didn't last long. There isn't a single eagle owl left now. The villagers believed that an eagle owl left the island every time someone died. When someone died, the deceased cried *squall squall* and the eagle owl cried *whoo whoo* as it flew across the moonlit night. Many on the island are still living, but all the eagle owls have departed. There's a blue lighthouse on one coast. Each night, the lighthouse and the little bulbs in various houses light up the island. From above, it looks like yellow light spilling out of a small hole, or a small yellow star. Imagine a star floating under a dark, undulating sea. That's Flugdatenschreiber. 50cc motorbikes rattle down winding dirt roads, the portable reed organ with the broken E key creaks nervously in the annex school, and a laundry pole taller than the wind stands in someone's yard. Flugdatenschreiber is no longer the Flugdatenschreiber with the ancient hieroglyphs or the Natural Treasure Habitat for eagle owls. For a long time, nothing has happened on this island. The fact that Flugdatenschreiber was able to remain so consistently unremarkable for such a long period of time is one of its miracles.

This is the story of a boy living in 37 Flugdatenschreiber, the house with the blue slate roof. The story begins with an airplane crash and fire in the cannabis field a few days before. One day, a yellow light plane lost its way, wobbled over the island, and plunged head first into the village. The plane got stuck on the lighthouse. The tail caught fire and fell into the wild cannabis field. Several hundred acres of cannabis were ablaze. The island was cloaked in thick, pungent smoke that kept rising from the field. The ravenous flames consumed everything in the field for two days until a downpour finally put out the fire. The islanders, high as a kite, sang and danced all night.

Spring comes late to Flugdatenschreiber. When the brisk spring winds sweep over the island—*whoosh*—every blade of grass stands up like a hair and falls back again. Men mend their fishnets with sunlight on their backs. In the afternoon shadow, fish cool their heads under the dark sea. Everything was as usual that day in 37 Flugdatenschreiber, the house with the blue slate roof, home to a seven-year-old boy who'd never left the island in his life, his stern grandfather, and his uncle who read a lot and knew everything.

That afternoon, the old man sat gutting fish in the yard with a cigarette between his lips. There were two oversized basins paved half-heartedly with cement. The boy lay under the awning, fishing out pieces of pear from a plate of raw oysters and eating them. The old man pinched the mouth of a long hose to sweep the blood off the yard. He looked over at the boy through the iridescent droplets of water in the air and shouted, "Sit up when you're eating!"

13

The boy wanted to lie there enjoying the somnolent smell of blood drifting in the soft spring breeze, but he had no choice but to sit bolt upright when the old man bellowed at him. It had long been the old man's wish to raise this "bastard child" to be a "decent human being." The old man used to put the boy in a basin and bring him along when he went to work in the field. Shooing the flies that kept landing on the boy's penis, the old man pulled weeds and vowed to raise the boy well. However, the boy found cohabiting with his grandfather much more exhausting than living with three biological fathers. Every time his grandfather roared at him, the boy wet his pants. He'd been toilet trained a long time ago, but couldn't help wetting his pants lately. The old man roared at him every time he wet his pants, which made him wet his pants even more often. The boy seldom cried. The old man appeared irritated. He kept yelling at the boy whose expressions were more grandfather-like than a grandfather's. From afar, the old man looked like an inadequately evolved animal trying to court a rock. In the backyard, the boy's underwear flapped on the clothesline. The boy gulped a piece of oyster and it slid past his pink tonsils. The oyster tasted like the cool shade. A pole the old man had carved stood in one corner of the yard. On its upper end, a dozen gobies looked innocently up at the sky under a veil of mosquito netting. The boy's gaze, fixed on one point in the sky, slowly began to move. Perplexed, he called out, "Grandpa!"

The old man was in the storeroom. He didn't answer.

"Grandpa!"

The old man poked his head out with a knife in his hand. Great winds gushed in and out of the boy's dilated pupils.

"Look!"

The old man's gaze followed the end of the boy's finger up to the sky. A yellow light plane was spiraling down across the bright, cloudless blue. The plane's inevitable plunge into the embrace of Flugdatenschreiber's insipid peace below seemed like the most natural thing in the world, like a wilting flower or a breeze. The old man followed the movement of the plane, wide-eyed. The boy said, "Oh . . . oh!" Islanders stopped their mending and weeding to stand up and look at the sky. Moments later, the plane crashed with a loud bang. Every blade of grass on Flugdatenschreiber stood up and fell back down. The boy's pants gushed around the front and turned a color as deep as true love. The old man looked at the hill with his hand on his forehead. The plane had smashed into the lighthouse. The tall lighthouse was visible from anywhere on the island. Plumes of smoke rose over the hill.

"Grandpa, what's that?"

"I don't know . . . . It looks like an airplane."

The old man made a strange face.

"And yet . . ."

The old man squinted as if trying to remember something.

"It looks like . . ."

The boy squinted, too.

"Like what?"

The old man remembered and spoke as though it wasn't a big deal, "Like an eagle owl."

The smell of burning cannabis wafted over them. It was heartwarming and powerful. No, it was fragrant and piquant. It made them feel good just as they were about to feel upset. It was a first for both the boy and the old man. Warm urine dripped like tears from the boy's shorts.

Two nights passed before the downpour finally ceased. People returned to work. The yellow light plane remained lodged on the lighthouse, like a stale loaf of bread. It was a cozy, peaceful spring day in Flugdatenschreiber, no different from any other. There was no news from the mainland. On the night of the fire, the old man danced before the boy, shouting, "I see your daddy's face, I see the green mountains from the song, 'Butterfly, Let's Go to the Green Mountains,' and I see your dead grandma's pretty butthole!" and promptly did three cartwheels in the yard. The boy clapped. The overjoyed old man lay down on the porch, put his feet against the boy's abdomen, held both his hands and raised him up to the sky again and again. Every time the boy took flight on his grandfather's feet, the boy laughed deliriously, *Hahahaha! Hahahaha!* The next morning, the boy looked ill from too much laughing the previous night. When they finally regained all of their senses, the boy and the old man regarded each other awkwardly.

The boy's uncle returned after the rain stopped. He said he couldn't have come sooner because the heavy rain cut off ferry service to the island. The old man dried fish and worked the field as always. He ran into the boy in the kitchen or the outhouse. The old man became bashful around him. Seeing his grandfather's embarrassment that had him blushing like a bride—he couldn't even make eye contact with the boy—the boy thought, "This is too much." He spent all day playing with airplane debris around the lighthouse.

Three days after the fire, the three gathered for dinner. The plane crash on Flugdatenschreiber was on the news. The gist of the story was that a plane crashed on Flugdatenschreiber, an island of unremarkable resources and scenery. The boy hiccupped.

"Mamma mia!"

The old man looked up from his soup mid-slurp. The boy shook his head as if to absolve himself of whatever accusation was about to fall upon him.

"What did you just say?"

". . ."

The plane and the cannabis field appeared on the screen. The fire had burned a giant heart in the field. It appeared that reporters had stopped by the island via helicopter while the entire village was high. Mainland folk were apparently faster and cleverer than the islanders. The man pushed the older man's dinner toward him and said, "Father, your dinner's getting cold."

The newscaster reported, "No bodies were found at the site of the crash, and we have no confirmation of the nationality of the

16

pilot or the cause of the accident. Officials say the plane may belong to an international crime organization, and may have been used to smuggle drugs or firearms. The recovery of the black box is crucial to the investigation at this point."

The old man spoke through half-chewed crab cake, "Where does he learn to use these words we never taught him?"

The man silently looked at the old man.

". . ."

The old man considered his son's silence a rebuke, which he instantly returned by snapping, "What?"

The man answered, looking at the boy who hung his head, "I think he just pissed himself."

⌒

The boy lay next to the man. His private parts felt refreshed after being hosed down. The man was absorbed in a news magazine article. The boy asked, intrigued, "Is it fun?"

"You don't read this stuff for fun. You read it to find out what's going on in the world. When you grow up—I don't care if you never read anything else—always read news magazines."

The boy smiled brightly and fell back on the futon. He hummed to himself as his thoughts began drifting off elsewhere. The inviting sound of pages being turned punctuated the early evening in the island village.

"Uncle?"

"Hmm?"

The boy looked up at the ceiling, his face aglow, and said, "Sometimes I want to die."

When did the boy last utter the word 'mom'? For him that term was as unfamiliar and difficult as 'Dnepr Kombinat' or 'Sodium Amide' or 'celluloid.' On top of that, the word required an explanation. Long ago, when the boy asked the old man about his mom, the old man retorted angrily, "You mom wasn't human."

That she wasn't human was all the information the boy had about his mother. No trace of her remained under the blue slate roof of 37 Flugdatenschreiber. Not a single photograph, article of clothing, or old, fine-toothed comb. She had disappeared like the ancient hieroglyphs of Flugdatenschreiber. The old man forbade the boy to even say the word 'mom.' But the boy's uncle remembered. He remembered how she'd become a widow months after she married, how blindingly beautiful she was, how sure and capable her hands were when she marinated seaweed, how fast she could run to the dock with her father-in-law on her back when he had fallen ill, and how the old man doted on her. She died while she was away supposedly visiting her family. She was found with a naked man in a burnt-down inn. All that survived the fire were some of her belongings and a half-scorched red underwire brassiere. The old man wailed with the boy on his back, "My son is not yet cold in his grave!" Since then, every time the boy asked about his mother, the old man yelled at him until the neighbors' shingles shook.

The boy idolized his uncle. The uncle had once been the most popular elementary school kid on the island. It didn't matter that the student body only consisted of twelve children. He was able to grow thanks to an encyclopedia set. When he was in the third grade, the old man spent a fortune on a set of encyclopedias. This was the result of two hours of coercion on the part of two sales people who had come all the way to the island by boat. The encyclopedia was printed by a phantom publisher whose very existence was questionable. This explained the poor paper quality, the strange layout, and low-resolution pictures. The theme of volume one was "The Universe." The man, then a third grader, picked up the encyclopedia larger than his torso, and opened it with a grunt. A bright universe opened before his eyes. The pictures of nebulae, planets, and the solar system shocked him. He felt as though the vibrating lights were speaking to him. The man began to peruse the encyclopedia. Some of the information was downright wrong, but no one could challenge him because there was only one man on Flugdatenschreiber who owned a set of encyclopedias, and that person lived at 37 Flugdatenschreiber in the house with the blue slate roof. The real reason the old man decided to invest in the set of encyclopedias was the "Couples Encyclopedia" for adults that came with it. The man happened upon the "Couples Encyclopedia" one day while rummaging through his parents' closet. The book was full of pictures of naked couples entangled in every position imaginable. When it occurred to him that the real appendix was the encyclopedia, not the "Couples Encyclopedia," he ran away from home in tears. Two days later, he returned looking very grown-up. The man grew smarter. He was once one of the finalists chosen from among twenty thousand applicants for a teen astronaut space program by a space association in a faraway place. If chosen, the winner would be trained in seventy categories over the course of a year and ultimately sent into space. All the islanders rooted for him. Some elderly man paid him to shout his name three times when the man made it to space. He came in second in the finals. His older brother drowned at sea soon after. Every time things didn't go well for him after that, the man would cry, "If only I'd won the astronaut contest!" Now he works at the ticket booth on the harbor where the ferry from the mainland docks. His job requires no skills besides punching holes in passengers' tickets. It's a mystery why he still carries himself like a valedictorian, but he still reads the encyclopedia and has an answer to every question the boy ever asks. To the boy, Uncle was a hero. Uncle's big words somehow made his opinions more credible.

The boy was still staring up at the ceiling, bright-eyed. Searching for words, the man blinked. He certainly couldn't tell the boy about the half-torched red brassiere.

"Do you want to hear about Uncle's astronaut contest again?"

"Sure," said the boy. "Later."

The man was discouraged. The boy pointed to the set of encyclopedias and asked, "Uncle, did you really read all those?"

Grinning as though someone had asked him his favorite question, one that he wants to be asked again and again for eternity, the man answered, "Of course."

The boy asked, his eyes watery, "You must know everything."

Barely containing his arrogant smirk, he said warmly, "Of course."

The boy carefully said, "Then if I show you something, can you tell me what it is?"

The man nodded.

"It's a secret," said the boy.

The man promised to keep his secret. He was so happy he had the opportunity to be a know-it-all again.

⌐

The boy presented him with an orange box. It looked similar to the tin box at the dock ticket office. The boy had pulled it out of the bamboo forest in the backyard.

"So, what is this?"

The man panicked. He'd never seen this object before, and had never said 'I don't know' to the boy before. The man circled the box, studying the expression on the boy's face. The surface of the metal box was smooth and stained with soot. The man sniffed the box and shook it. He believed he had seen it before somewhere, and that if he had, it must have been in the encyclopedia. Groping in the dark, he finally remembered its name.

"Black box!"

"Huh?"

"Black box."

"What's that?"

The man shrugged, "It means 'a box that is black.'"

The boy pondered this.

20

"So why is it orange?"

The man was taken aback. "Why is it orange? Why is it orange? Why on earth is it *orange*?"

He quickly made something up.

"What does your name mean?"

"Um, Grandpa says it means 'wise and brave.'"

The man replied, "So, are you wise and brave?"

The boy shook his head emphatically as if he had just had a revelation, "Ohh."

"So what is this thing?" asked the boy.

"This is . . ."

The man hesitated. A strange idea suddenly came to mind.

"You see, this is . . ."

The boy was full of anticipation as he looked at the man.

He answered soberly, "This is your mother."

The boy peed his pants a little.

"What?"

"Your mother."

The boy had believed everything his uncle ever told him up to that moment, but he didn't seem to comprehend this one.

"What?"

All sorts of information exploded over his head like the Big Bang. The man slowly began to explain.

"Think about it. In the beginning, when there weren't any living creatures on the planet, the air was filled with strange gases like methane or titanium or nitrogen. Get it?"

"No."

"Well, anyway, the air was filled with gases like that. The gases got mixed together, created electricity, and made fish and dinosaurs—you know dinosaurs, right?—and trees and stuff."

"Okay."

"And they went on to make lions and monkeys and lots of other things. So humans were made later—much, much later. So, who is the ancestor of humans?"

The boy remembered what the man had once said and
answered confidently, "Monkeys!"

"That's right! And the ancestor of monkeys?"

This required thought.

"Dinosaurs, silly! Dinosaurs came before the monkeys!

Dinosaurs came from fish, and fish came from methane and
nitrogen and gases like that. So if you think about it, humans come
from air, wind, sunlight, and stuff. Those are our true ancestors."

The boy looked confused.

"But air and wind made all sorts of other things besides humans,
see? So our ancestor could be tuna from the South Pacific, or a chair,
or a stainless pressure cooker. It could even be this black box."

"Why?"

"Because we have the same ancestors."

To drive the argument home, the man asked, "What does
Grandpa always say about your mom?"

The boy replied sadly, "He says, 'Your mom wasn't human.'"

"See what I mean?"

The boy nodded emphatically, "Ohh."

"It all becomes clear."

The boy pretended to understand. A little part of him wanted
to spare his uncle the embarrassment of losing face. There was no
way he was going to buy such a ridiculous idea as 'The black box is
your mom.' The man gave the boy a little nudge in the back.

"Go on, call her 'Mom.'"

The boy quietly looked at the black box. The rectangular
box was peacefully reflecting the moonlight. The boy turned and
looked back at the man, who nodded as if to give him permission,
as though he needed it.

"Mom . . ." His voice shook.

The black box did not respond. The boy called out once again,
"Mom . . ."

His eyes became blurry like a picture taken by someone with
shaky hands. The man put his arms around the boy's shoulders.

"That's it."

The boy's voice shook as he asked, "But why won't she say anything?"

"You see, if we are born as different species, we can't converse with one another. But if we stay close to each other, we may be able to find ways to understand each other. We'll figure out a way to communicate with Mom, too."

"Why?"

"These are the ethics of the universe."

The boy still looked confused. But his gratitude for Mom who finally came to see him and his faith in uncle's explanation made his heart ache a little. He squatted before the black box. He carefully embraced it as if brooding an egg. It felt cold at first, but the prolonged contact between her metal surface and his body warmed them both. The boy's small heart went pit-a-pat.

"Can I take it home?" asked the boy.

The man jumped and said no. Grandpa would toss it in the ocean. The boy looked devastated.

"What's wrong?"

The boy replied, "I'm happy."

A soft sea breeze drifted past the two of them. The man thought the breeze resembled one he felt with his entire body on the way home, a long time ago, just as he was about to fall in love. The boy stood there for a while longer calling his mom over and over again. The black box seemed a little bashful. On the way home, the boy asked, "Won't she be cold?"

The man replied in a hushed voice, "It's okay. Black boxes are by nature introverted and sensitive, so they don't like it when someone's too considerate."

The lonely blue lighthouse stood behind them. It blinked, emitting a small, warm light. The yellow light plane without its tail watched over them from a distance. The wings of the plane faintly cried, *whoong, whoong* as they sliced the wind. It sounded like an eagle owl crying *whoo, whoo* as it flew away, leaving the surviving behind.

A few days later, a chopper landed on the island with a deafening chatter of propellers, carrying intelligence officers in blue uniforms, researchers, and TV reporters. They pitched a tent on the highest peak and unloaded food, folding beds, tables, insect repellant, sun block, and so forth. One of the intelligence officers pulled out a pair of binoculars, looked down on Flugdatenschreiber, and saw the large heart-shaped scorch mark in the middle of the cannabis field. The intelligence officer blushed. These people had come to the island looking for the black box. Folks were growing very nervous on the mainland. Despite varying theories ranging from military conspiracy to scientific mystery to alien invasion, everyone passionately agreed that finding the black box was the top priority. The recovery of the black box was a routine procedure that followed all plane crashes, nothing that required passionate agreement to make it happen, but it was agreed to with passion nevertheless because no one had anything better to say except that the truth was in the black box. For several days, they all donned their white gloves and investigated the island, examining the crash site, collecting evidence, and interviewing villagers. They spent evenings on the hill, watching the crimson waves, getting sentimental, tearing up.

The boy spent day and night in the backyard. The old man didn't seem to care. The boy told the black box stories. He chirped on about the things he liked, the things he didn't like, what he had for breakfast, what grandpa said in his sleep, comics he'd been reading, the changes in his weight, and so on. The black box was a silent, attentive listener. It didn't agree, reprimand, or interfere, but the conversation couldn't have been more natural or comfortable. The man started to worry about the boy, but thought it best to leave him to it for a while. He wanted to give the boy more time.

24

Before long, intelligence officers came to 37 Flugdatenschreiber, the house with the blue slate roof. They asked the old man a few questions. Then, they opened the large earthen pots and inspected the shed. The boy held his breath as he watched their every move. The old man followed them around the house with his hands behind him and pelted them with questions: "Which country did it come from?" "Why did it crash?" The intelligence officers said they didn't know and retorted, "Could you please leave us alone?" The boy was about to steal away into the backyard when one intelligence officer stopped him.

"Hey, kid!"

The boy wet his pants instantly. The old man clicked his tongue, and the surprised intelligence officer inquired, "What's wrong with him?"

"Happens all the time! Sickly little 'un."

The intelligence officer wrote "Sickly little 'un" on his notepad and put his pen in his pocket. Then, he asked, as though he'd saved the most important question for the end, "Where can I get good sashimi around here?"

The intelligence officers stopped by 37 Flugdatenschreiber often. They asked questions they'd asked before and went away looking ruffled. The boy broke into a cold sweat every time they showed up. One intelligence officer would look at the boy and write something on his notepad. The day the man came home early from work, the intelligence officer was looking inside the large pot on the wood stove.

It isn't possible for a black box to disappear on an island this small. It's got to be here somewhere. We can't find it because someone's hiding it. That person is probably part of an unethical organization. This deed will not go unpunished, the intelligence officers declared before they left.

This did not happen in 37 Flugdatenschreiber alone. Their investigation at a dead end, the frustrated intelligence officers tirelessly grilled the villagers. The man huffed and puffed at their insolence.

Flugdatenschreiber

by *Kim Aeran*

Gobies lay on the large brass tray, all staring in the same direction. Their scales were peppered with chili powder. The old man de-boned the fish with his spindly fingers. Clouds hung low and moved quickly across the sky outside the window. The boy listened attentively to the news while sucking on a fish head. The gist of the story was that the plane crash investigation had come to a screeching halt. Faces of villagers flashed on the screen. They often digressed during interviews, and didn't appear to know what a black box was.

"The government has made plans to send a high-performance X-50s Detector, which will locate the black box by detecting a special alloy found in all black boxes," said the newscaster.

The man looked at the boy. The boy casually drank rice tea from a bowl larger than his face. He said, "Thank you for dinner" the second his spoon hit the table, and rushed outside. The man and the old man sat in the rippling light from the TV and watched the rest of the news.

The old man rose from his seat. "I'm going to the john," he said. "You clear the table."

The old man grabbed the flashlight and put on his muddy rubber shoes with the heels folded. The man nervously watched the old man. Not surprisingly, the old man heard strange noises as he was stepping outside the gate. It sounded like it could be the wind or someone murmuring. He tiptoed toward the source of the sound. It was coming from the bamboo forest in the backyard. The old man peered into the darkness with his animal night vision. He could make out the boy muttering to himself next to the earthen pot. The old man shined his flashlight on the boy. The startled boy fell on his bum.

"What are you doing here?"

The boy sprang to his feet and hid the black box with his body.

"Hmm? Nothing!"

26

The old man walked toward him still shining the light. The boy took a step back. The old man saw something orange between the boy's legs.

"What's that?"

"Nothing," said the boy, pressing his thighs together.

"Get out of the way."

The boy didn't move. The old man shoved him aside. When the old man tried to touch the black box, the boy jumped at him, crying, "No!" The old man realized that the object had something to do with the "black something" that the mainland folk were looking for.

"No! Give me that!"

Holding the black box with both hands, the old man bore down on the boy.

"You little rascal! What have you done? Don't you know they lock you up some frightful place for doing something like this? Hmm?"

The old man roared at the boy as though he was about to hurl the black box on the ground. The man heard the old man and came running out of the house. He seized the old man's arm, "Father, no!"

The old man dramatically pretended to look for a spade or a hoe and cried, "I'll break you in half!"

"Who said you can steal? Hmm?"

The boy's legs shook beneath his sopping crotch. The man pleaded as he shielded the boy from the old man.

"Father, I picked this up near the harbor today. I brought it home to give it to the mainland folk."

The old man looked at the man suspiciously.

"He was probably curious about it. I will put it back where I found it first thing tomorrow. Now calm down."

The old man looked at the boy and then the man and went back inside piqued. The man squeezed the boy's shoulder.

The man and the boy lay side by side on the sleeping mat. In the room across the yard, the old man alternated between dozing off and de-shelling clams. The man stroked the boy's hair and attempted to make small talk.

"Do you have anyone you like?"

The boy answered listlessly, "Huh? Long time ago."

"Have you ever kissed anyone?"

"No, what about you?"

"Of course, I have. I'm an adult." The man continued, "When you kiss someone you like, it feels awesome."

The boy seemed a little curious.

"What's it feel like?"

"Let's see. When you drop something heavy from the earth's atmosphere, the earth's gravity pulls down the object at an enormous speed, and the object burns up without a trace before it can hit the earth."

"Uh huh."

"That's how I would describe kissing."

The boy was touched. "It's beautiful!"

The man smiled.

"Sure is. Sometimes, pieces that broke off spaceships and stuff like that wander through the universe, get caught in the earth's gravitational field, and wind up circling the earth forever."

"Forever?"

"Mm-hmm. There's hundreds of 'em flying over our heads as we speak. We can't see them because they're too far away, but they're there."

"How exhausting," said the boy, pulling the covers up to his chin.

The man whispered, "Do you want to go see the black box?"

"Why?"

"To give your mom a kiss."

Whizzing sounds of bamboo swaying in the wind came from the backyard. The boy quietly looked at the man with a gaze unintelligible even to himself. It was impossible to figure out what premonitions it held.

The man and the boy crept past the old man's room and arrived in the backyard. The old man was nodding off before a basin full of clams, his hand clutching a knife. The man placed the black box in front of the boy. The black box looked tired. The bamboo forest danced—*whoosh whoosh*—in the wind. The wind was as heavy and muggy as a wet piece of cloth. The man finally spoke.

"The mainland folk will be here soon. You know that, right?"

The boy nodded nervously.

"They're going to take Mom away. They need her for something."

The boy hung his head.

"Let's send her off somewhere before they get here."

The boy replied, "I don't want to."

"Do you want them to take her away?"

". . ."

"If Mom stays here, she'll be captured. We must send her away."

"But where?"

"There."

The man pointed up at the sky.

"Mom will be able to stay in the earth's gravitational field and orbit the sky forever and stay by your side. Really. I promise."

The boy's face blurred. He kept digging at the earth with one foot.

"No?"

". . ."

After a while, the boy finally spoke, "What do I have to do?"

"Just kiss her. Then, you close your eyes and wait for a while. Before you do that, though, you must say goodbye to her."

The boy nodded. The man took a step back and said, "You can say anything you want to say to her."

The black box kept quiet. The boy began, "Mom."

". . ."

"Mom." The boy's voice cracked. A strong sea breeze passed between them. The boy continued haltingly.

"You've never called my name, you've never carried me on your back, you've never felt my forehead when I had fever, you've never come to fetch me when I was late coming home from school, and you were never there when I needed you. You won't pack my bags for me, you won't pull my rotten teeth, you won't go fight for me when I get bullied at school, you won't go on picnics with me, you won't be there for my first day of school, you won't nap with me, you won't pet me on the head when I win prizes, and you won't ever answer when I call you, but . . ."

The boy burst into tears.

"But . . ."

The boy's face was bathed with tears. The boy howled. The wind kept blowing. A bamboo leaf fluttered out of the darkness and landed on the black box.

"Mom's saying goodbye."

"What did she say?" The boy hiccupped.

"She said 'Take care,'" said the man.

". . ."

"She said to take care. Take care wherever you are, and that will make me very happy."

The boy howled again. *Waa*—The man quietly stood by the boy and waited for him to cry his little heart out. After a long while, the man whispered in the boy's ear, "You should say goodbye, too."

"What should I say?"

"Say, 'Take care, Mom.' Say, 'Bye-bye.'"

The boy wiped his tears on the back of his hands. The boy said to the black box that was solemnly crouching on the ground, "Bye-bye, Mom. Take care."

The child continued, "Take care wherever you are. And . . . that will make me very happy."

The man said to the boy, "Now, let's kiss Mom."

The boy slowly drew closer to the black box and held its cold cheeks with both hands. The boy looked at it for a while, closed his eyes, and kissed the black box, praying it would reincarnate as something softer next time. The boy's tears softly

30

drummed the orange alloy surface. Up in the sky, the moon was
bloating in the clouds.

At that exact moment, the old man dropped off and saw a bird
in his dream. The bird was inexplicably wearing a red brassiere. The
man looked up at the sky and murmured, "That looks just like an
eagle owl, just like it . . ." For a long while, the old man watched as
the bird with the red brassiere flew away. He suddenly noticed tears
on his face. The old man yelled, *Shoo!* up at the sky. He shouted
once more, as though the first wasn't good enough. *Shoo!* Looking
at the night sky with wet eyes, the old man muttered,

"Next time, don't go giving your heart to damn people."

The bird flapped its enormous wings under the moonlight
and disappeared—*whoo whoo*—to the far corner of the sky.

⌒

Once again, it is summer in Flugdatenschreiber. Somewhere
on this sun-parched island, on patches of green, amidst pedestrian
and time-honored labor, mysterious rumors and tedium,
and sometimes, a wind so cool it makes you want to call out
someone's name, people live who produce children year after year.
Flugdatenschreiber is its name. Men in rubber boots dry fish. In
the mid-summer shadow, fish cool their heads under the dark sea.
Not much has changed in 37 Flugdatenschreiber, the house with
the blue slate roof. The old man looks up at the sky as he guts fish,
and the man goes out to the dock each morning to punch holes in
ferry tickets. The boy has grown out of his old underwear, and has
long since stopped wetting himself. The tallest lighthouse stands
on the outskirts of the island. Lodged on top of the lighthouse is a
light plane, green with overgrown moss. It looks like a relic. Birds
sometimes nest inside its broken windows. The mainland folk
have all left. They picked up the black box someone left under the
lighthouse and disappeared with a deafening chatter of propellers.
The damage to the black box and ambient noise made it impossible

to make out what was recorded in the last thirty minutes before the crash. The pilot was never found, and the origin of the plane remains a mystery, but the plane accident was soon forgotten. The investigation team was able to make out one part of the pilot's message from the black box—one barely audible, "Goodbye."

Flugdatenschreiber

by *Kim Aeran*

Mouthwatering

by Kim Aeran

Translated by Jamie Chang

The alarm goes off. In the dark, her cell phone blinks urgently like a signal she needs to start her day. Daily she reaches for this small disaster like a foreigner caught in a storm at night and washed up on strange shores the next morning. She gropes around and grabs the light. Blue light spills from between her fingers. She lies there still as a corpse with the phone in her outstretched hand. She looks like Superman right before he rockets off. Maybe this is why she raises her fist high above her head first thing every day. She twists her body. All her joints creak. She buries her face in her pillow and grumbles in despair. Her despair is always one and the same: *I am tired*. Out in the hall, someone's morning paper hits the doormat. Hubae grunts.[1] 'I have to get to work an hour early today.' There are piles of manuscript paper scattered around Hubae's head. 'I have to pay a 20,000-*wŏn* fine if I'm late.' The pages contain standardized essays written by middle school students. Hubae grades one hundred and twenty 500-word essays every week for 1,000 *wŏn* a page. Hubae is still asleep, the pen in her hand. Hubae has red ink on her earlobe. She shuffles her sore limbs under the cover. 'The flu?' Outside, a motorcycle revs and takes off. She stretches and then quickly curls up in a ball, mumbling to herself

---

1. Hubae: refers to someone in the same field or school who is younger, less experienced, or lower in rank than the speaker.

once again, ***I am so tired***. She weighs her options. Should she sleep longer or not? If yes, for how much longer? A cab ride to work is 10,000 *wŏn*. 'I could get an additional 10,000 *wŏn*'s sleep and consider it a late fee. Or I'll just be late. Isn't the extra sleep worth 20,000 *wŏn*? But what about all the other, better ways to spend 20,000 *wŏn*? I've never been late to work, so why not just this once? Perhaps consistent diligence is a way of saving up in case of future mistakes. Paying a fine, after all, is a way of buying absolution. A little feigned apology should do the trick. They all saw me working like a dog yesterday, didn't they? But then who didn't work like a dog yesterday? What if I run out of free "Indulgences" the moment I desperately need one? In the time I was mulling over this question, I could have had an extra five minutes of sleep!' She tumbles down a deep gorge between therefores and buts, and disappears. Of course, she's not willing to take a taxi to work. She knows that it isn't determination but hesitation that gets her out of bed in the morning. In that moment of hesitation, she mistakenly believes that she has some control over her life. She snaps back to consciousness. She sits up like a madwoman, yelling, ***What time is it***? It's that universally hazy time in the morning between not-late-yet and may-be-late-soon—somewhere in that vicinity.

She goes into the bathroom. She sits on the toilet, happens to look down at her underwear, and is shocked. Her period. 'It's not time yet.' She pulls off her panties beneath her nightgown, squats next to the faucet, and fills the basin with water. 'It's Sports Day.' She has to run a relay today. She tried to get out of actively participating by volunteering to cheer, but she was told it was mandatory for everyone to compete in at least one competition. When the department head asked people to volunteer for the relay, she lowered her head as far as possible so no one would pick her. Nevertheless, someone raised his hand and said, "I would like to nominate Miss Pak." He said he saw her bolting to the station to catch the last train at night, and she was fast. She is miserable as she waits for her underwear to soak in the water. Winning a

34

competition at a company sports event was never something she wanted to do in life. Whether she wanted it or not, she had already competed in the preliminaries she never wanted to compete in, and received a Sports Day shirt. She somehow ended up finishing first in the preliminaries, which depressed her even more. The principal of the *hagwŏn* offered a two-million-*wŏn* cash prize for the winning team, and 500,000 *wŏn* for the best talent show team. She has to run the relay and perform in the talent show today. No one from her department volunteered to be in the talent show, and so it was decided that everyone had to dance. For many days, she spent her lunch hour on the roof of the hagwŏn building practicing the 'vertex dance' with the rest of her department. "Legs spread, arms spread! One, two, three, forward! Jab! Again, one, two, three, turn! Miss Pak! Forty-five degrees! You call that forty-five degrees?" Startled by the sudden, loud reprimand through the megaphone, she whipped her head around and lunged in the other direction, hit someone, apologized, and the beat went on, *Oom pa pa*. In the midsummer heat, her expression was permanently fixed as 'on the verge of tears' as she sweated buckets dancing on the hagwŏn roof that lacked a single patch of shade. Two things she hated more than anything as a child were group punishments and talent shows. The 'vertex dance' combined both. She hangs her head and watches blood from her underwear spread across the surface of the water like marbling. ***Should I skip work today***? She mulls this question over just long enough to think she has a choice. Moments later, she's quickly washing her hair in cold water.

There she is, running down the street, shielding her face from the morning light, her hand as small as a maple leaf. She's wearing cotton pants and an orange shirt. There's a logo on her shirt that resembles a globe, with the inscription "New Elite Academy 10th Anniversary." It's Independence Day, and there aren't many people out in the streets. There's an uncharacteristic peace around the sandwich stall and the free newspaper stand. A row of half-

35

awake people ride the escalator. As children, they probably didn't harbor such grand aspirations as going down in history, but they certainly didn't ask to be someone who has to work on public holidays, either. She joins their procession and laments, 'If only I had been motivated enough to demand after-school tutoring.' Almost instantly, she's embarrassed by her own thoughts. She knows too well that all parents make excuses for their academically challenged children by insisting that they "lack motivation" instead of admitting to their mediocrity.

The preparatory hagwŏn is located in Mok-tong. It's a corporate-scale hagwŏn with over a thousand students in the seventh grade alone. She's a Korean language and lit teacher for the middle school program. When she first started interviewing for hagwŏn jobs, she was surprised to discover that she had to name her own salary. One of the hagwŏn interviewers said, "We can give you as much as you want. If you want ten million, we can give you ten million. If you want six, we'll give you six. The important thing is that you are worthy of the price you name. So, how much do you want?" She sat on the leather sofa feeling like a small pill bug as she searched for an answer. Too little would make her seem incompetent, and too much would make her seem ridiculous. There was something strange about this salary system that the hagwŏn director maintained was "fair," but she didn't know what. She does know that what she felt at that moment, sitting on that leather sofa, was humiliation. As she presented her sample lecture for the interview, the administrative-level teacher who looked like he'd be worth six million a month slept with his head hanging back, mouth wide open. Their spontaneous demand that she do a sample lecture left her fumbling without any teaching material. For some strange reason, she couldn't say no to their request. She came home miserable, despite already feeling like a sell-out by looking for a hagwŏn job, which is easier and better compensated than the average office job. Anyway, she wound up choosing New Elite over the 'six-to-ten-million' hagwŏn.

She has the financial means to pay rent and utilities for her small studio apartment, afford health insurance, invest in an accumulative fund, and feed her high-interest savings account. She knows that in order to complete her accumulative fund payments, she must gallop like a horse and dance like a bear every day. From time to time, she feels she has received a certain part of her life as an advance. She is jealous of younger people who spend a year in silent devotion to civic exams and get stable government jobs in return. The security of being employed, the extra cash to go out drinking with people without feeling anxious, and the ability to make contributions at acquaintances' weddings and funerals all stop her from quitting the hagwŏn job. Every time she toys with the idea of quitting, payday always comes around like an apologetic lover.

The station P.A. system announces the arrival of the train. People inch toward the safety line. She takes a deep breath and resolves not to be a sissy. Periods never stopped her from taking the college entrance exam, showing up at her temp job, or going on college retreats. She's suddenly reminded of Hubae. Hubae sleeps during the day and works at night. Hubae got the essay-grading gig through her. When she offered her the editing job, Hubae, who had spent days going through jobsites on the Internet, her face dark as a storm cloud, she jumped for joy. At 1000 *wŏn* a page, editing would pay better than bussing trays. Less than a day later, Hubae looked up at her with bloodshot, teary eyes and said, "Ŏnni, Korean middle school kids are all retards." It's been three months since they've been living together. To this day, she doesn't know what prompted her to take Hubae in. If she had to give a reason, she'd say it was because she liked Hubae's voice. Or maybe it was the look in Hubae's eyes as she talked about this and that the first night they spent together. Was it the texture of Hubae's voice? Her face turns ashen. The train stops with a loud screech. She hops over the gap between the train and the platform into the air-conditioned car. The door closes. ***It's cold***.

Her co-workers always greet her in the morning with some comment on her appearance. When she first started working there, she took it seriously when people at the office greeted her with, "You changed your hairdo," "I like your bag, Miss Pak," "Where'd you get your skirt?" and so on. At first, this made her happy. Shy and proud at the same time, she would later check herself out in the bathroom mirror. It wasn't long before she realized that people at the hagwŏn discussed fashion obsessively. Fashion wasn't small talk, but a very important matter to be discussed with religious fervor. She grew wary of her limited wardrobe and the scrutiny by other female teachers. When someone paid her a compliment, she felt strangely indebted. She was often paranoid that everyone was looking at her and scoring her outfit as she entered the office each morning. She soon discovered that she had been worried for no reason. The teachers may have simply welcomed change of any sort because it gave them something to talk about. The first words she heard today when she entered the office, however, had nothing to do with fashion.

The department head calls her. During however many steps it takes to get to his desk, she thinks of all the things she may have done wrong. Nothing stands out. She is thorough and diligent, and always gets good scores on the quarterly teacher evaluations. The head asks, "You're in charge of class SH1 and CK2, right?" "Yes," she answers, bracing herself. "My Hubae—I know," he interrupts her. She keeps her mouth shut. "She marked perfectly fine words wrong!" She looks at the pile of essays on the head's desk. Hubae's loopy handwriting is all over the pages. She must have read them very carefully. Hardly any space is left in the comment boxes. "She changed 'for example' to 'for exemple,' and a 'because' here turned a perfectly fine sentence into a fragment. The parents of these children are highly educated people. Do you have any idea how many complaints I received today? Are you sure your Hubae is a Korean Lit major?" She doesn't know how to respond to that. Should she ask, to verify, "How many mistakes did she make?";

should she affirm, "Yes, Hubae really is a Korean Lit major"; or attempt damage control: "I'll redo them myself"? Finding the right response at last, she says, *I am sorry*. "Miss Pak. I know we only pay 1000 *won* per page, but the trust we lose when we make these mistakes is worth a hundred times more than that." He says Hubae can't have the editing work anymore. She keeps her mouth shut. He asks if he's been understood. She hesitates. He's waiting for an answer. She finally says, *I am sorry*, which means "I got it." She goes back to her seat. Her co-workers quickly pretend they weren't watching. She feels the cramps coming on. She sniffles. As she carefully dabs under her nose, Mr. Ch'oe asks, "Miss Pak, did you catch cold?" She nods. "Who catches cold in the summer?" Miss Kim chimes in. "Who catches cold in the summer? I do! Do you want to know why? You make me sit in front of the air conditioner the size of a house, that's why! You know I'm freezing my butt off here, and no one says anything about turning the air conditioner off or even turning it down a little, that's why!" She suddenly wants to cry like a child. Once, when she was coughing up her lungs, everyone expressed their polite sympathy, but not one person volunteered to sub for her. Hubae irritates her, too. "After I went through the trouble of printing out the 'Common Grammar and Spelling Errors' for her!" When she told Hubae to "turn off the light and go to sleep," Hubae would say, "No, I have to finish" and end up falling asleep like a baby, leaving the light on all night. The department head shouts, "Let's go!" She shoots him a quick sideways glance. 'Your *face* is a sentence fragment.' She asks herself how much she knows about Hubae, other than that she cannot spell 'example.' Like the time she couldn't remember a single word of French, which she had studied for three years in high school, her mind draws a blank. Mr. Ch'oe taps her on the shoulder. "C'mon."

Hubae was a good storyteller. It had nothing to do with great wit or knowledge. When Hubae told a story, she had a look on her face that seemed to say this story was the most important and meaningful one in the world. Every time she listened to one of Hubae's stories, she felt something quicken inside her, the way she felt after reading an atrocious translation of a philosophy text that was oddly moving.

The day she first invited Hubae to her place, all Hubae had with her was a small bag. The only connection between the two was an unbelievably vague and symbolic one—they had met before, having gone to school together. Like a traveler in a fairy tale, Hubae asked if she could stay the night. Hubae's voice was unadorned and gentle. She hesitated but in the end agreed to put Hubae up for the night. She didn't want people to think of her as a cold sŏnbae, and besides she didn't mind entertaining a guest for one night.[2] She laid out the futon for Hubae, turned on the heat for hot water, sent Hubae into the bathroom to wash up, and then seriously wondered why she had allowed Hubae to stay. Maybe she wanted to be a good person for a night. Maybe she was pleasantly surprised by such a boldfaced, innocent request after becoming accustomed to 'favors' that were thinly veiled 'deals.' That she jumped at the opportunity to put Hubae up for the night suggested that she may have been subconsciously wishing that someone would ask her a favor, even a rude one. When Hubae came out of the bathroom, she started to pelt her wildly with questions and offers. "You want something to eat?" "Do you want something comfortable to wear?" "The skin toner and lotion are here, this is the eye cream, and that's the intensive moisturizer." "Do you want a plump pillow or a skinny pillow?" When she ran out of things to say, she asked, without meaning to, "Would you like a glass of wine?"

That night, they pushed the futon aside and sat facing each other across a folding table. She put out a bottle of Chilean wine and two wine glasses, and said that she didn't know much about wine, but enjoyed it every once in a while. The two made an awkward toast and each took a sip. "Do you want to listen to some

---

2. *sŏnbae*: the opposite of *hubae*. It refers to someone in the same field or school who is older, more experienced, or higher in rank than the speaker.

music?" When she started to crawl toward her laptop, Hubae said that it was fine. They exchanged a few words—topics anyone could discuss with anybody without getting too engaged. Frivolous things about the weather. Politics. Movies. Hubae cracked a joke at some point, and they laughed together for the first time. "You appeared in my dream last night, Ŏnni," said Hubae. She looked puzzled. "You know how sometimes people you don't know very well appear in your dreams and make a significant contribution to the plot?" She nodded, "I know!" "It's really awkward when they appear in an obscene dream. You feel embarrassed and tense when you see them the next day, right?" Hubae smiled. She burst into laughter, "I know!" She felt relieved in a way. Hubae continued, "In my dream, you and I were standing in the middle of a summer field in some unidentified East Asian country. I had no idea why we were there together since we barely know each other, but anyway we were together. We stood in this spooky field looking up at the foreign night sky. Suddenly, I saw the Big Dipper, which hung unusually close to the horizon. Those were the only stars in the sky." She eagerly waited for Hubae to continue. "We headed toward the stars and were flabbergasted. The seven lights actually turned out to be seven little light bulbs on the roof of a brothel." She laughed out loud, "You're a liar!" "No," said Hubae with a sober look, "It's the truth." Hubae continued, "I remember feeling strangely relieved when I found out they were light bulbs." They talked about a lot of things. She threw her head back and laughed every once in a while, finding something hilarious. She lay on her side, deliciously tipsy. She thought to herself, this is so much better than being stuck in the backseat with a co-worker I don't like, engaging in forced small talk all the way to our destination. Perhaps this safe friendship with an expiration date made her feel generous. It was possible for anyone to be nice to anyone for a day. One could be as interesting or hospitable as one wanted for a day. Although she wasn't expecting it, she felt her kindness rewarded by Hubae's good stories. Hubae had a nice voice. They emptied the bottle of wine in no time.

Hubae left her leaning against a cushion with her eyes half-closed, and poked through her own bag for something. She seemed to want to show her something. She came back and sat before her. Hubae stretched out her palm. There was a small wooden box in her hand. The simple box had a muted sheen from years of wear. Hubae said quietly, "Ŏnni, I have a good story for you." She nodded. The box stirred her curiosity. "I came here because the creditors foreclosed on the place I was staying. They didn't say anything, but I could tell I wouldn't be able to stay there any longer." She braced herself. She was afraid she would be let in on a heavy secret in exchange for a hollow gesture. "When I was little, I used to move around a lot. As you know, I had a working student scholarship at school." She couldn't remember if Hubae had a working student scholarship at school, but she hoped that the story she was about to hear wasn't a dark and troubling one. Her studio apartment was too small for such stories. She smiled uneasily. Hubae continued in her unadorned voice. "I once took a trip to the city library with my mom when I was young. I don't remember exactly, but I think it took us over two hours to get there." She remembered that it wasn't until she was in middle school that she first saw the inside of a library. Summoning the memory of the library, Hubae also made the face she made years ago at the library. "That day, the moment I stepped into this enormous mass of silence with my mom's hand in mine, my heart began to race." Hubae looked at something beyond the reach of sight, the way a blind person does. She looked down at the box. She couldn't tell where this was going. "Mom sat me down at the library rest area, and told me to stay put for a while. She said she was going to look up some books. She gave me a pack of gum and told me to chew it if I got bored." She nodded. "I peeled a stick of gum as soon as Mom disappeared into the stacks. My mouth kept filling up with sweet saliva from chewing the gum, and I had to stop chewing and swallow the sugary water. I sat in the chair and watched people. I didn't know exactly what a library was, but I knew I had to be quiet." She nodded. "I waited for quite some time, but Mom didn't return. I was nervous, so I peeled another stick and chewed on it for ten, twenty minutes—until the sweetness wore off. In the end, Mom never returned." She felt she was listening to a pretty familiar story, and the familiarity of the plot made her feel a little jaded despite Hubae's misfortune. "Don't mothers usually abandon their children at the market or the train station? What kind of mother leaves her child at a library?" "I became anxious, so I started to blow bubbles. I blew bubbles, burst them—*pop*! I practiced being stunned. I was preparing myself in case something shocking was about to happen. Chewing the third stick, I wandered into the stacks. Since the library is a quiet place, I figured maybe Mom fell asleep somewhere. I looked for my mom. The shelves all looked the same to me, so I didn't know where I was going, but precisely because the place seemed like a maze to me, I was convinced I would find her there. I popped the fourth stick in my mouth because I was beginning to choke up. You can't say for certain that it's over until you've chewed the entire pack, you know? It makes sense, doesn't it? Mom wouldn't have left me with a whole pack of gum if she'd planned to come back before I was done chewing them all, now would she?" She nodded uneasily. "What was taking so long? How many books was Mom borrowing? The library was frightfully quiet. I peeled off the fifth stick of gum. The crumpling sound of the gum wrapper was overpowered by the sound of pages turning. I rolled the piece of gum covered in powdered sugar, and popped it in my mouth. Mom wasn't there. My heart was breaking, but I couldn't cry out loud. If I cried at the library, it would have been the loudest cry in the world." She listened intently. "In the end, Mom did not return." Hubae looked into her face. "This is the last piece of gum." Then Hubae pushed the box toward her and carefully opened the lid. Entranced, she leaned in to look inside the box. A flat piece of ginseng gum lay neatly in there. She felt like her heart had stopped beating. "Really?" "What?" asked Hubae. "Uh, nothing." Silence hung between the two as they sat face to face, staring at a piece of gum. She looked at the ginseng gum lying gracefully on the velvet lining of the box. The wrapper had turned soggy and discolored. Despite the ginseng content, the stick of gum looked like it would be toxic. What Hubae did next shocked her. Hubae took the piece of gum and ripped it in half without hesitation. "Wha, what are you doing?" she asked in shock. "This is for you," said Hubae. She turned blue. Like a person trying to dissuade a deserter, she pleaded, ***Don't***! Hubae beamed and said, "It's okay."

"What's . . . okay?"

The torn, exposed part of the gum trembled. "It's just gum," said Hubae. "Thank you, Ŏnni." She was bewildered. Everything seemed like a lie and the truth at the same time. Hubae's very existence seemed fake to her. Is she pulling my leg? Hubae probably has over a hundred packs of old ginseng gum in her closet of lies at home. Do they even make ginseng gum these days? The important thing was, apart from whether it was true, the story moved her. She refused many times before finally giving in and taking the half stick of gum. She put it in her receipt drawer on the dresser. 'It's just gum, and I can always give it back when Hubae leaves,' she thought. Anyway, of all the things that happened that night, there is one she cannot forget to this day: the conclusion of Hubae's story. It might have been those words that convinced her to live with Hubae. Hubae resumed speaking in her beautiful voice. "To this day, whenever I think of my mother who disappeared, or when I have to part with people I loved very much"—"Uh-huh," she reacted helplessly, the gum foisted on her. "When I look back on all those heartbreaking separations, the people I left, the ones who left me"—"Uh-huh." Hubae said with the most infinitely lucid expression on her face, "My mouth waters."

The bus departs. Cold air rushes out of dozens of tiny air conditioning vents. ***It's cold***. Also, ***I'm depressed***. She's not sure if it's the period, the cold, having company Sports Day on a national holiday, or the department head. The combination of the air conditioner and the smell of the bus makes her carsick. Looking out the window, she goes over the 'vertex dance' steps in her head. One, two, three, turn. One, two, three, step forward. When she practiced the steps in their tiny studio, Hubae doubled over with laughter. "Ŏnni! What?" Hubae cried, pale from laughing, "You can't dance!" The weather is fine, and a few tired teachers are snoring. The department head is seated in the front, sharing energy drinks with the team leader. They are determined to validate the existence of the Korean department today, as the general consensus about the hagwŏn is that the Korean department "doesn't do much" compared to the Math and English departments. Across the aisle, hagwŏn bus drivers are talking amongst themselves. It'll be another hour's drive. **Should I nap**? Sniffle. More phlegm. This is just great.

The morning after the night Hubae stayed over, she dressed and got ready for work, tiptoeing around. Hubae lay sleeping like a dead person. She watched Hubae for a long while before leaving the apartment. There was nothing more cruel than to wake someone and kick them out. She taught absentmindedly, attended a meeting, and returned home. When she opened the door, she found Hubae sitting matter-of-factly in the middle of the apartment with her packed bag. The apartment was pristine. Hubae seemed like a package, ready to be delivered anywhere.

"You'd already left. I wanted to say goodbye."

Still standing by the door, she nodded awkwardly. She didn't know what to do next. So . . . do I say goodbye now?—*Take care, I'll see you around.* Should I ask if she has enough money to get to wherever she's going? Without meaning to, she blurted, "Have a glass of wine before you go."

It must have been around then that it occurred to her to live with Hubae. That night, she emptied a whole bottle of wine and passed out before Hubae could leave. She woke up the next morning with a terrible flu. Hubae felt her forehead with her cool hand, called in sick for her, and quietly made soup. She peered at Hubae's busy movements from under the covers. Loopy from the cold medication, she told Hubae to stay until she found a place to settle down. Hubae said nothing as she sliced kimchi. That was three months ago. Hubae stayed at her place, passing the time cleaning the house while she was at work, to the point where it was unrecognizable, while downloading movies or American TV shows she might enjoy. Hubae organized the files like daintily folded towels, or put chrysanthemums in tall glasses, and also continued to look for work. She toted up sensible reasons to live with Hubae. Since Hubae was looking for work, it would be nice if she could chip in and pay half the rent. Hubae would feel more comfortable that way, and she'd be able to save on rent. Later, when she mentioned her plan in passing, Hubae asked hesitantly, "Would it be all right with you?"

Would it be 'all right' with me? What did she mean by that? The speech of the chairman of the board of trustees rang through the sky. Would it be all right with me? Wasn't that Hubae's way of pretending to be considerate when Hubae was really passing the responsibility off to me? Four canopies stand facing each other in the athletic field. The judges' tent is in the middle, and the others are all for cheering squads. The expressionless administrators sit under the shade in the judges' tent. She vows to stop thinking about Hubae. The emcee announces the raffle prizes: a kimchi refrigerator, a bicycle, an MP3 player, a soccer ball, and others. The field is stirring with excitement. The soundtrack for the National Warm-up Exercises blares through the speakers. Everyone awkwardly starts the marching motion. The music is accompanied by the demanding, "One! Two! Three! Four!" and the aggressive instructions, "Hamstrings! Deep Breath!" She's been familiar with the National Warm-up Exercises song since kindergarten. The song had a strangely exhilarating, refreshing, and then sobering effect on her. But today, she can't get over the hilarity of making rowing gestures with her arms to the most dramatic tune in the world as the man in the recording exclaims, "Whole Body!" The music ends, and waves of people sort themselves by color. There are five colors—red, orange, yellow, green, blue. One for each department. She is impressed by the size of her company. 'It's a lot larger than I thought!' The preliminary soccer games are in the large athletic field, and the three-legged race and kickball are in the small athletic field. The cheering squads divide into two or three groups and settle down behind the lineup. She sits by the soccer field with white inflated tubes in both hands. Male teachers from the Korean and Math departments stand in two rows and bow. The cheering squad on the other side cheers, and the Korean department cheers in response. She keeps sniffling as she makes clapping noises with the plastic tubes. The whistle blows, and the game begins. Light-footed young men spread out all over the field under the bright summer sky. ***Win***!

Hubae lived at her house. No one said until when, and it seemed unnecessary. She assumed Hubae would leave when she was ready to return to school, or had saved up enough money. They divided the chores, and saved on living expenses. She worked late every day except during school vacations. She would always text Hubae, "Should I pick something up on the way home?" or "Want anything?" The two sat on the floor and ate *Ttŏkpokki*, talked about their day, and divided up the bills.[3] Sometimes they would huddle in front of the laptop for a movie. She thought the best part about living with another person was eating together. The very fact that there was someone else eating with her made her feel like a normal human being, and the meal suddenly seemed to change from just another meal to the honoring of an ancient tradition.

The alarm was set and shut off several times as tiring, mundane days passed. Hubae's voice was still wonderful, but she didn't tell stories as often as she once did. They started falling into

---

3. *Ttŏkpokki*: spicy rice cake stir-fry.

patterns—patterns of life, relationship, and even the expectation of following patterns. This began around the time she first started coming home from work and standing at the front door thinking, 'I wish Hubae weren't in there.' She thought she knew Hubae pretty well, based on a list of her few bad habits. Like a reader waiting eagerly for the protagonist to die, she held her breath, waiting for Hubae to screw up. Of course, she didn't realize she was doing this. She rejoiced—*I knew it!*—every time she found a new flaw. Hubae often splashes water on the toilet seat. She doesn't use beauty products sparingly. She forgets to take the non-machine-washables out of the washing machine. She edits on the futon and leaves ink marks all over the place. She slams the door. She's too fond of tabloids. She stays on the phone too long and never uses the same towel twice. She dresses like she's twelve. Despite dressing like she's twelve, she criticizes my taste. She doesn't dry her feet completely on the bathmat and walks all over the futon with her wet feet. She began to dislike Hubae's habits. At first, she pointed them out nicely. Hubae admitted to her flaws sheepishly, but did not change. That was something she could not understand. She could not comprehend how Hubae could simply forget to change what she pointed out many times. Of course, she knew that there were things about her that Hubae might not like, but she honestly did not think that she herself made many mistakes. She started to dislike other things about Hubae as well. Hubae doesn't drink enough water. She holds her chopsticks funny. She has a corn on her foot that looks uglier each time I see it. Her face is too oily in the morning. She doesn't eat her vegetables. She prefers undercooked rice. There's something wrong with her. Is it because she doesn't drink enough water, doesn't eat her vegetables, and has an ugly corn on her toe? She started snapping at Hubae without meaning to. Hubae apologized and repeated the same mistakes. The worst thing, however, was the inkling that Hubae was copying her. It started with the way she dressed. Hubae made fun of the way she dressed, but started buying clothes similar to hers. She didn't think much of it at first, although she did sometimes pettily think that Hubae should be saving the money she was spending on clothes. Like any high-spirited young girl, Hubae was interested in clothes. Then Hubae started to parrot her way of speaking. Language belongs to no one; words are contagious and shared, but when one of her pet words or jokes popped out of Hubae's mouth, she felt robbed. She also disliked the fact that Hubae used her computer all day long. It seemed Hubae was leafing through the bookmarked sites she had spent so much time and energy organizing. She was particularly disturbed when Hubae looked through the music, movie, book, and philosophy sites that she had organized specially, and started talking about them as if they were her own finds. Hubae, who doesn't know much about music, picked a song by her favorite band as the background music for Hubae's website. Hubae joined a wine club and studied the history and types of wine. Hubae learned more about wine than she ever knew. When Hubae received her first paycheck from the hagwŏn, she bought her a bottle of wine with it. That night, when she came home to find the beaming Hubae and the late-night snack of wine and imported cheese Hubae had prepared for her, she was astonished. ***You drink wine*?** she asked.

Her department lost the soccer match two to nothing. She has been distracted all day. It might be the cold, the period, or the department head. The cheering squad is heading toward the small athletic field where women's dodgeball is starting soon. Women's dodgeball is known to be the most competitive and frightening of all Sports Day competitions. The Korean department in orange shirts is playing against the English department in green. The Korean department cheering squad leader tries to intimidate the other team by cheering loudly. "Go go Korean! Nice play, Korean!" Others follow his lead. She chimes in as well. The English department's cheering team leader shouts, "Oh, victory English! Oh, victory English! Oh victory English! Oh oh oh oh oh!

Ole ole ole!" Their booming voices take over the athletic field. A teacher from the Korean department rags on Yun Do-hyŏn more than audibly.[4] Yun To-hyŏn has nothing to do with the English department, but a few people from it look visibly annoyed. The ball starts to fly—*whizz! whizz!*—as soon as the whistle blows. The players rush this way and that on the court as they run from the trajectory of the ball. Gasps and cries of anguish come from both cheering squads. Deep down, she is also anxious for her team. Someone says, "Whoops," and one person is down. She's wearing a green shirt. The Korean department roars. She's genuinely happy as she claps the plastic tubes together. At first, she just wanted the day to be over, but she now finds herself wishing her department would win. Then the third-rate players bite the dust. The offense sniffs out these terrified players who don't know what they're doing, and "kills" them—*whack*!—with such vengeance that she feels sorry for them. A Korean teacher takes a hard blow to her lower abdomen and is out. The English department cheering squad shrieks. The Korean department cheering squad falls silent. Hearts sink with every move. The strongest players gradually take over the game. They duck with such grace and catch the ball with amazing speed to save their teammates. One teacher from the English department catches everyone's attention as she attacks, jumps, and rolls out of the way. For the moment, no one cares what kind of person she is—she's the English department hero right now. The Korean department cheering squad leader urges them on: "Korean team, P'ait'ing!"[5] The English department cheering squad leader scoffs in response, "Cheer up, English team!" The English department teachers cry, "Cheer up!" in unison. The inimitable pronunciation of "r" washes over the Korean department like a tidal wave. Things get ugly. When someone from the English department sprains

---

4. Yun To-hyŏn: Korean singer who sang "Oh, Victory Korea," which is parodied here.

5. "P'ait'ing!" is one of two ways Koreans often pronounce the English word, "fighting." Similar in meaning to "chin up" or "hang in there," the term is often exclaimed to convey messages of encouragement.

50

a finger, the English department jeers at the opposing team. An English department teacher, whacked squarely in the head, says, "FUCK!" as she leaves the court. Soon, both teams abandon civility altogether. "What the *hell* was that?" "Go ahead! Stand *inside* line!" "Learn the rules!" The insults are direct and meant to be heard by the opposing team. Judgment dispute. Indignant uproar. The ball ricocheted. That's cheating. That doesn't count. That teacher was hit, and she's not leaving. Throw her out. Mrs. Hong, the eldest among Korean department teachers and a mother of two children in junior high, shrieks at the referee through tears, "BITCH STEPPED ON THE LINE! THROW HER OUT!" the veins on her neck popping. Her hostility toward the English department begins to escalate. She vows to cheer in the future for all teams playing against the English department. The Korean department loses two to one. Unlike the English department people who are moving on to the next location in high spirits, the Korean department people depart in an atmosphere of tragedy. One of the teachers bursts into tears. Her cramps are back.

The afternoon games are generally finals. The athletes are rundown compared to this morning. Mr. Ch'oe complains about a blister he got playing tug-of-war. The cheering squads have turned a little tepid. She's getting ready for the relay. Although the Korean department's not doing so well, the relay earns the greatest number of points of all the games, so the tables may turn. Washing her hands at the fountain, she spots a few people in green—the color of the English department. They bother her. A few Social Studies people are on the other side of the fountain. Social Studies is so far behind she doesn't need to worry about them. She begins to perceive people by their color. The department head comes up to her as she is tying her shoes. He makes a fist to wish her luck before he disappears again.

The gun goes off. Runners dash. The empty center of the athletic field is swollen with energy pouring forth from the stands. The barely perceptible gaps between the runners widen. She becomes anxious as she watches the race. The Korean department goes from first to second to third. She's the last runner. The seventh runners take the baton and bolt toward the last runners. She bends down and gets ready. The Math runner passes her by like the wind. The Korean runner is getting closer. She is crouched with her back toward the approaching runner. Without looking, she snatches the baton the moment she feels it land on her fingers, and races down the track. She is surprised by her own speed. The source of this energy is unknown to her. She runs with all her might. She runs as though her life depends on it, like all the times she ran full speed toward the subway station to catch the last train. People in the stands lean in. She beats the Science teacher. Tension rises in the cheering squad tents. She desperately tries to catch up with the Math teacher who is in the lead. The gap is closing. All spectators are now on their feet. There are less than twenty meters left to the finish line. The gun goes off, and she comes in second. She's sweating through every pore on her body, and her heart is on the brink of exploding. Far off in the distance, she spots the Korean department head slapping his knees and sinking back into his seat. *I'm thirsty*.

Subway Line Five. She sits in the rumbling subway car. Her face is ashen as she holds a set of plastic containers with both arms. She got it for showing up on Sports Day. Other passengers glance over at her. She has no energy for embarrassment now. She tries not to fall asleep as she looks back on her day. The Korean department came in third out of five teams. Not embarrassing but nothing to boast about. She managed to remember all the steps of the 'vertex dance.' Considering the blood, sweat, and tears that went into the rehearsals, the audience response was polite at most. There was nothing sensational or stunning about the 'vertex dance.' Its only redeeming quality was that it's relatively easy to choreograph for a large number of people. The Social Studies department's 'sexy dance' received the most enthusiastic response. One of the departments sang an ode to their department head in the middle of the talent show, which prompted another department to do the same, which resulted in a string of not-very-heartfelt odes to department heads, one more tiresome than the next. After the talent show, when she was about to let the promise of imminent repose sink in, one of the hagwŏn bus drivers suddenly hopped up on stage and seized the microphone. It was right after the host asked, "Any last volunteers?" The atmosphere instantly became unspeakably awkward, but no one could jeer or stop him. The bus driver was, after all, a part of this hagwŏn and had every right to have his fill of fun on company Sports Day. But when he sang the national go-to song, the insipid "Southbound Train," people felt strangely uncomfortable. A few inebriated bus drivers off to the side were his only fans. The odd thing is, the situation reminded her of Hubae. The moment the bus driver climbed onto the stage, she thought, 'I want to stop living with Hubae.' If Hubae were to ask why, she couldn't very well say, 'Because you hold the chopsticks funny and you don't eat your vegetables,' but perhaps that was it. But she knows she isn't capable of uttering those words. She'll probably frown secretly, as she did the day before and the day before that, and never make it beyond telling on Hubae to the cataloger within herself who kept track of all of Hubae's foibles. She doesn't dislike Hubae. It's possible that the discomfort she feels around Hubae is a habit. She closes her eyes with her arms around the plastic container set. Her day in the sunshine has burned her nose red. When she thought it was over, the bus driver decided to sing. When she got her hopes up again, there was the company dinner, and when she thought there couldn't possibly be anything else left, they had to go out for drinks. All she wants now is to get home, throw herself on her fluffy bedding, and fall asleep.

She opens the door to her apartment. Light pours out from inside. Hubae is lying on the futon grading papers. Hubae turns to greet her. "You're home!" She unloads the plastic container set. "Whoa, did you win that?" She replies halfheartedly, "No, everyone who showed up got one." Hubae is delighted that now they'll have enough containers for all the side dishes. She glances over at the essays. "Are you still at it?" Hubae grins and answers proudly, "I'm almost done. The topic for this week is diversity. All the kids uniformly said that diversity is good and uniformity is bad. Isn't that hilarious?" She snatches the essay Hubae has extended toward her. "Look here." Hubae is alarmed. She quickly scans the essay. Hubae has corrected "for exemple" to "for example." She feels more rotten than before. "What's the matter?" Hubae asks. She replies, "Here." "Where?" "This here is wrong." Hubae studies the essay innocuously. She doesn't seem to know what she did wrong. "I know we only pay 1000 *wŏn* per page, but the trust we lose when we make these mistakes is worth a hundred times more than that." Hubae falls silent. She adds, "You should have asked if you didn't know." Hubae chews her lips. She feels dreadful about herself. She feels she has wronged Hubae, and the feeling upsets her even more. Awkward silence. Hubae finally says, "I'm sorry. I'll be more careful next time." She tries to figure out how she should tell Hubae that she's been fired. "Have you eaten?" "No, I just got up." "Why don't you eat something?" she says. "I'm going to jump in the shower. We'll talk when I get out." She goes to a corner of the room to change. She watches Hubae put away the essays. Her pupils dilate. She yells without meaning to, ***Are you having your period***? Hubae is puzzled as she asks, "Excuse me?" There is a coin-sized stain on her beige shorts. She quickly checks the bedspread. There is blood on the covers, too. She asks again, "Are you having your period?" Hubae gawkily checks her own buttocks and then emphatically defends herself as though she'd just been accused of committing a heinous crime. "I'm not due yet. This is weird. There's no way . . ." Hubae doesn't know what to do with herself. She reprimands her. "How could you lie there all this time and not know?" Hubae quickly picks up the covers and says, "I didn't know. I'll put this in the washer." "Why don't you go wash up?" She isn't happy with the way the Hubae is behaving. Hubae is treating her like a guest in her own house, and she's sick and tired of having to be the disciplinarian walking on eggshells. Like a student cast in the role of the bad guy because she was late on casting day, she doesn't give a damn about the play or whatever anymore. She wants to quit. Without her realizing it, the words slip out: "That's it." Hubae's eyes tremble. She can see all the stages of loss—premonition, resignation, and everything in between—flash through Hubae's eyes in an instant. It appears that Hubae has been well trained for this sort of thing. She can't think of what to say next. Hubae stands there, a large stain on her butt, looking at the floor. She explains, "It's just that I don't feel well and it's making me oversensitive. But I've thought this for some time now. I think it is best for us to not be together anymore. Let's take our time and settle things by the end of the month." Silence ensues. Hubae makes an effort to smile and breaks the silence at last, "Okay." She looks at Hubae who adds, "I agree with you. Don't feel bad, Ŏnni." She doesn't respond. 'Why is she telling me not to feel bad when I haven't apologized?' Hubae goes into the bathroom, holding a change of clothes in one hand and covering her butt with the other. She undresses absentmindedly. She can just see all the unpleasant times she'll have to endure until the end of the month. But once the hard part is over, she'll have her comfortable routine back. She can't wait to be lonely. She wants to spend weekends and holidays surfing the Internet or watching movies in her fluffy solitude, wearing whatever, getting up whenever, and eating whatever. When the occasional guest comes, she'll throw a feast for them. Corks will pop. It dawns on her that she hasn't been able to do that in a while. Hubae comes out of the bathroom. She goes into the bathroom to avoid the situation. Hubae will tidy up the room and have a late-night snack while she's in the shower. Should I take her out for beer? We might be able to ease the tension over fried chicken and meaningless banter. She turns the faucet. Hot water comes pouring over her. She thinks, 'These are the moments I'm grateful for my job: moments when I feel a relief, somewhat similar to fear, that I am satisfying conditions that make it possible for me to pay the water bill and enjoy its physical manifestation in the shower. Conditions that allow me to buy fancy bath soap, and feel refreshed.' Moments when she believes she has control over these matters. She soaps every inch of her body and scalds herself under the shower as she looks back on her long day full of incidents, not all of them pleasant. The important thing is that the day is over. The uneasy times with Hubae, too, will soon pass. She thoroughly washes the dirt out of her bellybutton and ear. Her hair whirls over the drain with Hubae's hair. The shower softens both her body and heart. She promises herself she'll be as nice to Hubae as possible until she leaves. She comes out of the bathroom with a towel wrapped around her body. She looks around as she wipes her feet on the bathmat. Something's off. An age-old forlornness sits right in the middle of the room like a guest. The futon is neatly folded and put aside. The bedspread has been taken off the futon. She looks around the room. Hubae's bag is missing from under the hanger where it always is. Hubae is gone.

It's late at night. There she lies on the futon holding her forehead with her hand as small as a maple leaf. Her phone alarm is set and placed by her head. The still, cozy darkness surrounding her seems to have been there for ages. It fits her body perfectly. She twists. She feels stiff all over. She put in a tampon earlier, so she'll sleep well tonight without worrying about possible leakage. She is reminded of Hubae who flinched at the very mention of tampons, enumerating their harmful effects on the body. She sniffles. She must be coming down with a cold. *I'm tired*. She lies neatly on the futon and breathes rhythmically. A good amount of time passes. Sleep won't come. She tries to fall asleep. She fears she will be faced with several times as many hesitations tomorrow morning as she was this morning. The more she encourages herself to fall asleep,

the more awake she becomes. Resigned, she gets up and powers
up the laptop. It would be a much better use of time to watch a
TV show than to struggle to fall asleep or torment herself with
over-thinking. She puts her laptop on the floor and opens a folder
saved on the hard disk. Video files of an American TV show she's
been watching lately come up with Korean subtitle files. Hubae
downloaded them. She opens the last file that says "Episode 24."
She plays the beginning. She's seen it already. She knows that
episode 25 is the last of the season. The episode was probably
uploaded on the site some time this morning. She can't decide. A
part of her believes downloading a new episode is too much work,
while another part of her really wants to see it. She badly wishes
to witness the end of a captivating story that doesn't dwell in the
present but runs headlong into the future—on to the next. She
logs onto the website where she finds downloadable video files.
She searches under "Episode 25," finds the file, and lightly clicks
on it. The download will be over in less than ten minutes. She lies
neatly on the futon again. The open laptop near her head emits
blue tides of light. Bytes, like innumerable dots of stories, fly along
electric fields like thousands of butterflies flying through a long
pipe from afar, and softly land on her computer. She lies as still
as the dead, waiting for the conclusion of the story to pile quietly
over the crown of her head. Suddenly, she remembers something.
She doesn't know why she all of a sudden remembered something
she'd forgotten for months. She gets up, walks toward the dresser
and opens the receipt drawer. She finds the half stick of ginseng
gum buried dolefully among motley receipts. She carefully picks up
the gum. She unwraps the paper and peels off the foil stuck to the
soggy gum. The gum sags wearily like flesh. She takes the gum to
her nose. The barely persistent trace of ginseng is caught by one of
her olfactory cells. The ginseng smells as deep and faraway as dust.
She pops the gum in her mouth without thinking twice. "My God,"
she murmurs, surprised. "It's still sweet." Her face is expressionless
as she lies back down, slowly chewing. The bittersweet taste of

ginseng fills her mouth with saliva. The taste ebbs and flows. She is curled up in a ball as she gnaws on the gum and waits for "download complete" until the sugar is all gone. It could be the dim light from the computer or the bitter taste of the ginseng that creates a rather curious expression on her face, which suggests she may or may not be sad. It is the dead of night, the alarm has not yet rung, nor is there any chance that it will.

Mouthwatering
by *Kim Aeran*

Pit-a-pat, My Life

by Kim Aeran

Translated by Jeon Seung-hee

When the wind blows, vocabulary cards gently flutter in my mind. Like fish drying in the sea breeze for a long time, they have been expanding outwards while shrinking in size. I think of the words that I pronounced for the first time as a child. This is snow. That is night. Over there is a tree. Under my feet is the earth. You are you . . . I first learned how to pronounce the names of everything around me and then copied their spellings over and over again. Even now, I am often amazed that I know the names of all those things.

When I was young, I picked up words all day long. I pestered everyone around me with my prattling, "What's this, Mom? What's that?" Each name was so clean and buoyant that it didn't stick to the thing it named. I kept on asking the names I had already learned the previous day and the day before that, as if asking for the first time. Whenever I lifted my finger and pointed to something, bits of print with strange sounds would fall, one by one. Like a wind-chime that swings in the breeze, something moved whenever I asked. That's why I liked the phrase, "What's this?" I liked that phrase more than the names I learned.

Rain is rain. Day is day. Summer is summer . . . I learned many words in my life. There were words that were used often, and words that were used not so often. There were those that took root in the earth, and those that scattered like the seeds of plants. When I called summer summer, I felt as if I could own it. Confident in this belief, I kept on asking. Earth, tree, and even you . . . This, that, and it overlapped and moved according to the breath in my mouth. When I pronounced 'it,' concentric circles spread out with the sound—sometimes I felt as if that width was the size of my world.

By now I know almost all the words I need to know to live. What's important is to gauge the area that words create while reducing their volume. To imagine a thousand directions of the wind instead of the four cardinal points when one says "wind"; to follow the shadow of the cross, growing longer as the sun is setting, when one says "betrayal"; and to fathom the depth of snow concealing the crevasse when one calls "you." This last, however, is one of the hardest things in the world, for the wind keeps on blowing, and I have never been young since I was born. Neither have the words.

The place where I first got mixed up with words was a village in the countryside, where the mountains were deep and the water clear. I learned my name and started toddling around the village, where a stream divided into several whirling branches. It took me three years to grow from a prattling baby to a child who could form a simple sentence, exactly how long my parents sponged off my mother's family. Most people in that village grew or made what they needed. That's probably why I learned mostly vivid words related to everyday life. I heard that the first word my cousin, who grew up watching TV every day, uttered was "LG." I worried my parents because I was slow to learn how to speak. Concerned that something was wrong with me, my mother asked other adults for their opinions. Father went to work in silence, saying that babies were prettiest when they couldn't speak. The foundations were just beginning to be laid for the Taeho Resort Complex in a nearby village, and Father was working at the construction site as a day laborer. My maternal grandfather, who was pretty quick with figures, built a house in front of his vegetable garden for the laborers who had rushed to this village from elsewhere. It was pretty drafty, with concrete walls and a slate roof. Four families could fit in that small, straight house. My family lived in one of the four units. A teenage couple that still looked like kids and a newborn baby were my family. Although the place was absurdly small for a family of three and its kitchen wasn't the best, they lived there without complaint, because they didn't have to pay rent or living expenses.

My grandparents had many children—six altogether: five sons and a daughter. Once I asked, "Mom, how did Grandmother end up with so many children? I heard that grandmother and grandfather didn't get along very well." Mother answered, embarrassingly, "That's right. I was wondering about it myself and once asked my mother. Well . . . She said that they did it very rarely, but she got pregnant every time." Mother was the sixth of six children. I heard that her childhood nickname was "Fuck Princess." She got this nickname because, growing up among foul-mouthed boys, she cursed at the slightest provocation, something people didn't expect from such a pretty face. I feel very close to Mother when I imagine that little girl going around the village, cursing precociously. It seems that her tongue has become gentler since she realized that she couldn't solve much by saying, "Fuck." Of course she still has a violent temper. Anyway, she had to realize it when she was expelled from school for getting pregnant, when Father was about to be beaten to death by her five brothers, when she had to silently endure the pickiness and ruckus in the restaurant, and when she had to stare at the medical bill—a problem she couldn't solve no matter how hard she tried.

Grandfather didn't like his son-in-law from the beginning. The biggest reason was that the "son-of-a-bitch who was still wet behind the ears" had made another "son-of-a-bitch who was really wet behind the ears." The second biggest reason was that Father, the head of the household, had no way to make a living. This was expected, though, given that he was only seventeen and still a student. When the two men met for the first time, Grandfather abruptly and rudely asked Father,

"So, what are you good at?"

This was after the whole storm of cries and skirmishes that had overtaken the family after the discovery of Mother's pregnancy had ended. Father answered, on his knees and completely embarrassed,

"Father, I am good at Taekwondo."

Grandfather groaned, dissatisfied. Although Father had gotten special admission to the biggest athletic high school in the province, such a talent was not very useful in life. Without a clue about what was going through Grandfather's mind and uneasy with Grandfather's silence, Father added,

"May I show you?"

He clenched his fists. It was a scene that could easily have been misunderstood, because it looked as if he was about to punch his father-in-law. After wincing in spite of himself, Grandfather calmly continued,

"I suppose rice comes out of your fists?"

"Well, after I graduate, I could find a job at a small studio . . ."

Father answered, although he knew that he had no chance of going back to school. Even though Grandfather hadn't expected a decent answer in the first place, he asked again as if giving him another chance.

"What else are you good at?"

Many thoughts passed through Father's mind.

'I am good at "Street Fighter," but . . .'

If he actually said that, he might have been smacked in the face.

'I am good at talking back to teachers . . .'

That didn't seem like an answer that would sit well with his father-in-law either.

'Then . . . what am I really good at?'

After agonizing like this, Father ended up saying to his father-in-law who was glaring at him,

"I don't know, Father."

Then immediately he realized,

'Ah! I'm good at giving up!'

After his son-in-law left, Grandfather said, sarcastically,

"He's good at nothing but breeding."

Unafraid of her husband, now that she was old, Grandmother grumbled,

"That's a talent as well."

With hair in the sesame-leaf style, Mother sat silently, assuming a prim air. Grandfather looked far away, as if more disappointed at his daughter's taste in men than her conduct.

"A man should know at least how to bluff, if he doesn't have money. He looks like such a simpleton . . ."

Grandfather was completely mistaken about this, however. Father was a simpleton, but a reckless and adventurous simpleton, i.e. the most dangerous kind of simpleton. That's why he squabbled with the officiant at his wedding and abandoned his wife like the bride in "The Myth of Chilmajae"[1] on her wedding day. That was also probably why, when I needed to know what our family motto was for a homework assignment, he calmly told me it was "Pung-u-yu-sin," even though he had failed in so many business ventures because he trusted his friends. He had this motto, which meant that trust should prevail between friends, framed and hung. He brought this framed calligraphy back from his trip to Pulguksa Temple. He had an old calligrapher in a souvenir shop write it out. Mother often made fun of this motto after condensing it into two syllables. People might have clucked their tongues, blaming her for treating her husband too contemptuously. This was a very natural deed, though, for a

---

1. "The Myth of Chilmajae" is the title of a poem by Sô Jông-ju, the renowned modern Korean poet.

woman who thought 'Pu-ja-yu-ch'in' meant 'One should always be on good terms with his rich (Pu-ja) friend.'[2]

Grandfather told Father to first finish his high school education. His advice to Father was to transfer to another high school which lacked students in order to get his diploma, as it was clear that Father would be expelled from the athletic high school. Grandfather told him that he would talk to the principal himself. No school was willing to admit Father, though, in such a small place where rumors traveled fast. They said that admitting him would ruin the school's reputation and discipline. Grandfather's pride as an influential man in the village crumbled in an instant. As there was no other option, Grandfather pushed Father to the construction site, maintaining that a man should go to work every day. He meant to teach his son-in-law that he should learn responsibility as the head of a household and how hard it was to make a living in this world. It wasn't a well thought-out suggestion, though, but a decision based on his wish to punish the rascal who had messed around with his daughter. Grandfather also didn't forget to preach to his son-in-law that he should prepare for the GED in his spare time, working during the day and studying at night. As Father was from a poor family, he lived with his wife's family, following Grandfather's advice. As the local self-government became active, people in the county were trying to turn the entire area into a resort under the banner of 'Taeho, an Entertainment City.' The most important project of this enterprise was to build a sort of natural amusement park, in which people could go sightseeing on a boat. In the long run, several villages, including my parents' home village, were going to disappear under water. Father went to work at the construction site with the migrant laborers living next door. People made fun of and adored him, calling him

2. 'Pu-ja-yu-ch'in' means 'there should be affection between parents and children.' 'Pu-ja' here is a homonym for another word that means 'a rich person.' 'Pu-ja-yu-ch'in' and 'Pung-u-yu-sin' are two of the five moral rules that should govern human relations in the Confucian system.

"Mr. Han." He got this name not because of what he did ('han'), but because his last name was Han. Village elders comforted him, patting his shoulder and saying, "It's ok. In our village, you're an adult once you get married." They also giggled, saying, "The Ch'oe family got a son-in-law for free." At first, Father was satisfied with his work at the construction site. The melodious and energetic conversations of other workers were refreshing and he could save face in front of his wife's family. He also liked that he could work off his raging teenage energy there. This felt better than sports, where he would get beaten every day, which made him want to quit. While he was working side by side with adults as their equal in a tough field, he felt like climbing a nearby hill and roaring, "This is the real world!" However, it took less than three days for him to realize how hard manual labor was, especially the extremely difficult and overwhelming physical labor one did for a living.

Father heard the news of Mother's pregnancy in a coffee shop downtown. It was a café, whose main customers were middle and high school students, near the inter-city bus terminal. Mother went on several blind dates there. A biker from the farming high school whom she met on a blind date came to her schoolyard one day and circled around it five times, getting her into huge trouble at school. The boy disappeared, kicking up a cloud of dust with a roar, after shouting "I love you, Mira!" three times while doing wheelies on his motorcycle. No doubt all the Miras in the school—Kim Mira, Pak Mira, Ch'oe Mira, etc.—were summoned one by one to the teacher's room. A blind date routinely ended up in the Karaoke Room. Mother observed with curiosity how boys who were timid and silent in the café became rather bold in the karaoke place. Students from farming or technical high schools would abruptly push aside the table and dance violently to the music of Sô Taeji or Deuce. The dark and musty karaoke room echoed with lyrics like "Time could never stop, Yo!" and "I have to be brave now in order to win you over." Girls silently put the microphone down on the table after singing the female part of a duet. Then a boy who liked the girl picked up the microphone and continued to sing the male part of the song. Boys were struck first by Mother's face and then by her singing voice. Often, when Mother put down her microphone, many hands rushed to take it. Not many boys from that village with five high schools including vocational schools captivated Mother. Boys from the farming or technical schools looked more liberal and magnanimous than those from liberal arts high schools. But the enigmatic pride of the boys from liberal arts schools was attractive as well. Father was the first athletic school student Mother met. She didn't meet him on a blind date, but in a very unexpected place. At any rate, Mother thought that Father seemed to have the characteristics of boys from both liberal arts and vocational schools. He had the pride of someone whose talent had been recognized, as well as the inferiority complex and simplicity of someone talented for sports.

The café wasn't very crowded. Both Mother and Father weren't wearing their school uniforms. Father had been wondering for a while why Mother looked so triumphant. He was also anxious that Mother was going to propose breaking up again. Besides, he was rather uncomfortable being there. He couldn't understand why girls liked to linger over one drink for two hours in a café. Enduring the awkward air, Father looked at Mother. Maybe because he hadn't seen her in a while, Ch'oe Mira looked as if she had grown more mature in the meantime. Whenever Mother wet her lips with lemonade, Father licked his dry lips as well. Finally, Mother resolutely opened her mouth.

"Come closer, Taesu."

"Why?"

"Just do it."

Father leaned forward. Covering her mouth with her hand, Mother whispered in Father's ear. The soft, fine hair on Father's earlobe stood up. Not paying attention to Mother's words and feeling only the soft steam of her breath, Father grinned. Soon, however, he turned pale.

"Why do you tell me this just now?"

Everyone in the café turned around at once to look at him.

"Fuck, why are you yelling? The thing I hate most in the world is a yeller."

Angry, Mother yelled even more loudly than Father. Father, who had been severely punished in the teacher's room some months ago for writing "hobbies: compromise, special talent: compromise" on his school aptitude card, hurriedly apologized to his girlfriend.

"I'm so sorry."

Then the two put their seventeen-year-old heads together to find a solution to their problem. But there was no solution. A few arrogant and self-satisfied looking teenagers were chain-smoking near them. Fumbling the tiny parasol stuck in the parfait and casting his eyes down, Father mumbled,

"Mira, I . . ."

Then he began mumbling about what a lousy person he was—he could never become a good father, he was too poor, he was afraid that he would disappoint others, and he just remembered that his family had a history of a cancer—words without heads or tails, without logic. Mother silently listened to him, then opened her mouth and gently said,

"Taesu?"

"Yes?"

"I heard that there's an insect that camouflages itself as bird poop in order to avoid being eaten by a bird."

"So?"

"You sound exactly like that insect."

The village economy was enjoying a temporary boom like a patient who had gotten an expensive infusion of extra nutrients. Excavators, ladder trucks, concrete mixers, and regular trucks were incessantly coming and going in this sleepy town. Around that time, sets of school supplies were distributed to every classroom at Mother's school. The construction company gave the supplies in fresh-looking plastic bags as a gift to all students in the school. H Construction Company's adorable logo was inscribed on the body of a ballpoint pen, a bottle of correction fluid, Post-it's of various colors, and a container full of pencil lead. It seemed that the company distributed them to all the schools in the area that would be affected by the construction of the tourist resort. Detergents and kitchen utensils were distributed to adults in the village as well. Like all freebies, however, they seemed to be a part of some shady deal.

One day, a friend approached Mother and asked her cautiously,

"Mira, what's the matter with you?

Her name was Han Sumi. She was Mother's long-time best friend.

"What? What are you talking about?"

"Well, you lie on your face all the time these days. Besides, you are very quiet during evening study hall."

Sumi, the class president, had to make a list of students who were noisy during evening study hall. She smiled ambiguously. It wasn't clear whether she felt relieved or troubled because Mira was quiet during study hall.

"I'm just fine."

Mother avoided Sumi's eyes. Sumi, a quick-witted girl, lowered her head intimately.

"Cut the crap. Why don't you tell me?"

Mother pulled away, hands in her vest pockets, saying,

"What's the matter with you?"

"If you are going to hide something, then don't show it."

"What do you mean?"

"How could you do this? I always tell you my troubles."

Mother pooh-poohed.

"What? That you're sad because you fell from first place to

third in an exam? I'm really thankful for your sharing such a momentous secret."

Hurt, Han Sumi bit her lips.

"Hey, what do you know about the loneliness of third place?"

Mother answered in that characteristically gentle voice she has whenever she's sarcastic:

"Sumi?"

"Yes?"

"Get lost."

Despite this conversation, their relationship was 'Pung-u-yu-shin,' not unlike Father's with his friends. They not only went to the same elementary and middle schools but also ate lunch and went on blind dates together. After her 'first experience,' Mother attempted to tell Han Sumi everything. No matter how hard she tried, she couldn't help feeling out of this world, as if she had wound up floating ten centimeters above the earth overnight. Sitting in the back of her classroom, Mother looked down on her classmates, jiggling her leg out of habit. They were all preoccupied with solving problems in their workbooks, heads lowered. Suddenly, a sentence passed through Mother's mind.

'Would they know that I slept with a guy?'

Like two paints floating on water, guilt and superiority intermingled and blended to form a strange design in her heart. Although she had lost something important, she felt triumphant all the same. Or, she felt as if she were alone in that classroom, living in a different time than the others. It was very confusing. A few days later, Mother called Han Sumi over to the refuse incinerator area. She wanted to make a clean breast of it, and, besides, she felt obligated to share her secret with Sumi. But when Mother finally managed to muster the courage to pronounce Father's name, Han Sumi suddenly burst into tears. Then she began muttering things like "Did you see the report card?" "It's so hard these days," and "I don't want to live any longer with this kind of class rank."

Mother had to keep quiet. It was a natural thing for her to do, since Mother knew how persistent and unrelieved Sumi's anguish had been. As the people of H Construction Company came in droves from the city to this village, they brought changes into the classrooms as well. The most distinctive change was in student rank. As executives and employees of the construction company and their children flowed in, there were more transfer students in the village. Many of these transfer students had studied ahead of the curriculum since childhood. The school seemed to be glad of this change, as it meant a higher average score. However, overnight the village first became third in class and the village tenth became fifteenth. Of course, the village lasts were still last, but they weren't happy, either. Being last among 45 was different from being last among 50. Han Sumi, who had never slipped below first in class before, had her pride deeply hurt. They had often seen tragic dramas featuring gifted students from villages who went to the city. But the misfortune of a gifted student being humiliated just by staying in her own home village felt quite unjust. They hadn't gone to the city, but the city had penetrated into them. Mother was somewhat worried about her best friend's depression. Although she didn't say so, she was always proud of having someone like Sumi as her best friend. Han Sumi studied even harder after her drop in class rank. However, strangely, even though her scores went up, her rank remained the same on every exam. After repeatedly trying and being frustrated, both of them entered the only liberal arts high school in the village. During the entrance ceremony, the top student gave the "Student's Pledge." Han Sumi, who stood among numerous 'average' students, lowered her head and kept on rubbing the ground with her foot. A teacher she didn't know scolded her for her bad attitude. Adults were saying this was the first time ever that a student from outside had given the "Student's Pledge" since the school's founding forty years before."Mira!"

"What, now?"

"If you really don't want to tell me . . ."

"Uh-huh."

"You don't have to."

"..."

"Instead, I'll tell you the method I use whenever I'm stuck."

Mother answered, making a face, "You are a dead girl, if you say like you did before that doing one's best is the best. Ok?"

"Gees, no, bitch! I know well that doing-the-best thing. I'm an example of someone who got screwed up by doing my best. I am! Right?"

Mother said in a softened voice,

"You'll still keep on doing your best, won't you?"

Han Sumi secretively pointed to a member of the firing club with her chin.

"She doesn't smoke because it's good for her body, does she?"

Despite herself, Mother nodded silently, after blinking several times.

"Anyway, whenever I encounter a difficult problem, I divide my notebook page into two columns and make a chart. I write down the good and bad aspects of the problem one by one. After that, strangely, the solution shows up by itself. If you feel stuck, try it."

Father was sprawled on the floor of his room. It was only midday. There was a yellowed world atlas on the ceiling. Paternal grandfather had pasted it there with his own hands when Father entered elementary school to encourage Father to dream big. After the meeting at the café, Father still had no answer for Mother. He didn't feel confident enough to propose having the baby, but he didn't have the courage to suggest an abortion. Father wasn't sure which was the right choice. He couldn't imagine how his life or that of the unborn child would turn out. There was only one thing he could vaguely intuit, namely that the weight of life he would bear from then on would be enormous. To speak frankly, Father hoped that Mother would decide everything. Then he could simply embrace her and say, "That was what I wanted." And he would be free of blame his whole life. At any rate, the most urgent problem was money. Whether they gave up the baby or not, they would need money sooner or later. But where on earth could he get it?

'Maybe I could try delivering newspapers or chajang noodles?'

Whichever work he chose, it would be a whole month before he could get his hands on any money, unless he received payment in advance. Besides, Father didn't have a motorcycle license. The most realistic solution was to borrow money from somebody. But none of his friends had that much cash. There was that boy in his homeroom who wore Calvin Klein shorts, but he was known as a tightwad. Father became depressed because he didn't have anybody to rely on, because he had regrets—'I should have restrained myself just a little'—, because the scandal would spread all over the village, and also because he was starting to think he might not be as 'cool' a guy as he thought . . . . Father looked blankly at the ceiling and stared at the world atlas, which was completely wrinkled from moisture. Five oceans, six continents, and six billion people . . . . Some random facts that he came to know, thanks to the cramming method of teaching, passed through his mind. Father suddenly imagined the origin of the six billion people. Naturally, the six billion dates, six billion sexual desires, and six billion sexual intercourses came to his mind. Immediately, his nether regions bulged despite his will. They were gradually swelling and soon became so taut that he felt like he was about to burst. Father felt like crying at that moment. Because of his desire that had senselessly reared its head in the middle of this conundrum; because of his premonition that he might become the slave of this desire all his life; and because of the fact that the thought 'wouldn't it be ok to do it once in the midst of this complicated situation?' came to his mind.

At the same moment Mother lay on the floor of her room facing downward with a notebook in front of her. After chewing on a ballpoint pen for a while, she decisively drew a long vertical line down the middle of a notebook page. She decided to write disadvantages in the left column and advantages in the right. Mother began filling in the left column.

1. I'll get scolded by Father and Mother.
2. I'll get kicked out of school.
3. People will point fingers at me.
4. I don't have money.
5. I don't have the ability to make money.
6. I'll get fat and ugly.
7. I can catch another illness during pregnancy and die.
8. I won't be able to do anything other than taking care of the baby for a few years.
9. I don't know what Taesu is thinking.
10. It can destroy not only my life but also Taesu's future.
11. I might not be happy.
12. I might become fat and Taesu could have an affair.

   . . .

The list grew longer and longer. And it became more and more negative and extreme. In her mind, there was already the scene of an impoverished and desolate house, an alcoholic husband, a rebellious son, and herself exhausted from crying. At first glance, the conclusion was already there. Mother, however, decided not to make a hasty conclusion and filled out the right column. Thinking, 'Right, this won't be everything. As people say, everything has its strengths and weaknesses,' she tried.

1. . . .
2. . . .

Mother was taken aback. She didn't expect that despite all the disadvantages she had written in the left column there wouldn't be any advantages at all in the midst of our human reality in which people were still vigorously 'breeding.' Of course, Mother knew something about 'the greatness of childbirth.' She wasn't unaware of such phrases as 'life is precious' or 'we should take responsibility for what we did,' things she learned from a TV educational program or in a moral or sex education class. But she couldn't write them down, because somehow they didn't ring true. As she was doing this not for others but for her own sake, she wanted to write only what she could accept wholeheartedly. In other words, she wanted to write the words she knew and believed . . . no matter how beautiful and right other people's words would be. However, she was afraid, with the notebook, in which right and left were diametrically opposed, open in front of her. Because of number 1 or number 3, or number 5 or number 12 . . . . However, the real cause of her fear lay somewhere else. Although she didn't know it at the time, she was afraid of a premonition of her great love for another being, an anxiety that loomed in its shadow, and her own feeling that she didn't know in which column she should write because she didn't know whether it was good or bad. While she was at it, she decided to make a list about Han Taesu. It was shorter than she expected.

Strength: Good-hearted
Weakness: Too good-hearted

She stared at it for a long time, because she wasn't sure whether this was good or bad.

I don't know which of the two minds, Father's or Mother's, influenced my birth more. What's clear, though, is that neither of them played a decisive role in it. Sometimes during our lives, the answer we so desperately look for appears from somewhere completely unexpected. Sometimes, the problem appears to be quite unrelated to the correct answer.

A few days later, the two minors got on a bus after making a conscious decision to go someplace far away to avoid other people's eyes. After looking around the streets of a city completely unfamiliar to them, they entered an ob-gyn clinic that looked relatively nicer and secluded.

"You have protein in your urine."

"Yes?"

"Was your blood pressure rather high before?"

"My father has hypertension, but I don't know about myself."

Mother listened to the doctor's words more politely than usual. The doctor said that Mother's condition could get worse if nothing was done. If so, Ms. Ch'oe Mira's organs could be permanently damaged and, in the worse case scenario, the lives of both mother and baby could be endangered. Surprised, Father asked, almost crying,

"What should we do, doctor?"

Mother was also waiting for an explanation, biting her lips. The doctor looked at the teenage couple who somehow looked dubious, shabby, and uneasy. After thinking for a bit, he said, in a businesslike manner, without finishing his sentence,

"Well, there is a treatment, but . . ."

Mother impatiently interrupted,

"What is it?"

The doctor glanced at the two minors again.

"Please tell us, sir!"

Father pressed.

"Well, the best treatment is . . ."

Mother and Father spoke at once,

"Yes?"

"Well, the best choice at this point is . . ."

The doctor who had been looking at the chart for a long time said calmly,

"Giving birth."

Even after that, Mother couldn't readily make up her mind. She didn't know what to do, seesawing between affirmation and negation many times a day. Time kept passing . . . My body kept on growing in a damp and dark space. I could hear the continuous thumps around me. I heard it not with my ears, but with my whole body. I tried to grasp the truth of that 'palpitation' surrounding me like a soldier trying to decipher Morse codes in an underground bunker. The code was as follows:

'Pit-a-pat . . . pit-a-pat . . . pit-a-pat . . .'

One might say it was like 'kung-kung' or 'dung-dung.' It was like the sound of a distant drum or loud footsteps. That sound rang out as if somebody with a giant body was approaching me with big strides. Each time I was ready to bolt like a reindeer, expecting an aftershock. But at the same time I also felt like dancing. Together, Mother's heartbeat and mine occasionally sounded like music.

'Bang tick tick . . . bang tick tick . . . bang tick tick . . . bang tick . . .'

Bang was Mother's and tick was mine. Bang was a fortissimo and tick was a pianissimo. Hanging from the long umbilical cord, I was preoccupied with that sound. Floating like a plump moon over my head, Mother's heart spread its bits/beats drop by drop like a tree spreading the color green around. They were bits, the basic unit of information; and they were the beats songwriters used to compose music. This bit and that beat were flying like leaflets, sending important messages to every part of my body. It was a truly seditious rhythm, and listening I really felt I was 'becoming somebody.' Cells receiving orders immediately began to act. After being hit by the bits/beats pouring down from the sky, organs sprouted and stretched. My liver swelled, kidneys ripened, and bones grew with a crunch. I grew quickly. Often in my dream, I met Mother in her dream and talked randomly.

'Mom . . .'

'Yes?'

'Mom . . .'

'Yes, go ahead.'

'My heart is trembling often . . . It trembles so hard it almost hurts . . . I feel as if I am breathing my last, that I am about to die . . . I cannot stop, though.'

'Baby?'

'Yes?'

'I, I feel the same way. My heart trembles often. Although it palpitates so hard that it almost hurts, I cannot stop it . . .'

It was about this time that Mother began wearing the maternity belt. Mother couldn't make any decision until then. As days went by, the maternity belt pressed me harder. Mother's breath became shorter as well. Sometimes, Mother's heartbeat was so fast that I couldn't keep time to it. Nevertheless, she went to school with a haughty expression on her face, without letting on. Then, one day, she couldn't button up her uniform any longer, and she cried, squatting in her room and embracing her book bag in her arms.

The rumor traveled in a flash. After hearing Father confess, paternal Grandfather came back home drunk midday and slapped his son across the face thirty times in a row. But Father didn't apologize during this slapping. Things weren't that different in Mother's house. Grandfather scolded Mother, cursing her with unmentionable words. His face showed winter's severity hiding summer's exuberance behind it. Nobody in the family defended her. Grandmother and uncles were all blaming Mother, avoiding her eyes. Grandfather got so angry while scolding Mother that he looked around and picked up a wooden broom. He had lifted it up high to bring it down on her with all his might when all of a sudden he stopped, trembling, with his hand holding the broom in mid-air. He was sad and angry at the same time, looking down at his last child and only daughter who, lying face down, was protecting her stomach instead of her head with her arms.

Pit-a-pat, My Life

by *Kim Aeran*

Interview with Kim Aeran

by Jamie Chang

Jamie Chang: Where do you find material for your stories?

Kim Aeran: My first collection of short stories was largely based on stories about my family or my personal experience, and the city—Seoul—played an important role in the second collection. Materials I draw upon tend to be on the periphery or in the magnetic fields of central events, not so much the events themselves. My stories tend to unfold in spaces where circumstances that are about to become a story or signs of stories gather. So sometimes, when I write about a city, I end up writing about everything minus the city, and when I write about fathers, the families I portray contain everything but the father. The basic material for my full-length novel was progeria—a disease of premature aging—but I couldn't tell what kind of story it was going to be until it was done. Come to think of it, materials for my stories have generally been things that attract my attention for reasons I can't explain rather than things that strike me as great ideas.

Chang: Which foreign writers do you admire? How have they influenced your work, if at all?

Kim: I like poems by Korean, Chinese, and Japanese writers from long, long ago—poems that, in the words of a classical Chinese literature specialist, are short but leave you with a profound thought. I was often captivated by a few words or sentences that had the power to transcend time and space in the blink of an eye. Like a snowy crevasse that looks solid but gives way under your feet. I could feel myself grow through these chance mental plummets (or ascents). I haven't committed to memory a collection of Chosŏn sijo, Chinese poetry, or haikus, but I still wish I could emulate the narratives and sentences I encounter in these poems. In terms of plot-driven tales, there's nothing more gripping than the Korean folktales, Aesop's Fables, and Greek mythology I used to read and listen to as a child. I guess their longevity attests to their power.

Chang: Congratulations on publishing your first full-length novel. How was your approach different from writing short stories? Which do you prefer to work on, short fiction, or full-length novels?

Kim: If writing a short story is being in a relationship, writing a full-length novel is being in a marriage. The experience was physically trying, but there was much more room to play around with things in a variety of different ways. I had fun. It gave me a chance to think about technical matters as well. I like the refined energy of short stories, but I plan to focus on full-length novels for the time being.

Chang: There seems to be a distinct contrast between the anxious, young, unmarried women and the strong mother figures in Mouthwatering. Could you tell us more about that?

Kim: I tend to have strong female characters, especially mothers, in my stories. This is perhaps because I grew up in a household full of strong women. As a woman writer, I don't have a particular fantasy about motherhood. I think the positive impression I had of the mothers I saw growing up influenced my portrayal of mothers in the earlier stories. It goes without saying that I respect mothers, but I think there are many different kinds of mothers out there. Some have monstrous ideas of motherhood, while others are devoid of any maternal instincts. This is because mothers are above all individuals with personalities. I plan to closely examine personalities in creating characters for my future works.

Chang: Why do you think Korean literature is not in demand overseas? I don't think writers should write with readers in mind, but what elements do you think are necessary for a book to be loved internationally?

Kim: I think poor translating conditions are to blame. There isn't a stable infrastructure or program to help translators and publishers. But I believe there's been a growing interest in these matters and that the necessary parties are in dialogue about finding solutions.

When I write, I don't think about how it'll be translated. It'd be nice if I could write books that many people can read and connect with, but I don't want that to be the reason I write. I want to write sentences that may not be easy to translate, but stir the translator's aesthetic impulse. Something that makes you think, "This is going to be really hard to translate. Nevertheless, I want to." The same goes for materials, descriptions, and themes. Before I can join the ranks of internationally recognized artists, I need to be more distinctive and true to myself.

Chang: You have occasionally dealt with social minorities in your stories. Is this an important issue for you that we'll see recurring in your future works?

Kim: I don't know what kinds of stories I will write or come across in the future. I don't even know if it's up to me. But I have a feeling that my future stories will have certain connections with stories I have written at one point or more than once. The story

of minorities is, of course, one of them. The important thing is
not how often these issues come up, but how I deal with them. No
matter whom I portray, I hope that they won't be used in my stories
as simple fodder or a token, and that I would be able to meet these
stories eye to eye. Research is easy, but reconstructing sentiment
is hard. Sentiment is also a marriage between circumstances and
individual characteristics. However, "other" is such a formidable
word. I must try not to lose my courage before this word, walking
on eggshells rather than being too confident, hoping that what I say
will never outrun what I write. I want to try to see people and the
world for what they are.

Five Poems by
Kim Un

Translated by Krys Lee

On the Snake

It doesn't seem that we'll reveal anything.

It appears we have the same particular fantasy. About the tongue.
    About the street the tongue licked clean. It seems we should
    come to the same conclusion about a snake that's all gloss. The
    moment the tongue moves

Words pass. Toward air,

we cock our ears and music passes. Though I floundered in the air,
    we talked again about our expressions after we listened several
    times and knew it was music.

From moment to moment we speak bleakly. About the tongue.

About music and screaming, we speak with a forked tongue. When
    we wake up, all day long we disguise ourselves with the snake's
    brothers that lie in a heap near our heads. When we're scared,
    we have the habit of covering ourselves with hats. Our hair takes
    off its skin and sneaks out. The snake sticks out two-forked and
    three-forked tongues, and gets away. To try and take off its hat.

Music passes. Though I fell in the air and floundered, you wear all the expressions of someone trying to put on the hat. It doesn't seem we'll reveal anything. About the snake.

I have briefly depicted the tongue.

MEETING

You wait anxiously.
I go to meet you but
I don't know where one of my feet is walking.
Do you know who one of your hands is greeting?

Bumping someone's shoulder then bumping it again,
My feet strut to their inner world.
If these feet look unfamiliar,
watch my walk. Is the final destination of this stride,
with everything below my knees entirely omitted, your house,

or beyond?

A person's hand is waiting.
While I press the doorbell, there is the sudden
sound of your moving feet.
I open the door

and we hold each other from behind.
In front of me I hear your faraway sounds.
From over your back, my feet have just arrived.
Immediately I take off your clothes.

The too small world of the hands and feet rest at last,
lying down on another bed.

Helen, What Do You Hear?

The sound of sirens passes.
I tap her fingers.
What do you hear?
I hear it near my head.

I mimic a baritone sound.
I tap her fingers.
What do you hear?
I hear it near my ankle.

I wave a leaf I picked up from a park.
What do you hear?
It seems like an empty space has formed nearby.
If you tickle me a little more, soon
it will be the time for the kittens to wake up.

Soon after, a truck passes.
What do you hear?
The smell of sweat rises to the top of my head.
What is happening on the other side of the globe?
I hear hundreds of combat boots or
the smell of hundreds of people hating.
It just arrived at my belly button right now.

Next door, I hear nails being pounded in.
What do you hear?
I often sneak looks at a scene where someone's waking up.
Behind a window that stays fogged no matter how I clean it,
A man casts glances at me.
If he just beams, I continue to hear
my sweat-soaked dream from age nine onwards.

Don't resist, don't resist, my fiancée—

Don't be surprised. I am only breathing.
What do you hear?
A pair of shoes in the cabinet said,
I have never seized my feet before.
I mean the sound of ankles fleeing.
Don't misunderstand.
Until now, I didn't say anything.
What do you hear?
Why does the solitary caterpillar keep slipping?
Though it is most certainly green,
It is yellowish, multicolored, and looking for a time to leave itself.

Why do you hear?
You can't hear or see
Or even speak, so why do you express yourself?
I think only about the departing mother bird's stiff beak
holding a caterpillar.
Are there babies in the bird's belly as it sits on the nest it built?
Is the caterpillar also in there?
Today, the sun rose squirming
A little late.

Then she tapped my fingers.
That was her way of thanking me.
To thank me for the questions
That she cannot hear, she asked,
What do you hear?

I've never seen a more certain event than this.
The sentence does not occur after the event, but
after the sentence, the event occurs. One sentence is quite wise.
One sentence is quite foreboding. And one sentence is
somewhat responsible for what it says. It has become a bit more
    unfortunate.

Who is offering a hand in front of you? Is it a begging or helping hand?
Or the head of a group whose greeting
on the first meeting mistakenly assumes equality?
They are the same in that they represent the group, but they are
    not equal.
It is not even fair. Someone's hand is larger. This sentence
will begin a trivial dispute. It is surrounded by a great doubt.

As promised, war broke out. "Grandmother passed away."*
With this sentence, thousands of lives will be minutely weighed.
Life and death, these are too simple.
Enemy or friendly forces, these are too clear.
Prisoners of war press in from all sides.
Both the enemy and friendly forces
carry the roar of the cannon in their mouths and proclaim.
Until I hold a white flag and silently wave it,
the guns stay cocked. Bang, the sentence begins.
Thump, the flagpole breaks. Drip, the person who stops crying
on command, I'll proclaim. This sentence was signed
and a period added to that sentence and they cremated the corpses so
anyone could know who the bodies were. Only after the ashes were
scattered was our morale,
higher than a collapsed building and buildings,
lowered onto a piece of soulless paper.

They calmly drift down. As the sentence compels,

the water is azure, and momentarily, the hue of blood, and the sea

reveals a mouth that isn't sufficient for swallowing

all the corpses. One or two sentences are lacking.

The prisoners of war have returned to nearly all the continents.

All those sentences are thrusting to an end.

Most constitutional laws are being newly written.

One sentence is quite decisive. Another sentence makes room for
    exceptions early on.

Someone's steaming breath blurs the event. These words control
    the event.

I haven't seen a more certain reason. The chaotic political
    situation is used

and new sentences are completed. A sentence harboring logic
    and fallacy.

As in the past, future, and now, the sentence of this moment is the

most important. The night's stars are completed with this declaration.

Holding logic and fallacy together, the sun shines, the stars
    circle the edges,

and the moon doesn't move. Words that destroy moment to
    moment then

return. Earth is expanding while the country is in decline. The
    universe dies of the cold

and a star removes unneeded embellishments in order to burn to death.

When it's a chore to speak,

the words "Big Bang" leap from the scientist's lips.

On a radio program the same words leap out again.

In a few accidental seconds, the size of the words

expands by hundreds of billions.

Even deep in the Andes Mountains, these words were discovered.

In a flowing gutter's entrance, the words are discovered again. Eddying,

the water is sucked down the drain hole. From someone's lips, smoke and gas and so yet another sentence is transported to

someone else's even bigger lips. In the beginning

there was the sentence. Just before, issuing commands,

and just after, possessing all of the explosions and massacres

    and mercy,

this religion. The sentence completes the commands. Legal council

speaks for the voice we cannot hear. When your detail-oriented hands

can't keep up with the mountain of paperwork,

you strike three times with a gavel and you strike the prison

    bars repeatedly

and your voice tries to escape just a little further by bellowing.

Though most can't escape the clutches of the law,

the circumstances of the sentence, which holds

both logic and fallacy, are a little different. Though it may have

little compassion for someone's circumstances, another person's event

might have great influence. This sentence is unnecessary.

Even if this sentence was omitted, it would be fine.

These words control the event.

This steaming breath erases the sentence.

I haven't seen a more certain reason than this.

The reason why it has to live. And for most, the reason to stay silent.

* The code used when Germany invaded Poland on September 1, 1939.

We apologize but we are dots and beings of bulk.
We are spherical and we do not remain at
regular intervals from each dot. We grow distant and disappear,
and disappearing, we gain a changeless size. We naturally
achieve symmetry and we enjoy that each side of our face has a
    different personality.
The ground made of skin is wide and far and whirls about in
an unknowable cigarette smoke. There is no world as unknown as
    the senses,
but there's no more defined muscle than the three-dimensional
    world. We see,
hear, touch, and divide the objective world and another clearly
    different
objective world into different spaces. We grieve and create
both the growing star and disappearing dust. We came from
    nature but
we don't deny the nature that came from us. Like amoebas,
we do not reflect on our instinct to reflect.
We are completed houses with large holes drilled in them.
We see our surrounding world and inner world simultaneously,
    and draw.
Not knowing where the earth is, we find our room
unerringly in our hometown. There,
we open the room as if someone were inside and find one dot.

Lip Sync

by Park Chansoon
Translated by E. K. DuBois
and Nathan A. DuBois

Still out of sync. Should I shorten Recurvirostra avosetta to avocet? I turn the jog shuttle to the left once again. On the screen, a blond woman in a beige jacket with black binoculars around her neck is speaking. She looks fairly old, but her voice is fast and confident. I try to synchronize the translation with her lips. "One avocet was spotted in Minsmere in 1946." Too long. The image of a muttering voice actress on her way out of the dubbing room comes to mind—phew, that was tough! I bit my tongue trying to cram it all in.

I change "Minsmere" to "Here" since a subtitle indicates the location, and replace "1946" with "46." "One avocet was spotted here in 46." Too short? A few more words would do it. It would be better to add "extinct" to clarify why the English people were so thrilled to have the bird return. "One avocet, formerly presumed extinct, was spotted here in 46." I type and hit Enter. It's about the right length but now it doesn't fit her gestures. I rework the sentence once more to match the woman's movements. "Though formerly presumed extinct, one avocet was spotted here in 46."

Her voice is rhythmic, like a dance. "*Re˘cur′vi˘ro′stra˘ a′vo˘set′ta˘* was′ spot˘ted′ in˘ Mins′mere˘ in′ 1˘9′4˘6′.*" The original sounds like a couple of lines of Shakespearean iambic pentameter. "To˘ be′ or˘ not′ to˘ be′: that˘ is′ the˘ que′stion." There once was a translator who insisted on translating Shakespeare's works with the original meter, even if it took her entire life. There is no way that the woman from Minsmere is going to keep her Shakespearean rhythm. Forget the meter. I'm not even close to translating the style. That line alone made me sweat.

Going on like this I will never make enough money to pay the hospital bills, now three months overdue. Only after getting current can I move my husband to another hospital. Otherwise, he will go on a blacklist and then no hospital will take him. I only took this job translating, researching, and interpreting for a documentary in the first place because it paid well.

"If you're that desperate just pack up your stuff and move in here. There's even a sink and stove."

I remember Yun, the producer, blurting this out last night while we were having sex on the worn-out sofa. He said it as if he was doing me a huge favor. Just the same, it was a long-awaited and thrilling rendezvous following our trip to England. The thought of my husband made me hesitate at first, but before I knew it I was accepting Yun's embraces. Sometimes Yun comes to mind before my husband, even though we were initially just coworkers. Even so, after suggesting that I should move in, he sprang to his feet, turned around, and re-dressed himself all before I could pull up my panties.

"I really don't know why you are so obsessed with that invalid. You said that even the doctors told you he should go home or to a nursing facility."

My relatives say the same thing. The security deposit for our flat went to pay hospital bills long ago. Truthfully even I don't understand why I am doing it. Thinking back, I wonder if Yun was sincere when he told me to move in.

Just as he said, there is a small sink in the corner of the editing room. There is a leftover ramen cup with some used chopsticks in it. The dim basement editing room is about ten feet square and crowded by machines, a desk, and the sofa. There is a pair of editing VCRs and an old computer on the worn-out metal desk. There is also a stack of beta tapes of the England coverage converted from 8mm. The actual production process takes place in another room that we rent as needed, and this room is just for editing. Yun's blue jacket lies where he casually tossed it over the sofa. I pick it up and hang it on a coat hook on the wall. Y-Special, our production logo, is printed in black on the white wall. One corner of the Y is torn off and another letter is stained.

Suddenly I feel like getting some fresh air and having a cigarette. I walk upstairs and go out on the roof. The sun is setting between the buildings. I exhale cigarette smoke and look around. To the north is 63 Building and Trump Tower. The image of Yun shouting towards Yŏido while eating grilled pork and toasting with soju is still vivid in my mind. That was three years ago, at the opening of the production company he started with his coworkers after he got laid off from a cable company during a restructuring.

"Yŏido in three years!"

Producing shows for major broadcasting companies is his dream. Only 63 Building and Trump Tower are visible from this seven-story commercial building in Tangsandong, but the network broadcasting companies lie beyond. The lights of Yŏido, therefore, signify the major broadcasters. For me, someone who makes a living translating cable TV and videos, which pays only a fifth of what major broadcasters do, translating for the big companies feels far off, like a world beyond the clouds that I will never lay my eyes on.

Yun cried his lungs out for "Yŏido in three years" but his dream was thwarted until recently. His partners left one by one for other work and now only he and one of his younger colleagues still remain. But these days he's whistling in high spirits because his project proposal was nominated for a grant from the Korean Broadcasting Institute. It looks like he's also planning to enter the Banff World Television Festival, a famous international TV program contest.

I go down from the roof and sit in front of the editing screen again. The next scene is about reed beds and marshes. The woman with the lively voice narrates. "The Royal Society for the Protection of Birds formed an artificial marsh and created extensive reed fields for this one bird. Flocks of avocet that had not lived here for decades began nesting in Minsmere once more." I type and hit Enter. It's difficult to hear each word without a script. Perhaps the work is taking so long because I do not know much about the avocet. What sort of bird merits such compassion from the English people?

Actually, I didn't even see a feather of the bird while I was in England because Yun and the cameraman depended entirely on me for everything from the moment we arrived. I am a translator and interpreter by profession, but I was up to my neck researching filming locations, setting up interviews, and creating surveys. Even when the crew went to film the bird, I was booked with other appointments and could not go with them. So I didn't actually learn anything about the avocet at all. Maybe I should watch a BBC documentary first.

I insert a tape called "The Return of Avocet" into the VCR. A very bizarre-looking bird shows up on the screen. The first thing that catches my eye is the bird's long, black bill. It's more than half the total body length—long enough for other birds to play jump rope with. If you ever see a bird swinging its own bill and playing jump rope with other birds that would probably be an avocet. The end of the bill also curves upward. That must be where the name Recurvirostra comes from. The narrator says that the bird's nickname is "Cobbler's-awl," since the tip of a cobbler's awl is curved and has a hole for stringing thread to sew shoes. Why does this bird have such a bizarre bill?

"Most birds have straight beaks like the magpie, downward curving ones like the parakeet or eagle, stout ones like the sparrow, or flat ones like the spoonbill."

Even Yun, a nature specialist and environmental documentary expert, said that he had never seen a bill like the avocet's. But the curve is not so unfamiliar to me. Where have I seen it before? My cell phone rings as I wonder about this. It's my husband's regular caregiver, telling me that she has found a substitute for the weekend.

I barely catch the bus as it's about to leave.

For three years already, I have been working every weekend as my husband's caregiver, but I decided to find a substitute this weekend since I will be very busy with my translation work. Just the same, I have to meet the sub and make sure that she can manage a critical-care patient.

I sway to and fro as I hold on to the handle in the bus. Looking out the window, I catch sight of towering buildings and construction sites here and there. Every one is competing to be the highest. Tall buildings block my view as the bus enters Yŏido. This is the place of our dreams, Yun and I. The towering forest of buildings is suffocating, perhaps even more so after our ten-day trip in the secluded English countryside.

On the bus ride east from London there were many houses just two stories high, sitting comfortably here and there in the woods. Even the houses seemed to be on vacation. It was mid-January when we reached Minsmere Nature Reserve in Dunwich, Suffolk, but the weather was mild enough for us to go without coats. The biggest trouble was the English accent. I tried to get used to it by watching *The Full Monty* several times before the trip, but it was no use since my ears were accustomed to Hollywood English. I couldn't help but hear the English accent as a completely different language. How frustrating it is to make a living from language and yet fail to understand it!

I get off the bus and go into the hospital, which reeks of disinfectant. The hospital is several decades old and many attached buildings cluster around each ward. The hospital expanded wherever there was available space, so the passage to my husband's room is like a maze—through the main entrance, along the corridor, up and down the elevator, and finally down a rambling hallway.

A nurse pushes a dressing cart down the hallway. My husband's bed is the first one on the left in a six-person room on the seventh floor. It's dinnertime so the patients are sitting up and eating from their trays in bed. Only my husband is lying down. From a nutrient pouch hanging on a pole next to his bed, his meal drips down one drop at a time and trickles through a tube in his nose. Even after many attempts to train him to swallow, he still kept getting food in his windpipe, so the doctor decided to switch to a feeding tube instead.

"We've got to do it. There's a risk of pneumonia."

The doctor put a feeding tube in my husband not long after he was hospitalized for a stroke. If the visible, external part of the tube is three spans of an adult hand, the internal portion, beginning at the nostril, passing through the esophagus, and entering the stomach, must be multiples of that. Food travels through the tube, which serves as an extension of his throat and mouth. The translucent, slender, and soft plastic turns orange when he drinks carrot juice and purple when he drinks grape juice. It's fastened to the tip of his nose with a bandage, and taped and hung around his right shoulder. The feeding tube curves like a bow, and he pulls it out whenever his caregiver takes her eyes off of him. It's simply a wonder that he has the strength to do so.

I take an envelope of money out of my purse and hand it to the caregiver. It's two weeks' worth of payments, so the envelope is full to the point of bursting. My eyes fall on the money, which I borrowed from a friend, rather than on the man with the oxygen and feeding tubes in him. How much longer can I keep this up? I feel suffocated. Why can't I, just as Yun said, be free of this patient? Even my relatives pat me on the shoulder and say, "You've done enough."

Perhaps my husband and I still have some unfinished business. I can understand his stammering speech quickly and interpret it clearly, but I also know that I have a critical attitude towards him. Even today, while I stood in front of the ATM after asking my friend to wire me some money to pay the caregiver, I felt like screaming "I can't take it anymore!" But I knew that there was no one to hear my cry.

Lip Sync

Chansoon

AZALEA

Caregivers only accept cash, and I can borrow money from my friends just so many times. Ever since my husband started his own business I have been petty with money. I resent him for this. So how, with such a heart, can I look with affection upon this patient? But as soon as I turn away I hate myself for looking at him so callously. I try to keep my hopes up by thinking that my husband and I are still young and the day will come when I will spread my wings; but the thought of overdue hospital bills always turns my world pitch black again.

"He must have injured his spinal cord as he collapsed. It doesn't make sense for him to be paralyzed otherwise."

I want to forget the doctor's words.

After transferring her duties to the substitute the regular caregiver comes back in and speaks to me. "Call your office as soon as you get a chance."

I turned my cell phone off earlier, so Yun must have called the hospital. Maybe today's meeting on the west coast didn't go well? While I am hesitating to return Yun's call, my husband opens his eyes and looks at me. He moves his lips into an indistinguishable expression, neither smile nor frown. He doesn't speak well because of the stroke.

"Whe di yo ge ba? Ho wa yo wor?"

When did you get back? How was your work? The last letters are always broken off of his words. As if reading lips, I quickly repeat his questions and answer him.

"When did I get back? Yesterday. How was my work? The English accent made it very difficult."

It's times like this that I shine as a dubbing translator. Whether relatives or friends, no one can carry on a conversation with him as quickly as I do. One time his friends came to visit him, but they got caught up in the meaningless details of every phrase.

"Ther i a caf-tri dow-sta. Pu i o m ta."

His friends listened attentively to what he said over and over again, but no one figured him out.

"There is a cafeteria downstairs. Put it on my tab."

His friends were amazed at my lip reading and said that I wasn't a dubbing translator for nothing.

My husband has a habit of asking me, "Di yo ea?" Whenever I visit him in the evening he always asks me, "Did you eat?" Though he never was the breadwinner, either on his feet or on his back, he never forgets to ask if I ate.

When my mother passed away several years ago my husband and I became each other's only living immediate family. In my mother's opinion we were both good-for-nothings who shared the same bad habits.

"Like husband, like wife. You are as alike in your laziness as you are in your long fingers and toes."

Mom used to click her tongue in disapproval. The thing she hated the most was that neither of us had a steady job but lived very *freely*.

"Everyone says that a freelancer is 'a freelesser.' Talk about freedom—you are leashed to the phone!"

Mom knew instantly that I was out of work whenever she saw me fidgeting on the sofa. Several years ago my husband lost everything we had, including the security deposit for our own home, so we moved into my mother's new apartment. She scolded us for spilling cigarette ash in the house, and for stashing dirty laundry all around our room. She would say sarcastically that we had the cleanest house in the world. Every time she came home, from the moment she stepped through the gate, Mom would start sniffing for cigarette smoke. One day, she snatched the cigarette pack out of my purse and threw it into the trashcan. Her shrieking shook the house.

"How can you both be so damn alike? You only make pennies and yet you sit around on your ass all day long sucking on those damn cigarette butts!"

"There she goes again." Just when I was about to cover my ears, my husband's manly voice resounded loudly.

"It's ok. She'll quit when she wants to. Leave her alone."

I do not know why he defended my smoking habit for me. Perhaps he wanted me on his side? Or maybe he thought that a person, man or woman, shouldn't lose heart while fighting to survive in this harsh world?

My cell phone rings. It's Yun. As I come out into the hallway to answer the call, an intern enters the room with a device for removing phlegm. Yun's urgent voice leaps out as I flip the phone open.

"Did anyone from the town call while you were in the office?"

"No, at least not when I was there."

He must have heard that there would be an answer today. Depending on whether we have the town's cooperation or not, we can be eliminated from the grant nominee list. Yun and I cannot afford to fail. This grant is our last chance. I suddenly remember that there are no more diapers or sterilized gloves for phlegm removal. I tell the caregiver who is on her way to wash the nutrient pouch and syringe that I'm going to the medical supply store. I head to the elevator. It's full of patients in wheelchairs going out for evening strolls. I take the stairs instead and go to the medical supply store. My cell phone rings again as I come out after buying what I need.

It's the nurse in charge.

"Where are you? Come up right away."

"What's happening?"

"Just hurry."

I have had many emergency calls over the last three years, but this time it feels serious for some reason. My heart begins to race.

The doctor in charge is in the room along with several interns. RNs are moving about busily and the heart monitor has returned again.

"What happened?"

"Well, I was exerting some pressure on the patient's abdomen to take out the phlegm and . . ."

The intern cannot finish her explanation, so an RN continues.

"She lightly tapped the patient several times, and he began to vomit violently."

My husband, oxygen tube in his nostrils and his face deathly blue, moves his lips urgently. He might have been waiting for an interpreter. "Where does it hurt the most?"

"Ca brea ca brea ches hur."

"Can't breathe, can't breathe. Chest hurts."

The RN is nonchalant even after I interpret what my husband said. "It's common among stroke patients."

The RN crosses his arms and casually gazes at the monitor as if there is nothing to worry about. An RN in the previous hospital treated my husband just with medical patches for two weeks even though he was crying out in pain "Ma, ma si hur." She said that it was just a muscle cramp, but later they sent my husband to the internal medicine department and tortured him by flipping him this way and that, extracting almost two liters of water from his lungs.

84, 160, 90, 38, 115, 49. Blood-oxygen levels are drastically low and the others are dangerously high. His breathing is hoarse and labored through a thick layer of phlegm, like the breathing of a man carrying a large rock up a hill.

"What are you talking about? Call a respiratory physician. And a cardiologist, too. His lips are deathly blue. The last time this happened he had a heart attack and caught pneumonia."

The RN nods to one of the interns who then runs to the nurse's lounge and after a moment returns again. "Neither of them can come right now."

"Send him immediately to the ICU," I plead.

The disapproving stares from the families of the other patients in the room are like piercing daggers for depriving them of their sleep.

My husband is now apparently unconscious and shows no response as they wheel him away on his bed. Just the feeding tube which connects to his stomach through his nose and becomes one with his body sways to and fro along with the jerky motion of the bed. The tube comes out through his nose and stretches into a long arc around his shoulder. It's a familiar curve. The arching bill curves backward like a bow.

"You can see him when the basic procedures are complete and he is stable. Stay in the family lounge or someplace else nearby. It'll probably be six in the morning," the nurse in the ICU says and closes the door.

I sit vacantly on a chair in the hallway for a while but then get up. I cannot stay here all night. I have to make the most out of the few hours I have in order to meet the deadline.

When I get back to the editing room I notice a news tape on the desk. Yun must have gotten it for me while I was out. Whenever I urge him to borrow clips he just rolls his eyes and mutters, "Do you know how pathetic I feel when I ask for clips as a no-name producer?" I insert the tape into the VCR and tap the play button.

The scene of a bird standing in a muddy salt marsh near a small fishing village on the west coast appears. The bird diligently whisks the water with its long bill.

Anchor's lead-in: "This is a clip filmed by a viewer. I would like to introduce an exotic visitor to Korea."

Subtitle: Sunset Village, a fishing town in South Chungcheong Province.

The name of the person who filmed the clip follows the subtitle, and then comes an interview with Dr. Lee, an ornithologist:

"*Recurvirostra avosetta* is characterized by its bow-like curved bill. It's a rare and distinguished guest that only visits every several years. The avocet stirs its bill in the water and feeds on shrimp and lugworms. Sometimes it prods into holes in the mudflat with its curved bill and catches soft crabs and clams."

I insert another news tape from January 2004. Woo Island in Jeju Province appears on the screen followed by a winter view of Hadori Beach and Seongsanpo Port. One avocet strolls leisurely in the water on its long legs. There can't be another bird in the world with such a long bill. Why does such a cumbersome thing persist? As far as I know, unnecessary parts of the body diminish over time according to the laws of evolution. If that is so, does it mean that its bill is still essential? Perhaps the avocet needs that long bill to sniff around the world, like the man on his sickbed used to do when he was youthful and filled with curiosity. The interesting thing is that only a single avocet was found on the west coast and in Jeju, both times after several years.

Ornithologist's explanation:

"The upward curved bill seems to pierce the hearts of the people. Avocets usually live in flocks in England, Spain and the Mediterranean region, but somehow one of them lost its way and flew to Korea by accident. Hence the term vagrant bird."

Anchor's lead-in:

"It must have gotten lost on its way from Europe—through Greenland, Siberia, and to Asia."

Vagrant bird. I want to raise an objection to the ornithologist's comment about the lost bird. This bird is not lost. It just loves to wander and that's why it flew to a curious country in the east. The reason why its nickname is Cobbler's-awl is not just because the bill is curved upward. It signifies that the bird is diligently poking around and always working somewhere, just like a cobbler's awl. Or maybe it was persecuted in its motherland and deported and is seeking asylum here.

"How much did you do?" asks Yun, holding me in his arms from behind. "You're not bogged down thinking about the invalid are you?"

I do not respond.

"How come you don't answer me? Stay that way and you'll go bankrupt and be out on the street at thirty-five. I heard he went back to the ICU?"

He must have called the hospital. Letting his words fall aside, I stand up, pry his arms from me and say, "I never asked you to pay the hospital bills for me, so back off and stop lecturing."

I would not have worked with him if I had known he was going to preach like this. Since Korean movies became popular they took over cable TV and naturally my translation work dried up. Korean movies like *Haeoondae*, *Thirst*, and *Take Off* suit the taste of Korean audiences, so there is no reason to seek out unfamiliar and culturally distant foreign films. This means that I am in no position to be particular about my work, especially when my debt snowballs day by day. My heart, which was running towards Sunset Village and the avocets just a moment ago, was pressed back inside those concrete walls when Yun appeared. What does he know about my marriage?

Once, early in our marriage, my husband and I took a day off and went to Chŏngnŭng. He looked so handsome in a sky blue t-shirt with a camera around his neck. We rode bikes together, and I let go of the handlebars and spread my arms out wide. I also rode the bike backwards. Once, I even spread my legs way out and held the seat with both of my hands, putting my weight on the seat. My husband took one picture after another. I wanted to show him the ultimate trick that I learned when I was young: hopping on one wheel across stepping stones. I heard that there is a special bicycle for tricks but I had had enough practice with cardboard boxes already. I once saw a famous film where a kid flew past the moon with an alien on his bike, so jumping a few stepping stones would be no problem. I pulled up the front wheel and hopped two stones in succession on the rear wheel.

The next stone was further away though. As I held my breath and got ready to hop again my husband prepared to take my picture and record the jump. I gave it all my might, but that was the problem. I put too much force into it and the bike sprang from the stone as I landed. I was thrown into the air and fell, breaking my leg. My husband put me on his back and ran to the hospital. After, when I was in a room and wearing a plaster cast, we put the curtain around the bed and savored a delicious kiss for a while. The picture of me in a pink t-shirt and blue jeans, floating above the stepping stones on a bike, is still hanging on the wall in my studio.

My husband and I had always been adventurous, but my husband's publishing company could not run on that adventurous spirit alone. He had to shut down the company after he lost his pension and the security deposit for our house, but he still could not give up his lingering dreams. Actually our real problems were only just beginning. He couldn't find a proper job, so he often traveled abroad and called me. "Hon, I'm in Indonesia. I want to start a clothing factory." Or "I'm in Beijing now. Chinese people have never heard of *galbi*, so I'd like to start a *galbi* restaurant with my friend."

I wasn't averse to risk, but he seemed in a very precarious position to me, like a child near water.

I sit in front of the editing machine and press the rewind button. Yun, who was writing a manuscript, comes close to me and rests his hand on my shoulder. Suddenly his hot lips are against mine. I turn my body and put my arms around his neck. Was I too harsh to him earlier? He is after all the only one who cares and brings me work. But no. I have a sick man to take care of. Even while kissing, my head aches from the alternating faces of my husband and Yun. I wince unintentionally. Yun cares less about how I feel and he is already groping under my sweater and raising me up, leading me to the sofa. I kiss him back and let him lead me.

Yun is a producer with initiative. He gets programs approved even when everyone says that it's impossible. He has a fierce driving force once he resolves to do something. Is that what attracts me to him? With him in my life I feel like he could get rid of every burdening and worrisome problem. He was never married so he isn't gentle and caring like my husband, but he has a peculiar power that grabs others–a charisma that saves me from my monotonous life of yesterday in today and today in tomorrow.

For a moment I find comfort in his embrace. Our heavy breathing compounds and amplifies in my ears. Suddenly, a thought flashes through my mind, that my husband, the man in the hospital, should be the one breathing with me. I stand up abruptly and slip away from the sofa. Yun gets up, disappointed but not angry. Awkwardly I sit back down in front of the editor. Yun comes over and stands by me, a little at a distance.

"Sorry about earlier. I didn't come here to tell you to move him to a nursing home. But I will tell you that this is going to be a hit. I just know it."

He draws an arc from his nose, upward into a curve like a bow. It's the bill of an avocet. He begins to speak as if reciting a line from a play.

"A seaside village at sunset, into the nest of an avocet."

He has the wits to get himself out of trouble. It's a little like Shakespearean meter, but I cannot help but laugh at his awkward intonation. His ability to approach a translator is extraordinary. Is he so fixated on the bill of the avocet that he already forgot that I rejected him just now? His voice is full of confidence.

"The ornithologist and I talked to the fishermen today and visited the town hall. Several months ago they were worried about the bird flu, but they're relaxing now that they know the bird is from Europe. I met the opponents of the project and told them they'll have more tourists once the area becomes a habitat for migratory birds. It's all set now."

I feel uneasy. I always worry about people who are overly confident. One of my favorite novelists wrote that a man is more prone to become a lunatic if he is overly confident. I turn my head to look Yun in the face. "Aren't you taking things too lightly? Those fishermen make a living harvesting clams and crabs. Why should they give up their existing livelihood and take a risk by making reed beds and salt marshes?"

I tell him that bird watching has become less popular because of the bird flu, but he just ignores my words of warning.

"How does one bird motivate the English people to give up their huge carrot and canola farms for reed fields and marshes? That area is the size of 1,326 soccer fields!"

He is well informed about the sanctuary for migratory birds in Minsmere.

"They made waterways and sluices in the marshes to regulate the fresh and salt water, all for a bird that leaves when there's no salt in the water. They also imported special horses that graze reed grass in order to keep it from growing too high. Do you know how much money they make yearly from admission fees? That bird is art. Don't you agree? Huh?"

Yun leaves without waiting for my response. Who was it that said no matter how objective a documentary is it becomes subjective the moment one decides what to film? "Reflect indeed on your attitude and actions for the sake of truth and reality." I would love to remind him of his own motto, which he recites every time he meets with program writers, but I can only stare at his back as he walks away.

When I look at Yun I delude myself into thinking that he's the same man who is lying on a sickbed in the hospital. My husband was confident too when he was persuading me about his business.

"I could work as a salary man for a hundred years and get nowhere. Hon, I'll make sure you don't have to worry about money ever again."

I hardly knew anything about the publishing business, but I was certain that he would make a lot of money printing good books. No, I was relatively certain.

After hearing Yun, I think that men generally are prone to absurd dreams. Why are they so unrealistic? Are they illogical? In the end, does it mean that much to be realistic or logical? One documentary I translated stated that men have shorter life spans than women, so they tend to play their ace cards earlier in life. I hate to generalize about people, whoever they are, but if the theory is right, I prefer the risk-takers. After all, countless ventures, hits as well as flops, have been undertaken by people just like them.

I cannot focus on my work. The ICU will cost several times more than the regular room, and the money from Yun's production is my sole source of income this month. I also had a serious run-in with an administrator at the previous hospital. My husband still had half a month to go before checking out, but I kept getting pestered for not making arrangements with another hospital.

"Honestly, even doctors can't make exceptions for you. The medical insurance premium from the government is slashed after the first two months. Besides, you haven't paid your hospital bill for more than a mon—"

"But I am going to settle with you before I leave," I interrupted.

"We've experienced numerous cases of families abandoning their relatives," she persisted.

"You think I'm just a deadbeat who's going to stiff the hospital and run off?" I snapped at her, glowering fiercely.

"You never know. This year alone there are more than forty bodies in the morgue that families disowned, though some are unidentified or without next of kin. But even when we find the families, they don't try to claim the bodies." Her tone became slightly insolent. "Pakistani families are wretchedly poor but they sell everything they own to get their sons' bodies returned, even without cremation."

I almost screamed when she said that. What a nasty bitch she was! What did she think I was? I stomped out of the hospital, forcing myself to contain my seething rage.

I turn the jog shuttle. The avocet's mating scene appears on the screen. A male avocet is standing beside a female, courting her by slapping the water with his bill and shaking his body as if dancing. He repeats the same dance on the other side of her. The female only stares haughtily straight ahead. The male hops on top of her. He opens his long bill and shouts something. He resembles a slender tenor as he sings through his upward curved bill.

Plut, plut, plut, kluit, kluit.

Perhaps he's a little heavy. The female closes her eyes and gently clamps her bill shut. It must be bearable judging by how she closed her bill. It even looks like she is softly smiling. Their two bodies become one in the next scene. Four legs tangle together as they face each other in a half sitting position. They become one body.

Plut, plut, plut, kluit, kluit.

How should I translate this?

Onomatopoeia always makes me wonder. Koreans hear frogs calling gagol, gagol while English speakers hear ribit, ribit. We hear cats calling ya-ong, ya-ong and they hear meow, meow.

Judging from the louder and clearer noise, the avocets must be singing together, unified in body and soul.

Plut, plut, plut, kluit, kluit.

Their cries sometimes sound like heavy breathing, and at other times like a mellifluous melody. Sometimes it's like a flute. The long bill is a curved wind instrument. The melody, like one of Mozart's flute concertos, is clear and merry. Do only birds make this kind of sound? Do humans, becoming one, make melodies like this? How does it sound when I make love to my husband, or Yun?

Earlier on the sofa, when I got up in the middle of things, his sagging shoulders made him looked dejected. Is it because we are not truly one? I sometimes think we fit together pretty well. Is that why I was callous to my husband in the hospital, even though I was in sync on the surface? My husband and I. Yun and I. Are we not yet one in the deepest part of our hearts? It's like how the mouth and gestures of the person on the screen are in perfect harmony, but the voice-over is still out of sync. When will my husband and I savor a heartfelt kiss again? How long will Yun and I maintain this relationship? The happy avocets do not seem like they will ever stop singing.

Plut, plut, plut, kluit, kluit.

I eject the documentary clip and insert our coverage. I listen to the reserve custodian's explanation several times, then I translate and type it. "The avocet has a habit of holding its wings open." A bird appears on the screen holding its wings out straight. Its curved bill, turned upward, seems prominent, as if it has some sort of mission. "The avocet demonstrates this posture just before going after something big. He is gathering all of his energy into his bill. It's uncertain what made this bird so excited, but in the next moment he shoots downward like a bullet, driving his bill and head beneath the surface of the water." The phrases "holding its wings open" and "driving his bill" strike me. At the same

110

moment, the bird cries out. *Plut, plut, plut, kluit, kluit.* This time fast and urgent, completely different from when it was mating. The sound is like a sharp needle.

How should I translate that desperate song?

"We don't know if the bird spotted his prey or something else that was worth risking his life for. A bird with such an ornate bill may very well act impulsively like that, not knowing that there is a rock below."

Birds with crippled legs and broken wings lie on the salt marsh and mudflat. Even though they are on the ground, they still hold their long, black bills upright.

"These ones are paying the price for taking risks. There is always an opportunity cost. It is the same with the lives of men."

As I am thinking that avocets lead a dramatic life for such fragile-looking birds, I hear the sound of a new text message. A sudden surge of hunger comes over me when I see that it is well past 9 PM.

"At the bus stop. Waiting." It is Yun's number.

He was urging me to get to work just a second ago, and now he's calling me outside?

"It's over." Yoon gets up from the bench where he was sitting. "There were more nays in the referendum." My heart sinks as the meaning becomes clear. Yun is wearing just a corduroy jacket. No coat or scarf. And the fierce winter wind is blowing.

"I just received a call from the town. The problem is the present profits from the mudflat, not the bird flu." Yun gives a hollow sigh.

"It's all over."

After blurting out these last words his head drops. He looks smaller than he is. What I was worried about happened in the end. I remember an old man muttering behind me last time I visited the fishing village. "It's all well and good, but who is going to feed us in the meantime? Are we supposed to just suck on our thumbs for a couple of years?"

We wrote the proposal after visiting every corner of the fishing village on the west coast.

"It's too cold. Let's go in somewhere."

Yun shakes his head.

"Then let's walk at least. I'm freezing to death."

I hold his hand tightly and we head towards Yŏido.

"Yŏido isn't far."

The empty street makes me feel even colder. I look up at the northern sky. The first full moon of the year is rising between the tall buildings. The lunar halo is clear tonight and the moonlight gently streams down. 63 Building and Trump Tower look like castles made of bricks of light. After I have been staring at them for a while, the lights come together and float, glimmering before my eyes. Amidst the trembling lights shimmer the silhouettes of enchanted avocets thrusting down their heads and bills. The birds open their bills and shout something. I involuntarily make the sound along with them.

Plut, plut, plut, kluit, kluit.

The falling avocets smash their wings and break their legs. They lay scattered upon the mudflat. The long, slender bills of the fallen birds overlap with the image of the tube that my husband has through his nose. Before my blurry eyes an avocet strides slowly towards me across the mudflat. Before my eyes the lips of my husband slowly move.

"Di yo ea?"

I speak in sync with his lips.

"Did you eat?"

Five Poems by Kim Kyung-Ju

Translated by Chae-Pyong Song
and Anne Rashid

THE BLOOMING PUBLIC PHONE

After work the female factory workers open
the cold locks of their bikes they had parked together.
When large snowflakes like white rice fall outside of the window,
the female workers on the night shift at the wig factory
jump over the wall and rush to the public phone on their breaks.
They press down the snowflakes one by one with their
    pocketbooks.
The more uneven their teeth are, the more brightly they wave.
In spite of the wind blowing in through the gaps in makeshift walls
and the dusty light bulb, the snow heaps up.
When they press their frozen ears to the receiver
shaking off the encrustation of old numbers,
the clear signals are transmitted—
of the first love that had been cut off like a fingernail
and even of Mother's hearing aid wrapped within a handkerchief in
    a drawer—
they all plunge into their hearts.
Each of these signals is stitched into their hearts.
When Chang the foreman puts chains across each alley and leaves,

the female workers take off their white cotton gloves;
their cold fingertips are puffy.
Every place where injuries occur, seams become crooked,
sleepy eyes become hazy over heaps of hair that await weaving.
All night underneath sewing machines the women call out
paper, rock, and scissors
to decide phone privileges; their calls bloom and wither,
but the radio static continues on.

Only as I hang out the laundry
after returning to my hometown
do I realize that Mother still wears red flowery underwear.
One snowy day, she kept me near her
as she diligently chose underwear for her family
from a cart at the market.
As the speaker boomed
into the expansive sky, ample like her bottom,
Mother picked up a pair of light panties
and rubbed the warm cotton on her cheek
till the fabric became a damp red.
The flower pattern that she rubbed with her fingertips
made Mother still feel alive as a woman.
Today, cheeks flush with the memory of that red flower pattern.
As Mother proved whenever she started over again
with her newly washed underwear,
those flowers won't wither easily,
just as the underwear in the market was still new
no matter how many handled it.
Onto her hanging underwear, one by one
a few flying snowflakes descend and gently take on the red color.
From the wrinkled flowers, a clear flower water drops, drip drip—
a pair of Mother's old panties
that might have felt shy within the drawer
next to a snowball-sized moth ball.
Into the mossy smell of skin, the sunlight softly settles.

A STRANGE TALE

I burned the map
so where
do all the buried volcanoes flow?

There is a dream of conception
one only dreams once more after birth.
Will the narratives that replace sleep
become my tomb?

I see a doll that sits in a room vomiting a strange cord.

To a human being who has flown out into the earth
and slowly floats to his own dream of conception,
there is a blood only he can bleed again
when he crawls back into the womb.

THE HOLE

I clean up the hole

The hole hatches an egg

Desiring a hole,

I have written a few books

The hole has no work today

Exhausted, the hole's sympathy is at risk

Clearing away the hole, I ran down the stairs

The hole is the life of the inner room

Looking down at the hole is the time that pushes an object

The hole where a toilet should receive all from top to bottom

There are holes that ask the color

The hole's surroundings are suspiciously drying up

The flowers that bloom away from the hole are heartbreaking

The hole with today's efforts recognizes more distance than depth

The hole floats within the hole

Nowhere hurts in the hole

It appears only the hole hurts

Waves walk toward heaven bleeding profusely, shouting, "Hole,
    please save me!"

The hole floats up in the air

The life of the hole that floats in the air

Snowmen appear in a straight line

The hole

The city where the hole appears

The time when the hole is not read like the way Benjamin Péret's
    poetry is not read

The time when people are afraid of the hole's haunting has passed

The flower that blocks the hole dies early

The writing that pursues the hole with all its efforts

The writing that describes the hole

The writing that consumes the hole

I am injured by the hole

I scoop up something from the hole

After leaving the hole, I can't believe in the hole

The hole evolves, leaving the hole, because it no longer believes in it

If there is such a thing, my life has already been ruined

I look down at the eye in the hole

I follow it down with my eyes

Like a well, four directions

Rise up after breaking the hole

Where do I live?

CHRONICLE

At flower tea time I color my teeth
with the water of old tea
It rains when I, fingers wet with saliva,
pick up the golden yellow feet
of insects from a book
It rains like the evening I ran after
my lost tooth in the stream as a child
The rain falls in the in-between and
I listen to the inside of the rock
I place in this "between"
the isolated language
in which rain falls
When I feel sorrowful from watching my childlike face,
I listen to the inscription of the tooth that slowly floats in water

Wings

by Park Hyoung-Su

Translated by Sora Kim-Russell

When my friend K of the beautiful bald head died, this evil-looking hag showed up at the funeral with her kid in tow and put up a big front, wailing about how she was O's mistress and therefore deserved to be treated with respect by his surviving family, so I approached her carefully and took her by the arm and told her this was not the funeral for the great O, where even mistresses were welcome, but the funeral of my friend K of the beautiful bald head, and though he was bald, he was barely thirty and a bachelor, whereupon the old hag glared at me as if to say "We'll see about that," then polished off a bowl of *yukkaejang* and slipped out.

Anyway, this has nothing to do with any of that, but I can see into the future. The future that I will talk about from here on out takes place 170 years from now, that is, when all the rational people got the heck out of the solar system and the earth became a hotbed of radioactivity, cockroaches, and Freemasons: the year 2175. Humankind failed to protect the earth and, having learned from that failure, was mucking up the universe at a ferocious pace. How that was possible, I have no idea. I can observe their behavior, but I do not understand their science. The majority of their generation was in the same situation. Science has always been an art reserved for the few.

I watch them from Planet Earth, October 2005 A.D., 170 years before their lives. As it is fall, the sky is blue and the occasional passing breeze carries the scent of dried filefish being roasted. Right now, it is not quite four in the afternoon. I always grow bored around this time. Not lonely, not lonesome, not alone. Just bored. Bored, so I sit at my desk. I close my eyes and ponder as much time as I want. The hag from K's funeral keeps trying to leap out at me, but she's come to the wrong place. Or maybe she was just really jonesing for some *yukkaejang*. I manage to shove her away and get back to pondering time. That is how I see 170 years into the future. What? Am I weird for saying I can see the future? It's not that extraordinary. Anyone can travel to any place and any time if they want to. I mean, if they really, desperately want to. You close your eyes and spread your arms, desperately.

What I see is an eighty-four-year-old woman who works in a basic education facility on a colonized planet in the outer reaches of the universe. It's not my fault she's so old. Let's turn our eyes for a moment from the distant future to the more recent past. The eighty-four-year-old woman, obviously, was born eighty-four years earlier. Her father was a handsome man committed to a life of bachelorhood, and he worked as a programmer for the governing council on an artificial sun. One day, he returned home and decided to end his life. He leisurely swallowed some pills and lay down. Just then, a horny yogurt delivery woman came by and raped him as he lay dying, a spaced-out look on his face. At the moment of his death, an extraordinary number of tadpoles burst forth from the tip of his penis. One of those tadpoles became this future woman.

The dazzling development of organs grown for transplant was not good for lactobacillus. Yogurt was rendered a superfluous part of the human diet, and the woman's mother, who had staked her life on yogurt sales, likewise was reduced to rags. When the girl turned six, her mother sent her away to a poorhouse on the distant rice planet. High-density water covered twenty percent of the surface of that tiny planet, and the air was thick with the scent of moss. The three moons that hung in the sky were, because of their mineral compositions, red, redder, and flaming crimson.

To overcome the depression transmitted to them by those three moons, the poorhouse staff popped cheap, seventh-generation Prozac like it was food. The poorhouse inmates ate every bite of their ever-inadequate food rations like it was medicine. That's how poor the rice planet was. It was a desolate rock without even a single local specialty, nothing in the way of mustard leaf kimchi or pumpkin taffy. Everyone looked down on that planet.

The girl grew into a beautiful woman. Among the poorhouse staff, the XY chromosome carriers all wanted to sink their tadpoles in her. But the woman was not interested in spending her life there. Despite her lowly birth and lowly place in life, she had more pride than that. At the age of sixteen, she enrolled in a teacher training school. It was a strict place, but she was at least able to eat her fill. For fourteen hours a day for four years straight without a single day off, she studied the history of science and the proper comportment for a teacher. In other words, fourteen hours a day for three hundred and sixty-five days—five times four is twenty, leave the zero and carry the two, six times four is twenty-four plus the two from before leaves four and carry the two, three times four is twelve plus that two leftover makes fourteen, then add to that five times one is five, six times one is six, three times one is three, which gives us four thousand and ninety, and multiply that by four again, four times zero is zero, nine times four is thirty-six, leave the six and carry the three, four times zero is zero plus the leftover three that slips down to take its place, and four times four is sixteen for a total of sixteen thousand, three hundred and sixty—wait, where did I mess up? Anyway, we're talking about a shitload of time spent studying. At the age of twenty, the woman was employed as an instructor at the basic education facility. There, she began teaching perfectly established scientific facts, the kind that required no further curiosity and no experimentation. Things like how it was impossible to assemble two organisms that were more than 87 percent identical, or how human beings were incapable of flight, whether through genetic, biological, or other means, and so on.

The children thus taught were able to quickly access a higher level of science in lieu of wrapping capes around themselves and leaping off of walls.

The year the woman turned twenty-seven, a twenty-year-old man was newly assigned to the facility. He was a teacher who specialized in the common human language. He was an enormous man, ill-suited to the gravity on the rice planet, and instead of teaching standard writing in class, he mainly taught the students emotional modifications to writing. The language that flowed from the giant's mouth gave his listeners a peculiar feeling. His colleagues took no small discomfort from their inability to clearly define what that feeling was. It was the same for the heroine of this story. But there was something special about the giant that other people didn't have in those days. Whatever it was worked on the woman. She came to like the giant.

The giant was the first to profess his feelings. He mumbled a brief, peculiar vow that he had inherited from his home planet and reached down to embrace her. Though the woman trembled a little, she did not back away but meekly gave herself over to him. That is how the woman who only taught precise scientific facts and the giant who taught an obscure emotional language fell in love. The two of them shared a love so deep that it is difficult to explain to minors. But as I am an extremely bashful person, I am not going to spell out that embarrassing scene in excruciating detail. You'll have to imagine it for yourself.

The giant was from the corn planet, which was governed by an ideology of universal equality. Though the woman was seven years older than him, he used the familiar form of speech with her. Even with people a hundred years older than him, he used the familiar form. The higher-ups hated people from the corn planet who were in the habit of shouting ridiculous bullshit, like "We are as equal as the grains of corn on a cob." It was not long before the giant was charged with failing to keep up and was sent to a different educational facility on the planet. It took a whole day just to get there, even using the fastest form of transportation. They saw each other once a month. The giant would stick his arms out and hug her as soon as he saw her, while she would pretend to gasp for air and be smothered by him, though she secretly enjoyed it.

One day, the woman was shocked to find the giant standing right before her eyes. When she was done gasping for air, she asked how he got there. "Did something happen?" They weren't supposed to meet that day.

"No," the giant said. "All day today, I kept missing you. Even while teaching the little kids, I thought about you. After work, I sat at my desk. I closed my eyes and spread my arms and thought about how badly I wanted to see you. My body slowly began to float. Then I flew through the air to be with you."

When he was done talking, the giant hugged the woman again. She wasn't upset about it or anything, but she felt a little confused whenever the giant said things like that. One time, he even told her he had just gotten back from visiting her when she was a little girl at the poorhouse, twenty years in the past. He took her in his arms and whispered sadly that she was just skin and bones back then and that her frightened face had looked so pale. The woman often muttered, "I don't get you." Each time she said that, the giant would look mystified and ask, "What? Am I weird for saying that?"

Their love lasted approximately 10,000 hours. After 10,000 hours, the giant was dead. Though his death had not been confirmed, the odds of it were very high, as he had fallen into a deep pond in the embryo zone of the rice planet. He had taken his students there on a picnic. One of the students snuck into a restricted area and fell in. The giant rushed to help him but in the end was unable to save himself. The troublemaker who caused the problem was executed on the spot by a government official, and a rescue team of monkeys—so highly trained they could even ride bicycles—was dispatched. The giant's body had sunk to the bottom of the abyss. The water was so dense no living creature could survive in it. The giant was presumed to have died instantly when all of the cells in his body simultaneously shut down the moment he was submerged in the water. The monkey rescue team rode back on their bicycles.

Two days later, the woman arrived. She did not cry. She did not even fully comprehend what had happened to her. She went to the spot where the giant had fallen in and touched the water. The surface of the high-density water danced beneath her fingertips. There was no wind, and a spectacularly red moon floated above her head. The woman tried with all her might to part the surface of the water. People who saw her thought she was drowning in grief. The atmosphere in the vicinity of the accident site had almost zero sound wave loss. Sounds that originated there took forever to vanish. They would circle the pond and return to their point of origin at two-day intervals. So the local council fired off a symmetrical sound wave once a week to completely cancel out the sound. The woman sat motionless at the edge of the water and listened as the giant drowned two days earlier. The chattering voices of the mischief-makers and the voice of the head teacher giving the children incessant warnings reached her ears. Then, there was a sudden uproar. Beneath the blood-red moon, she heard a child sob and call for help, the water's surface part, the water close again and engulf something, and a deep, deep swallow. But she dismissed it as nothing more than sound. She could not accept the fact of the giant's death. A thick fog descended unexpectedly. The weather god seemed to have been driven a little crazy by the crimson moon. Veiled in fog, the woman sensed that a long, long period of ill fortune was approaching.

After returning to her residence, the woman submitted a petition to the council. She was asking that the giant, assuming he was down there, be pulled out. The only entity with that kind of power was the council. Anything and everything required for daily life was had through the council. There were no private electric companies, subway construction companies, or broadcasting companies. Even the place known as a court of law and the occupation of judge had vanished, not because there were no longer any conflicts, but because human beings had already experienced every possible scenario by then. Simply by perusing the staggeringly large number of judicial precedents stored by the council, they could determine what had to be done when someone did something wrong. That's got nothing to do with this story, but anyway, the woman submitted a petition to the council. Anyone could petition the council. Plus, the woman was an instructor, which meant she was an employee at a facility run by the council. Two hours later, she received a rejection notice. She took it in stride. It would cost too much to retrieve the giant. As I said before, this was because of the immense density of the abyss. Still, the woman did not cry. She spent the next fifty years that way, not crying.

During that time, the world grew wider, and the cost of travel even cheaper. The woman toiled hard to save her money. She did not eat, dress, or bathe properly. Her life revolved around money. She had a good reason for saving up. She grew as gaunt as she had been during her days at the poorhouse. Her clothes grew tattered. She developed some wicked BO. Now, the XY chromosome carriers no longer wanted to sink their tadpoles in her. Not when the place was lousy with pretty AI robots ready to spread their legs, after all. The latest models had monitors in their chests so you could play computer games while having sex. Of course, those robots were extremely expensive. But after the magnesium deposits were discovered in the starch zone, the rice planet enjoyed unparalleled prosperity.

The woman applied for a leave of absence from work and submitted a much more elaborate petition to the council. At last, she received a modest grant and permission to exhume the body. The woman packed her bags and headed for the starch zone. She set up camp in the exact spot where she had heard the giant's shouts. The work crew, which had been promised hefty compensation, parted the surface of the water and sent down sturdy alloy robots. They found the body easily, thanks to the high-sensitivity magnesium lenses attached to the ends of the robots' feelers. But the body could not be raised to the surface intact. The absolutely incomprehensible pressure and density of the abyss had created razor-sharp diamond blades that were hidden everywhere. It would take alloy technology from one hundred years in the future to bring the giant's massive body to the surface. Despondent, the woman saw on the screen the body of her old lover lying facedown on the floor of the abyss. Due to the water's density, he had not decomposed at all. Turned slightly to the side, his face had the same smile—the one that looked like he was dreaming—that she had often seen half a century earlier. Fortunately, the woman was finally able to accept her beloved giant's death. She did not say a word. She knew she would burst into tears the moment she opened her mouth. Her face did not even change. She knew she would burst into tears the moment her face moved. She did everything she could not to cry. She knew that once she started crying, she would not stop crying for the rest of her life.

Finally, the woman reached a decision. She would take a little bit of the giant's flesh without leaving a mark. Faced with their doom at having to go in among the diamond knives, the robots went nuts, screaming in high frequency, but the woman did not budge. She shredded seven pricey alloy robots before managing to retrieve a tiny piece of flesh, no bigger than a grain of rice, from the giant's forearm. She took that grain of rice to a council hospital. The extracted DNA was planted in her uterus. She selected the average body size for the general population of the rice planet, so that the gravity would not be too arduous, and chose male for the gender. The baby was born nine months later. This all happened 165 years from now, in the year A.D. 2170.

Yes, a baby was born. The woman was seventy-nine years old at the time. Nowadays, if you were to tell a kid, "Your mom is seventy-nine years old," they'd flip out, but in the woman's time that age was not at all too old for raising kids. For reference, the

128

woman's yogurt delivery mother was ninety-three at the time she forced herself on the council programmer. At any rate, the woman matched the frequency of her own life to her child. She no longer longed for the giant. In those days, not longing for the dead was seen as proof of spiritual evolution. She believed the time of ill fortune that she had sensed at the giant's pond had now come to an end.

The woman went back to work. She resumed protecting her young students from wild, useless thoughts, from myths, legends, romantic tales, and daydreams, just as she had before falling in love. She spent her entire salary on her child and herself. She bought clothes and fixed her wrinkles. The woman once again became popular among the children and XY chromosome carriers. She even hummed from time to time. She bought a convection meter and installed it in the child's room. The device measured minute changes in the flow of gases around a physical object each time it moved and reconstructed it as a three-dimensional image. Though it appeared in black and white, the movement was quite smooth. Plus the images took up very little space, so they could be stored for an eternity without having to replace the memory. When she played back the data on the receiver, any physical object disturbing the air in the room—i.e., her son—would appear in vivid detail down to the last strand of hair. Even at work, during her spare moments, she would take out the receiver and look at the image of her child. He was gradually beginning to resemble someone. The woman was happy.

When he turned four, the boy entered preschool at the educational facility where the woman worked. With his bright and ready smile, the child was popular even among the teachers. He was clever, unlike other clones. There were many clones on the rice planet, but most of them exhibited severe developmental disabilities. This was unavoidable, as clones were originally developed for combat. But they turned out to be unsuitable for use even as cannon fodder because of their chronic and universal synesthesia. The clones could not distinguish clearly between sound and smell. They experienced color and taste nearly simultaneously. But the child had almost no developmental disabilities. He had none of the symptoms of synesthesia that would have caused problems in his daily life. Whenever he asked a question—big, pretty eyes shining—the teachers melted. One told him he would be a great teacher himself one day. The woman was happy when she heard that. She planned to raise him to be a teacher.

Of course, they were not entirely without their problems. The child was excessively enamored with myths. He was extremely fond of legends and often fell hook, line, and sinker for the wild stories concocted by the crafty magnesium miners. Sometimes, he spoke a strangely modified language, which perplexed the woman. But she put it down to his age. She believed that in a few years, when he started the regular curriculum, it would be but an embarrassing memory that he would want to forget.

Then the boy turned five—that was the year 2175. The woman turned eighty. It's not my fault she was so old. Time had passed. That year, the woman had her left eye and a faulty joint in her right leg replaced. Her pancreas was still good for another three years or so. The fact that there were foreign objects inside her body bothered her for a few days. But as she knew that she could not fight time, she decided it was better to get used to it.

Then, there was this day. An old lady from the flank zone requested a visit. The woman looked at the visitor request data, rendered in binary code, and wondered what the old woman was so pissed off about. She skimmed over the background information on the visitor. Then she ran a search on reasons why the old lady might want to see her. Only one possibility came up. The old lady's young clone was in the same class as her son.

Two hours later, the front door scanner buzzed. The woman checked the monitor beside the door. The old lady's body was full of cheap plastic organ transplants, and her coat read, "Christians Go To Heaven, Unbelievers Go To Hell." The scanner estimated the old lady's age to be two hundred years. Yup, the admirable scanner had guessed right. She was exactly two hundred years old. And in the year 2005, 170 years in the past, she was thirty. At the age of thirty, what should have been the flower of her womanhood, she was having frequent, noisy fits of hysteria in apartment 1001 of the Chŏngnŭng P'ungnim Apartments, exactly one floor below where I live. To be totally honest, I'd like to bite her to death. Her hysterics are truly horrific. If she were to fling herself off a ledge as a gift to my cat whose birthday is next week, it would be fantastic. But unfortunately, she does not die. And, like Frankenstein, she will keep swapping out her organs, living like a dog until 2203 A.D., when she will be bitten to death by a drunken hobo. That hobo was a former dentist who was reduced to rags overnight because of one genius.

Anyway, in the year 2175, the old lady was there, standing in front of the woman's door. Sticking to her side was her girl clone, face covered in dirty scratches. The girl hopped from foot to foot like she was about to poop her pants. The woman opened the door. The old lady came in all worked up, wagging her finger in her face. The woman was caught off guard. The old lady ordered her to "get that child" and bring him to her. The woman courteously invited her into the living room so she could hear what had happened first. The old lady blew her off rudely, just as she had treated me back in 2005, the simple-hearted guy living above her in the Chŏngnŭng P'ungnim Apartments. But the woman also had eighty-four years of experience dealing with countless rude people. Plus, she had spent ten years in that miserable shelter and endured half a century cursed by the memory of a man's corpse. In the end, the old lady went to the living room.

After taking a seat, the old lady seemed to calm down. But then she suddenly burst into tears. The reason was simple. The old lady made a career of taking her clone to funerals and bursting into tears—every generation has one or two such people. Making a show of tears before getting to the point seemed to be a habit for her. The woman handed her a tissue to wipe her tears. The old lady used the tissue and tossed it aside. Negative ions and disinfectant automatically sprayed out of the wall, which had detected contaminants. The old lady allowed a sufficient amount of time to pass then opened her mouth to explain the purpose of her visit. This time, halitosis remover and air freshener sprayed out of the wall.

It was a real quandary. The woman could not believe what the old lady was saying. But the lady was stubborn. "Get that child out here now," she demanded. After barely managing to restrain the old lady, the woman asked the tiny, idiotic-looking clone, "Did my son really do that?" The girl looked at the old lady, then at the woman, then at the old lady again and nodded. The old lady pulled a crumpled monitor out of her pocket and thrust it before the woman's eyes. On the screen was an image of a half-broken, palm-sized blood purifier. It wasn't something expensive or important that was worth making a fuss over. If it was broken, she could just buy her a new one. But it was wrong to destroy other people's property. If the child broke it, she would have to scold him. The woman stared hard at the flexible monitor. Then she quietly rose.

The child was sleeping peacefully. She did not want to wake him. She had given up fifty of the most beautiful years of her life to have him. She was prepared to give up all of her remaining time if it were for his sake. But that was not the problem at hand. She had to find out if it was true, no matter what. She shook him awake. His breath was sweet. He blinked and sat up. "Yes, Mommy?" That's what he said in his sleepy voice: Yes, Mommy?

When she saw the woman bringing the boy out, the old lady pitched another fit. The woman ordered her to calm down. It was not her usual way with people. She was already beyond offended. The woman turned the flexible monitor on the table toward the boy. She pointed at the object on the screen and asked, "Do you see this? Did you break it?" The boy blinked and peered at the screen. He spoke clearly: "I never touched that."

The old lady opened her smelly mouth wide and hollered like a crazy woman. The wall toiled to churn out negative ions and disinfectant and halitosis remover and air freshener all at once. The old lady did not trust the child one bit. She shook her finger at him and spoke harshly. The woman could not believe it. She loved her child so much that she had always assumed everyone else felt the same way. The woman put her hand over a button on the table. It was a warning that if the old lady did not calm down she would report her to the council. Finally, the old lady sat down again. The woman closed an electromagnetic curtain between the old lady and herself. Then she turned her chair around to face her son. Her heart was racing, but she did not want him to see how upset she was.

The woman looked into the child's bright, serene eyes. Then she looked at the old lady through the electromagnetic curtain. The lady snarled and glared at the boy, slapped her clone, glared at the boy again, and slapped her clone again. The clone started to cry. The old lady looked pleased and struck the clone again then yelled, "Your kid chased my child all the way to our zone, stole her blood purifier, and stomped on it until it broke!" The synesthesia caused the old lady's clone to register her shouting as the smell of shit instead and plug her nose.

"Did you do that? How could you do that?" The woman said the words she didn't want to say in the tone of voice she didn't want to say them in. But if she didn't, the old lady would protest. The woman acted as if she knew exactly what the child had done wrong and was prepared to gladly forgive him for it. It hurt her to act that way. What was she saying? She wanted to hug her son. But that would only get the old lady more riled up. She took her son by the shoulders, shook him slightly, and asked him again. "How could you do that?"

The boy looked at the old lady, looked at the old lady's clone, and looked back at his mother. "Mommy, what are you talking about?" The boy's voice trembled. "I told you I didn't do anything. I didn't go that way today. I left the facility and went toward the starch zone. I came home from there."

The woman turned her head to look out the window at the fading autumn garden. Though it was no more than twenty-five meters square, the garden looked huge due to the light configuration. In the future, after he was grown up, her son would be able to do a lot of things in that space. She turned her gaze back to the old lady, who was shaking her head in disbelief.

The woman said, "It seems that one of these children is lying. In that case, I have an idea." She pulled the receiver for the convection meter out of her bag. "My child carries a convection meter on him at all times. We can look at this to find out which way he went."

Despite saying that, the woman did not want to review the data with the old lady. Of course she believed her own child. She trusted in his existence, in his loveableness, and in every word he said. But as she was careful in all matters, she was beginning to doubt him. She knew where the starch zone was that he was talking about. A kind man named Allejandro lived there. In his early thirties, the man looked exactly like Seong Beomsu, one of my younger friends from college who is getting married at the end of the month. Congratulations, Beomsu. But Allejandro, who is the spitting image of my friend Beomsu, was an Egyptian stonecutter in one of his previous lives. In the following life, he was a German miner in the 1890s, and in the next life, he worked in the Aoji Coal Mine in North Korea in the 1970s. Now he was enjoying his fourth life in the magnesium mines of the rice planet. This is totally off the subject, but Allejandro worked hard, swapping out his lungs forty-three times due to miner's lung, before passing away in 2522 A.D. He then became a guardian spirit of the magnesium mines of the northern starch zone of the rice planet to protect the frail miners from magnesium ghosts, which show up all the time. A hacking, coughing guardian spirit. Congrats, Beomsu.

Incidentally, the woman knew that her son liked Allejandro and went to see him often. Because theirs was an era in which all forms of discrimination were considered an evil, she did not tell him to stop seeing him. She only told him to wear an air purifier to protect his lungs. The boy said he had gone toward the starch zone. And that he had come directly home from there. She would know whether this was true or not once she checked the convection meter.

The woman changed the high frequency curtain to a hologram monitor and transmitted the data from the receiver. The image appeared in black and white. First they watched the route the boy took in first-person perspective. The boy was clearly headed toward the starch zone. The woman felt proud. On the other side, the old lady's face turned red with disappointment. The woman wanted to get rid of the old lady as soon as possible, so she fast-forwarded through the playback. She switched the perspective to third person. Now the boy became a tiny dot roving about this way and that between empty fields, orchards, and low buildings. He kept a regular pace and did not stop anywhere in the middle, so the dot's movement looked extremely graceful.

The old lady snapped when the dot disappeared for a second time. She insisted there was a gap between where the child disappeared and where he reappeared. That much was true. But the convection meter had merely clicked off for a moment, to protect others' privacy, as the boy had entered a public space. The woman explained this to the old lady. Then she explained how it was beneficial to the public to have the device set to that mode. But the old lady was not convinced. Instead she argued brusquely with the woman, claiming it was decisive proof that the child was guilty. The old lady had never owned such a well-mannered device as the convection meter, so she did not even believe that such a thing could exist. And that's why I feel like I'm going to lose it each time I see the woman from apartment 1001.

Anyway, upon hearing that, the woman said that if they checked the convection meters that were installed in public, rather than the data on her personal device, it would prove that her son had passed through such-and-such a spot before returning home. Then she adjusted the receiver to contact the council. She was connected immediately. The woman moved the pointer slowly so the old lady could follow along.

And then it happened. This was the moment for which I exist. What fun would it be to sit at my desk under the pretense of seeing the future and merely relay a story taking place 170 years from now? Even my seven-year-old nephew can do that. A few days ago, he came to me crying and predicted that there would be no more dentists in the future. He was right. Because of one genius born in 2027, dentists all over the world were rendered penniless.

Anyway, I have a few words to say about this moment that will take place exactly 170 years in the future. To be precise, I am talking about the mentality of the woman and the old lady sitting in the living room. As I am a famous writer, I am exceptionally tuned in to other people's minds. First, the old lady. The old lady is currently in quite a precarious situation. The way things are going, it is clear that damned clone of hers has lied again. To make matters worse, the woman sitting before her refuses to get angry and scuffle with her. Instead, she is methodically displaying proof of her child's innocence with the use of a cold machine. Based on my superior skills, I would say the old woman is on the verge of screaming, "You bitch! We've messed with the wrong adversary today!"

Of course, "bitch" here refers to her clone. Next, the woman. The woman is tired. She is getting nothing out of demonstrating her child's innocence to the old lady. Even if she hangs her head and gives up, she'll just be throwing her son under the bus. The best thing for her to do is hear the old lady out and send her off quietly. It does not please her in the slightest to hear her child say he is innocent—just as it does not please her to know that she has two arms. The reason I insist on profiling them this way is simple. Because of what the child says in that moment, both of their attitudes will change radically. So what could the child possibly say? What he says is: "That's not how I got home."

The look on the woman's face as she took her hand off the pointer and looked at her son was one of utter confusion. "What?

That's not how you came home? Then, how did you get home? Is there another path?" The woman kept repeating herself, changing her words a little at a time.

"No, that's the only path. Except for the path through the carbohydrate tunnel, I mean."

Realizing that the tide was turning, strangely and without warning, in her favor, the old lady put her hand on her clone's knee and began to look pleased as punch. Still, she did not rush to act. Nothing was certain yet. The child's route as it appeared on the monitor was incomplete, but it was still clear he had not gone in the direction of her clone. She scowled patiently at the child.

"Then, what did you do?" the woman asked gently. Being a well-educated teacher, she was capable of this. Were she the old lady, she would have immediately thrown her son over her knee like a toad and lit into his hide. But even as a teacher, she couldn't help but worry. "What happened?" The woman asked again, gently.

"I came home a different way," the child answered simply. An anxious look came over the boy's eyes.

"You came home a different way? How?" The woman's voice rose a little higher. But in that moment, the woman still had not lost all trust in her child. Of course, he had come home another way. Nothing was coming to mind just yet, but there must be a ton of ways to get home, a bunch of different paths. He just chose another way, a different path than usual this time. That it had to be today, of all days, was odd, but that didn't prove he did anything wrong, the woman thought. It didn't matter in the slightest that she could not think of any other paths that led home. The woman had faith in her son. She had faith in him the way I have faith in the power of money. From the mouth of the boy in whom her faith was ironclad, the following words came spilling out.

"I flew home."

The woman closed her eyes and sighed. Twice, briefly, she let out a sigh. The child continued. "I flew home. When I was going through the carbohydrate tunnel, my legs hurt. My legs hurt, so I thought, I want to go home, I want to go home to Mommy. I closed my eyes and thought hard about it, and my body floated up off the ground. That's how I flew through the sky and came home."

The old lady decided the time had come for her triumphant overthrow. She gathered all the fire in her belly until the flames reached the peak of their destructive, fighting power. Her face reddened, and her biceps quivered like slime eels. The woman was aghast at the sight of her, but there was nothing she could do. She hung her head.

"Please forgive me. It seems my child was in the wrong. I will replace the broken item immediately, with something better. As a token of my apology, I will also send you a new flexible monitor. Please forgive my son, as he is young and does not know any better," the woman said. It was a crazy move. And like me, when I tried to hold my head high and stand up against the lady, she was crushed.

The old lady demanded that she send the items immediately, while she watched. That shrill voice had not rusted in the slightest over 170 years. The woman felt sick to her stomach, but she summoned up a ferocious degree of patience and stayed calm. She ordered the items from the council as the old lady watched, nodding her head. What? She ordered them from the council? Yup. The council even has a market. The prices are crazy high. But it's also crazy reliable, so people use it when they need to purchase important items. The costs for running the council are mostly covered by the market. Well, not that you really need to know that. Anyway, the old lady took a good look at the price of the items the woman ordered. They were three times that of the original objects. The old lady looked pleased.

The woman, feeling like China after all the pandas were stolen, saw the old lady to the door. She bowed, and bowed, and bowed some more. When she returned to the living room, the boy had his head down. She sat across from him. She couldn't believe what had just happened. In a firm voice, she told the boy to go to his room.

AZALEA

Wings
by *Park
Hyoung-Su*

138

"Think about what you did wrong. Don't talk to anyone. Don't look at anything. Sit there in the dark. That's right. In the dark."

The woman was surprised at herself. She had never once spoken to the boy that way. She would never have thought she was capable. The boy tried several times to say something. But the woman was not ready to hear anything he had to say, and the boy knew it. Eyes brimming with tears, the boy went to his room.

The woman sat in the living room for a long time. It wasn't fair. The boy was the one who had done something wrong, but she was the one in pain. By locking the child in a dark room, the woman wondered, who was really being punished? Was he sorry for what he had done? Did he resent me for it? How long should I wait before giving him a hug? When I go to hug him, she wondered, will he come to me? The next thing she knew, she was standing in front of the boy's room. She shook her head and went back to the living room. She collapsed into a chair. He can't do this to me, she thought. How could this happen? How could he lie to me? She had no strength left in her, which made even sitting difficult.

Just then, the woman realized the boy was standing behind her. She did not turn her head, but she knew he was covering his eyes with his hands and crying. She briefly pondered whether his tears were a sign of remorse. I have to tell him to go back to his room. Or, on second thought, I should hug him and tell him never to do that again.

But that was not what the child's tears meant. Standing behind her, the child said tearfully, "Why don't you believe me?" Tears continued to spill from his eyes. His face looked like it had been furrowed by the summer rains.

"What? Am I weird?"

When she heard those words, the woman felt her mind go blank. A terrible lethargy swept over her. It was because of the child. Because he was repeating the exact words that someone else had said long ago. Those words tore open memories that had been sealed tight inside her most painful place, like it was nothing. The woman remembered it all clearly, as if it had just happened. Half a century ago, on a day they weren't supposed to meet. She had asked him how he got there. Not because she actually wanted to know, but because she was grateful and delighted. Half a century ago, the giant had responded that he flew to her because he missed her so much. You flew? With that giant body of yours? It was the first time she'd ever heard something so silly. She never thought she would meet someone else who said things like that. She thought it was buried inside her forever. She was wrong.

Though the woman was sitting across from her son, her eighty-four-year-old gaze fell on someone she had met in her twenties. She had tried long and hard to forget the giant. As I mentioned earlier, not longing for the dead was accepted as proof of spiritual evolution. But that was always a virtue unattainable by humans. One part of the woman's heart that could not be policed had never stopped touching, hearing, and tasting the giant. She was plunged into confusion with no clue as to how she should act. It was not something you learned with age. The boy rubbed his cheek against her shoulder and spoke again. She was barely able to make out what he said. "Come out to the garden, Mommy."

She struggled to rise. The boy led her out to the garden. She felt like she was walking in a dream. The evening was silent with the moon dipping below the horizon, and a bluish strand of atmosphere flowed like a legendary snake through the shade of the stars. Just like this early autumn evening near Mt. Bukhan, 170 years earlier, where I sit writing this story.

The boy led the woman to the middle of the garden. He let go of her hand and backed away until he reached the other side of the garden. The woman felt dizzy and nauseous. She could not look directly at him.

"Mommy," the boy called in his sweet voice, "I'll show you. I'll fly to you, Mommy." The woman's head was swimming. Every time she took a deep breath, her chest felt hollow. A sour galactic breeze seeped between her ribs. Her vision wavered. She covered her eyes in surprise. Tears flowed without warning. With a sigh, the woman began to sob. She had held the tears in for so long that it hurt to cry. Because she was covering her face, she did not see the other side of the garden. She did not notice when her son disappeared.

Then, suddenly, she felt someone reach his hand down from behind her. It was as soft and warm as feathers. Quietly, she turned. Arms reaching down from above wrapped around her sweetly. The woman gave herself over to them. It was not unfamiliar. It felt just like when that incredibly huge giant had held her. She was comfortable. She was happy. But when she thought about how she had once been fulfilled by that sensation, her whole body smarted, and she felt crushed. She wanted to do whatever it would take. She wanted the giant's dreamy smile, broad chest, and his strange vows back. She wanted compensation for all that was taken from her and for the time trapped at the bottom of the abyss.

But, but that was all.

Desire was the only thing the woman could do. She did not move. She did not open her eyes. She refused even to take the sweet hand that was held out to her. Because she could not accept the things that were happening to her. She had been schooled for too long, and had schooled others for even longer. Flying through the sky, traveling to other times—these were impossible. If they were possible, why hadn't she just returned to a younger, more beautiful time? Why couldn't she fly back half a century and return to the arms of the one she loved? If she could do that, were she allowed, she would bury herself in time with that fine giant and never return. But that choice was not available to her. She could not bring herself to lower her hand from her eyes to confirm what was happening. Her faith in the impossible had plagued her for too long. She had lost even the ability to waver between this way and that.

Five Poems by
Sin Yongmok

Translated by Eun-Gwi Chung
and Brother Anthony of Taizé

INSIDE THE GLASS DOOR OF THE
SŎNGNAE-DONG CLOTHING REPAIRS

In an alley bent like a carp's backbone,
the sunlight, too, is bent. Time, a hunchback too,
has a hard time going far, so between galvanized iron walls sits
a sewing shop with a low glass door.
At nightfall when earth's tilt coils the sunlight
sometimes girls
glanced at it from a distance but
only saw their white faces printed there,
reflected off the dark behind the glass,
and no one walking up the alley after turning into a sheet of paper
ever wondered what lay inside the glass door.
Sometimes to hem the legs of newly bought trousers,
someone pulls at the door handle resembling the cover of a fairy
     tale book,
but the old wife's not there
just the husband spitting out a bit of thread, who greets briefly
with amphibian eyes, and if someone shows
the desired length of the trousers with thumb and forefinger,

pretends not to understand,
just vibrates his gills, then soon,
as if to train someone's needle's eye in biting
begins a backstitch that looks like an ellipsis.
There is a wave inside the glass door
that suspects no one coming out
after checking the needle rake,
which, forever straight, becomes even finer on the two fins
lying on the sewing machine.
Threads buoyantly float about
and a carp that lives on thread is hidden there.
Sometimes a newspaper comes flying and knocks at the door
but the door does not open. If it allows time in too often
the carp's scales will grow dry, so the glass
obstinately clamps shut its dentures and hangs on.
Next to the bent alley, there's a sewing shop.
Since all the people of Sŏngnae-dong
had become thin as paper,
no one peeped through its glass door,
but they could not avoid having their footsteps bent
whenever they passed the store
the way a fluorescent tube is bent in a fish tank.

In a thousand years' time, this will be a sacred shrine.

Apartment.

To be allowed to lie down in these magnificent remains,

he endured hard labor

and painful contempt—

my descendant may read that on a board in front of the janitor's lodge.

The management office where I went down

to pay the maintenance fee, clasping my remains

that would later be pictured in the guidebook.

The Roman catacombs where the faithful sleep layer upon layer;

like photos hanging after devoutly taking over the throne. One

    morning, sitting on the toilet,

I thought of the apartment residents

who must all be doing their business dangling their hands

a few meters up and down or apart.

Sun powder being sprinkled like the blessings of persecution,

the cloven foot of a camel setting off across a stony desert,

a woman's face like a dry tongue,

children chewing grains of sand,

in the catacombs where all of them live with their share of destruction

in each body, each room, night comes.

Between one cloud and another, a banquet is being served

and sheets of time transforming earnestness into holiness

hang beautifully in every window. If an era

ends like this,

I will be a martyr.

There's no roof on the bird's nest.
The solitude, as it buries its beak under a wing
and withstands storms, and the stillness of feathers soaked then drying
must have nurtured its wings, then

an instant comes bearing fate on its back.
At the heart of the city,
the wind's upper and lower jaws
are clamped unremittingly
on a black plastic bag as it suddenly goes soaring up,
marked with signs of tooth decay

the air's black target, its center open everywhere.

The whirlwind circles the nest,
and the solitude has ripened into horn

so as it aims just one blow at the sky.

birds wheel in search of a weak spot.

Reveal the bright air's dark windpipe! If I can attack that spot
beyond the wind's back teeth,

I could happily set off,
sacrificing a whole lifetime, limbs shorn off like horn.
Therefore, ah, Death,
set fate free.

Creatures sleeping with their backs to the sky, solitude's tomb is the sky,
and just as the sudden black bag digs its own grave in the sky,
in order to reach that spot,

birds never tile their roofs.

A FLOWERPOT

One day a flowerpot was delivered.

I've
come into some land. Soft
soil, I
will be buried there.

As I pass in front of a flower shop, behind the window
caskets are disposed entrancingly. Trees and flowers grow like
    lovely burial mounds,

Sunlight and winds admiringly seep into 70 square meters of solitude,
now orchids blossom there and hunch-backed time is enjoying a
    kind of honeymoon.

My grave is fragrant.
Though not like a butterfly performing the dances of a distant land,
    one day I will set my soul afloat in the void where flowers once
    fell, in that clear height.

If I hug the roundness and wait, maybe I can grow old painlessly. If
    disgrace is pruned away like a flower stalk, maybe harsh longing
    can die a natural death, maybe.

One day,
a drunken foot broke the flowerpot in passing.

The cobweb is the butterfly's body. It is the flap of wings drawn in
the void by a butterfly that passed through the spider's stomach.
It is the void a butterfly gifted to the spider. It is a rice bowl
handed back after eating. The wind nods and permits the void's
fluttering earthquake arising as a butterfly calls a butterfly.
Sunlight telling by its blazing impact that if you dig down into
the bottom of hunger, longing emerges like a stone. Between
spider and cobweb, there stands the butterfly's life. Something
passing through the spider's body, erect as a cobweb, that is the
story of my mother who hates my older brother for resembling
Father, that is the reason why love comes to me with its face
changed every time. A butterfly goes to a butterfly and shakes
the world. Shaken, it attains cold-heartedness.

Frank and I

by Cheon Myeong-Kwan
Translated by Kevin O'Rourke

Let me begin at the end. I never met Frank, but my husband regaled me with so many Frank stories that he must have thought I knew him well.

The two boys grew up like brothers in back-to-back houses. They went to martial arts together, and when they were a little older, they combed the neighborhood together and indeed every nearby neighborhood. Twenty years ago Frank emigrated to Canada where he set up a small auto repair shop. The boys were cousins; Frank was the son of my husband's father's elder sister. He changed his name to Frank when he decided to go to Canada.

That's all I know about Cousin Frank. My husband's lengthy stories about him follow a pattern, more or less as follows: The boys sling their guitars across their shoulders and head for a fun part of town. Some beautiful college girls gather around them. Just by chance. The boys aren't much interested. Predictably. The girls make the move to mix. They have to. The atmosphere mellows nicely. That's when the local heavies appear. Invariably. There's a lot of them. They pick a fight. Naturally. Frank puts up with the abuse. Patiently. He remonstrates. Gently. They don't listen. They begin to harass the girls. Shamelessly. Frank puts up with the abuse and continues to remonstrate. Unequivocally. Of course they don't listen. Their fists fly first. Wham! A punch lands. Boom! Another fist flies; another punch lands. Phew. Frank puts up with it. He continues to remonstrate, patient to the end. Please, he pleads, please, for the last time, the very last time. Earnestly. The heavies snort in derision. Swish, another punch flies. Smash! The fist of justice strikes. A lightning jab. The heavies are scattered across the floor. Poetry in motion. Mercy, mercy; let's get the hell out of here; the heavies take to their heels. The girls applaud. Frank smiles sheepishly. Before the smile disappears from his face, the heavies pile back. This time there must be twenty of them. Minimum. They have sticks, steel pipes, motorcycle chains. Cowards. One of them points at Frank. Their leader steps forward. He has a knife scar on his face. Monstrous. Tattoos, too. Ugly. And a fish knife in his hand. Blue-glinting sharp. He spits through his teeth, sneers, lunges with the knife, cuts callously. Frank feints. That was close. A moment later the leader of the heavies is dumped to the ground. His lieutenants rush to the attack. As one man, but through empty air. Pipes swing, knives fly. The heavies are scattered across the ground. Justice is the victor.

My husband's stories about Frank's deeds of derring-do always end the same way. Frank is a man among men, the just among the just. I don't know if it's true, but he insists that Frank never lost a fight prior to going to Canada. My husband always called him Frank. It allowed my husband to be Paul or Richard.

He once showed me a photo of Frank and himself, taken in the martial arts gym before Frank joined the marines. Stripped to the waist, they face the camera with laughing faces, fists raised like a poster for a fight. My husband is slightly bigger but Frank with his dark skin looks tougher. Firm fleshed, no flab, they have the air of young men who have not yet attained maturity. "When were you ever that slim?" I ask. "Look at the photo!" he says. In the old days, he claims, he could fly up walls like a character in a martial arts movie. Between the time the photo was taken and meeting me, he put on twenty kilos, and in the fifteen years since we were married, he's added another twenty. 1.85 meters and over a 100 kilos, you

152

might think he's a bit of a monster but not so. Despite his size, he's cute and charming; he cries regularly watching TV dramas. He likes to perform for me, imitating famous entertainers. His party piece is what I call the "Dangle Dance," which he does after getting out of the bath. He puts his hands on his shoulders, shakes his butt up and down and from left to right, and lets his pepper and nuts dance freely under his considerable belly—as if they had a life of their own. It's cute and disgusting at the same time. No matter how angry I am, I can never watch him without bursting into laughter. Just imagine! A giant of a man, over a hundred kilos, stark naked and shaking his ass and pepper.

Then he lost his job. The streets were already full of the unemployed. The threat of bankruptcy hung over people's heads like a dark, thick shadow. At first I wasn't too worried. With five or six skills certificates in his pocket, I figured he'd be able to get a job, but I discovered that people with much more than skilled worker certificates were unable to get work. He sent his CV here and there, asked a few influential people for help. The reply was always the same, "It's not a good time."

He graduated from a technical high school, went from there to a technical college and ended up working for a small company that made hairdryers. One day he came to the sports section in the department store where I was working. He wanted to buy a tracksuit. We didn't have his size but I promised to get it for him if he would call again. He dropped in a few days later and asked me on a date. His size was a big talking point among my co-workers in sales, but I fell in love with his sheer bulk. I thought it was a compelling attraction.

After we were married, he changed jobs twice; once to an electric razor manufacturing company and once to a company that made electric rice pots. The electric rice pot company was his last job. When he got fired, our son was already in elementary school and we were burdened by substantial tutoring fees and monthly mortgage repayments. In bed at night, a sense of desperate crisis oppressed us, as if a monster were striding across us at the head of the bed.

I made a number of enquiries before eventually getting a job as a cashier in a shopping center. My work experience in the department store before I got married was a help in getting the job. This was a good break for us because my husband's rat's ass salary meant we were always struggling to get by. If he could get a job now and we had two salaries, things would improve. That didn't happen. Several months passed and he was still goofing around the house. He didn't even seem much interested in getting a job. This put me under enormous pressure. I began to nag him and in the end he moved his butt and started to look for work again, but work wasn't easy to come by. Our debts had mounted meanwhile. With less than a million a month coming in, we simply couldn't cope. Add to this the accumulated red ink from idling for so long. Things were going from bad to worse. A job immediately was the only solution to our difficulties.

That's when Frank entered our lives. I got home from work late one night, feeling like pickled leeks, only to find my husband positively glowing. He had been waiting for me, and as soon as I sat down, he went into machine-gun mode in a rapid-fire account of all that had happened today. Here's the gist of the story.

Frank phoned. The men exchanged greetings. Business is good, Frank said. Put on a lot of weight, it's a worry, he said. Over 120 kilos now, he said. Asked my husband how he was. Just passed the 100 kilo mark, he said. Not that, Frank said. How are things in general? My husband hesitated. Been out of work for a year, he said. It's a worry, he said. Can't sleep, he said. Can't eat properly either, he said. Can't understand why I'm not losing weight, he said. Frank burst out laughing. Surely you're not down on yourself because of something silly like that. Might be all for the good. What could be good about it? Are you trying to give me a hard time? Nothing of the sort, Frank said. I'm talking about a golden business opportunity. What opportunity? Importing Canadian lobsters.

What are lobsters? Sea crabs in Korean, Frank said. He knew what sea crabs were. I have no money; it can't be done without money. Don't worry about money, Frank said. I'll buy the lobsters here and send them to Korea. All you have to do is sell them. You can keep whatever you make, just send me back my original stake. Is that really all I have to do? That's all, Frank said. It's what we call doing the right thing, he said.

My husband finished his account of the phone call. I looked at him with a blank face. I'd never eaten lobster in my life.

"Do they sell lobsters in Korea?" I asked.

"What do you mean?" he said. "Not everyone lives like us, you know. Other folks have lobster once a week. Some even eat lobster every day. Never miss a day," he said, clenching his fist confidently.

"Is lobster really that tasty?"

Next day we took our child to eat lobster. My husband had three portions, the child had two and I had one. Half my month's salary went for the lobster. Having eaten lobster once, my husband fell in love with it. Next morning he was out and about doing a survey of the market. Once a day he had a prolonged phone conversation with Frank. The other half of my salary went for international calls.

A month later. My husband said he would have to go to Canada himself. "Is that really necessary?" I asked anxiously. "Absolutely necessary," he said. He'd have to see for himself the price of lobster in Canada, meet Frank and work out a detailed sales plan. And he asked me to arrange the money for the trip. He added that Frank, of course, would send the plane ticket if he asked him, but this trip was for himself, and he couldn't ask Frank, however close their friendship—after all he's offering the lobsters for nothing—he couldn't ask him to send the plane ticket as well. That would be really brazen.

I had to ask my brother—he runs a fishing store-to lend us the money. My brother told me on the phone that customers were fewer these days, that he was barely getting by. It's killing me, he said. People aren't fishing any more, he said. And when I asked him what they were doing instead, he said he was wondering about that too. I explained my husband's lobster import project in the grandest terms and assured him that three months would be more than enough to pay back the money. My husband watched anxiously as I negotiated the loan with my brother. He gave a whoop of delight when I told him my brother had agreed to lend us the money.

"Great, great, that's great," he said rubbing his hands together. "All we have to do is get to Canada, bring home the lobsters and all our problems will be solved."

My husband prepared for the Canada trip in a fever of excitement. He was like a kid going on a school outing. This was his first trip abroad. He bought travel books on Canada and prepared a lot of winter clothes. Canada is so much colder than Korea, Frank said. He'd die of cold if he thought in terms of current Korean temperatures. My husband listened to Frank's advice. He kept buying things he thought necessary for the trip, and the phone calls to Frank were increasingly longer. He bought a heavy duck down parka, woolen mittens and gumshoes. He heard that cigarettes were expensive in Canada so he bought five cartons of Korean cigarettes. And he bought anti-diarrhea pills, anti-fever pills and painkillers. Among the various items he bought were nose plugs for swimming. When I asked him why he bought the nose plugs, he said blankly, "Are they nose plugs?" He had no idea why he bought them, he added.

When we went to buy the plane ticket to Canada, we discovered there was nothing left in the bank. I had to call my brother. Once again the world was killing him. He'd discovered that people were more into scuba diving than fishing. So in the future he'd have to have scuba diving gear as well as fishing gear in the store. The money squeeze was deadly, he said. I exaggerated a little as I elaborated on the lobster import project.

"Don't worry," I said. "When we get the lobsters from Canada, all our problems will be over."

Without being aware of it I had begun to parrot my husband's speech habits. My brother kept telling me that he'd have to have the money back in three months so that he could have the scuba diving gear in the store ahead of the summer season.

One way or another we got the plane ticket. Preparations for Canada were more or less complete. My husband bought an English conversation pocket book and studied English whenever he had time. This was in case he had to travel around in Canada without Frank. He handed the book to our child. The child was to ask questions in Korean and he was to answer in English. "How do you say *komapsŭpnida*?" the child asked.

"How do . . . how do you . . . ."

"Well, what's 'Where's the Sich'ŏng?'"

"Sich'ŏng . . . sich'ŏng . . . Give us a hint."

"Sich'ong is City Hall. There's your hint."

"Ah City Hall . . . that's right, City Hall. I know it now . . . City Hall . . . City Hall . . . ."

That's how it went mostly.

The day came for my husband to leave for Canada. I had to go to work so we said goodbye on the way out in the morning. He said he'd call from the airport before he left, put his arms around me and kissed me. I hurried out; the back of my nose was stinging.

Soon after I got to work the calls began. He couldn't find his sunglasses. Had I put them somewhere? I put them in the small bag, I said. Have a look there. OK, he said and hung up. He called me seven times on his way to the airport. And he called me twice from the airport. Once he couldn't find his ticket; once he couldn't find the diary with Frank's number. Customers were milling around me; every call brought a sinking feeling.

I told him to stay cool. Begin at the beginning, I said, and search carefully. He found the ticket in the toilet where he had gone for a pee; he never found the diary with Frank's number. Frank was supposed to be at the airport in Toronto when he arrived. If he needed Frank's number, he said, we had it in the phone diary at home. He assured me everything would be fine, told me not to worry and hung up. As soon as he hung up I began to feel uneasy about how he was going to make the long journey to Canada and back and get the lobsters safely home.

When he phoned again, I was deep in dreamland. Huge lobsters were swimming slowly, their pincer claws propelling them through deep seawater. The hard shells were uniformly stuffed with white meat. The phone rang. I wondered how I could hear the phone in the midst of the tranquil sea. Suddenly I opened my eyes. The phone kept ringing at the head of the bed. I looked at the clock. It said four in the morning. It had been seventeen hours since my husband got on the plane for Toronto.

I lifted the receiver. It was him all right. I asked if he had arrived safely. He'd been in Canada for three hours, he said. He was calling from the airport. He hadn't met Frank yet, he said. What happened, I asked? He didn't know what had happened, he said, but he wanted me to look up Frank's number quickly. Still half asleep I began to rummage through the diary. It took a while but I found it and told him. Sorry for waking you up, he said. Don't worry, he said; go back to sleep, he said. He hung up. I tossed and turned until dawn, completely frazzled; I didn't sleep a wink.

A few hours later, I dragged myself to the shopping center. I was just about to begin work when the phone rang. It was my husband. Had he met Frank, I asked. He hadn't met him yet, he said. He'd phoned him, but there was no answer; something must have gone wrong, he said. If Frank phoned me, I was to tell him he was waiting at Exit 13.

After I hung up I remembered that there was no way Frank could know my cell phone number. I made several mistakes with the cash that day. I kept bungling around, tore a fish wrapper and had mackerel flapping on the top of the cash counter. All day long the fish smell hovered over it.

After I got home from work and put the child to bed, I got a phone call. The caller said he was Frank. At first I couldn't believe

158

that this was the voice of Frank, the great righteous hero my husband spoke about. The voice went wing-wing like a mosquito; the pronunciation was sloppy and vocal quality weak, thin and quivery. He had gotten my husband's arrival date wrong, he said, was late getting to the airport and failed to meet him. I explained that my husband had been waiting for hours at Exit 13. There's no Exit 13, he said; the exits are A, B and C.

I was in shock. Where the hell was Exit 13? Aware that I was upset and worried, Frank tried to calm me down. He can't have gone very far, he said; he has to be somewhere in the airport. Finding him is just a matter of time, he said. No need to worry. Wait a while and we'll have news. Maybe you'll get a chance to come to Canada later on, he said. He hung up. The unease that had raised its head before my husband left for Canada slowly began to choke me.

I got no phone call for a week. I was dying to know if he had met Frank and if the lobster project was going ahead smoothly, but the murderous cost of international phone calls kept me from calling. Everything will be fine, I thought. I tried not to worry. But as time went by my unease grew.

 The weekend passed. On Monday morning I called Frank. No one answered. I kept calculating the time difference between Seoul and Canada and called repeatedly. Vague feelings of unease grew into concrete worries. Suddenly someone answered the phone. A voice filled with diffidence slid from the receiver. "He-hello!"

I knew immediately who it was. "What's going on?" I cried angrily. "Why didn't you phone?" So relieved that it wasn't a foreigner, he answered me in fine clear tones. Met Frank that day at the airport, he said. Came home to his house, had so much to talk about we went out to the club and had a two-day session. Drank a skinful, he said. Went fishing together next day, he said. Tomorrow we plan to look into the lobster import project.

"There's a problem though," he lowered his voice.

"What's the problem?" I asked, already tense with an acute sense of foreboding.

"Consuela's really angry."

"Consuela? Who is Consuela?"

"Consuela is Frank's wife. Well, not really his wife as they're not married. But they live together. Since I got here, she says, Frank has had no time for her. All we do, she says, is go around drinking. She's very angry, she says. When we went fishing, we left her behind."

"Is she Canadian?"

"No, she's Mexican. Over 100 kilos too."

I had a vision of two 100-kilo Korean men and a 100-kilo Mexican woman sitting together on the sofa eating cereal and watching TV.

"So what's the problem?"

"Frank hasn't said anything to me directly, but the impression I get is that Consuela resents me staying here. You know yourself how big they are on privacy over here. So it looks like I'll have to get a room tomorrow in a hotel downtown." His voice got lower and lower.

"You can't," I cried disconsolately. "There's no money,"

"Not to worry. I'll get the cheapest possible place. We might need some money in the long term though. Of course if I mentioned it to Frank, he'd pay for the hotel, but you can't be sponging all the time."

The money thing made the hair stand up on top of my head.

"So how long will it take?" I said, making an effort to stay calm.

"We'll have to get a move on. Two weeks at most. Not to worry. Everything will be fine. Goodnight honey," he said and hung up.

What the hell time was it in Toronto that he was saying goodnight already in the morning? A cold sweat ran down my spine.

The shopping center had a huge sale to celebrate five years in business. Housewives stood in queues from early morning to get free gifts. Working hours were extended by two hours. By the time work was over I was so exhausted I hadn't a thought left in my head. I felt like plopping down on the floor. As soon as I got home I fell down on the sofa and slept. I didn't even bother to change my clothes.

The phone rang at first light. Half asleep I lifted the receiver. He was staying in a hotel, he said. He had investigated the price of lobster and discovered that the profit margins could be greater than we originally thought. On the other hand, he said, the hotel was more expensive than expected. He had used almost all the money and could I send him some more?

"How much do you need? I said.

"Well, for a start I need 700 dollars urgently. I can get by on that."

"All right," I said, still half asleep, and I fell back asleep straightaway.

Next day on my way to lunch I passed an ATM machine in the shopping center and remembered that he had asked me to send more money. This quickly brought me to my senses. I did a rough calculation of 700 Canadian dollars in Korean money. It was the equivalent of a month's pay, enough to send me into shock. I couldn't ask my brother to lend us the money. I was too ashamed to ask and anyway I didn't think he'd be willing to lend us more.

That afternoon I used cash advances on two credit cards to send the money. Thoughts of the enormous interest and service charges drained the blood from my body. It couldn't be helped. All I could do was pray that everything worked out.

For the next week I heard nothing. I was dying to know whether he got the money and when the lobsters would arrive in Korea, but I was afraid to phone. I had the uneasy feeling that if I called first, all I'd get would be bad news. A few days before the sale ended my husband called. For some reason his voice was very subdued. Things could take longer than we thought, he said. I made an effort to keep calm. I asked was something wrong. He hesitated. "Frank's had bad news," he said.

"What bad news?"

"Consuela's left."

"Why did she leave?"

"Seems she has another man. An emigrant from Chile, he's a football coach in an elementary school."

"Chile? You mean that long, skinny country?"

"Yes, that's right. They've been seeing each other for more than a year. She's fallen for him head over heels. Frank didn't know."

"So?" I pressed my hand on my heart to control the trembling.

"So the pair of them ran off to Vancouver last night. They took the money Frank had set aside to buy the lobsters and they took the car."

"So what's to be done?" I said. I thought I'd burst into tears at any moment.

"Frank borrowed a car this morning and took off after them. I'm to look after the shop until he gets back. He knows where they've probably gone, he said. He'll have them back soon, he said. I'm to wait, not to worry."

Wait, not to worry! My God! The power drained from my legs and I sank to the floor. Toronto to Vancouver was ten days by car, he said. Consuela, Frank, Chile, Vancouver, football coach, lobsters, lobsters . . . .

Lobsters were in my dreams that night again. They waved their huge pincer claws slowly in the depths of the sea. When I got close and touched them, the shells fell off. The flesh underneath was black and rotten and gave off a strange smell. The rotten flesh fell off and spread through the water. I tried to grab the pieces in my hand but they slipped through my fingers, wavered in the water and disappeared. When I awoke, I was in the grip of a boundless desolation; I lay there vacantly for ages.

He called again a few days later. I borrowed a bit here and a bit there from co- workers in the shopping center and from friends and managed to scrape together 1,000 dollars, which I sent to him. He calculated in dollars rather than *won*. I got used to this quickly too, but every time I borrowed, it felt as if the blood in my veins was drying up.

Frank was back from Vancouver. He couldn't find Consuela and the football coach. Don't worry, he said. He'd get some money together very soon and buy the lobsters. The exchange rate was

162

down, the price of lobster was falling; the later we bought, the greater the profit.

One good thing was that since Consuela had left the house, my husband no longer needed to stay in a hotel. He was living now in Frank's house; he was a help to Frank, he said, in his hour of need. It was good, he said, to be with his friend when he was needed. On the other hand, Frank was unable to deal with his broken heart so the pair of them went to the club to drink every night. I urged him not to get distracted, to get the lobster project going as soon as possible.

Had the affair come to an end at this stage, everything would have been fine. Unfortunately, the situation got even more complicated. While drinking at the club, Frank had a run-in with a black man. There was no opportunity to let tempers cool; Frank was like a cranky child itching for the scrap. The he-man marine, never beaten in a fight in his life, massacred the black man. Frank was carted off to the cop shop, the black man to the hospital.

A few days later, Frank posted bail and got out. The problem didn't end there. The black man Frank beat up had come from LA to Toronto to sell drugs; he belonged to a prominent LA gang. He was going to shoot Frank, he said. He and his mates began fine-combing the city trying to find Frank. A frightened Frank hid at home; he had no time to worry about lobsters or anything else. God save us!

"I'm sorry, love, I had no idea things would come to this. Had I been there, I'd have stopped him, but I was in the toilet when the row started."

I broke down in tears. He used every pretext he could find to comfort me.

"Don't worry," he said. "They'll go home soon. They'll get tired of looking and go home. What choice do they have? It's so much colder here than in LA. You know how black people are in the cold. I know them from my time here; they go around with handwarmers when it's even slightly cold. And I just heard the forecast. The weekend is going to be much colder."

I had no idea how vulnerable black people were to the cold. While hoping the gang would go back soon to the City of Angels, I couldn't help wondering how many rows Frank and my husband had caused when they lived in Korea. Suddenly the future with a husband like that stretched very bleakly in front of me.

I was in big trouble now with credit card debt, worn out taking calls from bill collectors. My nerves were ragged; I regularly shouted at the child and in the store I couldn't greet customers warmly. After a huge row with one customer, I was called up by the boss and given a thorough dressing down. I went into the toilet, locked the door and burst out crying. Lobsters with their big claws were chewing chunks out of our happiness.

To get back to the story. The bad times were not over yet. On two occasions in the meantime I'd sent 1,000 dollars, and the black gang had not gone back to LA. In fact, a new gang member had arrived in Toronto. My husband phoned.

"Something terrible has happened, love," he said.

I wasn't that surprised. "What's happened now? I asked indifferently.

"Frank's come from LA," he said. He always began a conversation with Frank.

"What do you mean?" I said. "Frank's in Toronto, why would he come from LA?"

"Ah, not Cousin Frank," he said. "Mafia Frank."

"Mafia Frank?"

"That's right. The guy Frank beat up, his boss is called Frank, same as Cousin Frank. He's actually a cousin of the guy that got beat up."

"Frank? Cousin? I'm all confused. So why has Mafia Frank come?"

"Why else? He's come for revenge. He's a big shot hoodlum in LA. On the FBI blacklist. They always take care of people that try to screw them. Recently two Colombians stole drugs from them. They followed the pair to Bolivia; killed them without mercy. Frank got away because there was no evidence."

164

My God. A gang leader called Frank from LA had now entered the scene. How was an ordinary housewife from the other side of the world supposed to make sense of all this? A cool clinical mood came over me.

"And so?" I asked.

"And so, you ask? And so we can't go out; we have to have our food delivered to the house. Yesterday Frank put seven extra locks on the door."

What next! Who the hell was this Frank who put the fear of God in our two 120- kilo-plus legendary heroes, men who were afraid of nothing in the world and unbeaten in a fight in their lives, so much so that that they put seven extra locks on the door?

"And by the way, Mafia Frank grinds his teeth at the mention of a Korean. Seems he got it rough at the hands of a Korean gang in LA. They pointed a gun at his head and told him to crawl between their legs. Then they force-fed him kimchi. Cousin Frank obviously needs a change of scenery."

I told my husband to forget about lobsters and everything else, pack his belongings and get back here to Korea. He said he could get the plane ticket at any time, but with Frank in such danger, he felt he had to stay by his side to protect him. That was the right thing to do, he said. The right thing to do my ass, I said. There's no more money to send; we are completely broke. Come home or get shot by the LA gang, whichever you please, I shouted and I hung up.

I dreamed the lobster dream again. The lobsters were much bigger than in the earlier dreams. Their pincer claws were almost as big as a man. For some reason the lobsters were dark like black men and they growled at me like wild animals. Because of the water the sound was even more threatening. The lobsters pursued me. Naked and terrified I floundered in the water trying to escape, but I could make no headway. The lobsters were very fast. They harassed me with their huge claws and chopped at my arms and legs relentlessly. I couldn't breathe. I screamed but no sound came from my lips.

The story continues. Mafia Frank and his lieutenants searched every corner of Toronto for Cousin Frank. My husband kept tabs on the gang's movements through a first-generation Korean employee at Mafia Frank's hotel. One day at daybreak, Cousin Frank left Toronto and took refuge in a friend's house in Ottawa. That left Mafia Frank and my husband in Toronto. As Cousin Frank and my husband were cousins and both were fat, my husband wasn't free to circulate at will in Toronto.

While I was under enormous economic pressure in Korea, my husband was whiling away the time in Frank's house in Toronto. We prayed earnestly that Mafia Frank would forgive everything and return to the warmth of LA. If Mafia Frank went back to LA, Cousin Frank would be able to come back from his friend's house in Ottawa, get his hands quickly on some money, buy the lobsters and send them to Korea. All our problems would be solved.

I don't know who was listening to our prayers up there but in the end we got some good news. Our trustworthy Korean waiter in the hotel informed us that Mafia Frank had finally given up on the idea of revenge and was packing his bags to go home to LA.

That was the last message I got from my husband for some time. I interpreted the lack of communication positively. I figured he was busy buying lobsters and finding out details of import procedures. Believe me, that's what I wanted to believe. However a few days later a phone call from my husband reduced my expectations to rubble. Mafia Frank was still in Toronto, he said. The reason for this was classic: romance had been added to the mix. Mafia Frank had packed his bags and was about to leave the hotel for LA when he fell in love with a white Swiss girl working at the front desk. A climactic development.

The girl's name was April. Mafia Frank sent his lieutenants home and extended his period of residence in Toronto. Every night he dated April. They had dinner together and went to a show. He had lots of girls in LA, and they were mostly a lot sexier than April, but he preferred April—she was a bit more intellectual and she had that elusive European aura. He began to like Toronto more and more. His LA lieutenants rang him repeatedly telling him about a backlog of pressing business and guys that needed to be dealt with, but a man in love was not about to listen. He thought he'd like to wind up his Mafia life and begin a new life in Toronto with this elegant, white Swiss girl. His dream was our despair.

We had one hope left: April wanted to live in LA. Unlike Mafia Frank, she entertained the vanity of a more dramatic life in a vibrant, exciting city like LA. Her vanity was our last hope.

It was more than two months since my husband had gone to Canada. All talk of Cousin Frank had ceased since he ran away to his friend's house; his place had been taken by Mafia Frank.

Frank, Frank, Frank . . . . Damn it. My husband talked about Frank so disgustingly often that now the name sounded like the name of a friendly, respectable neighbor. But Mafia Frank and Cousin Frank were names of deities who held our hopes and fears in the palms of their hands.

Fortunately, Mafia Frank decided to let April have her wish. He was used to a city where gunfire and bloodshed were commonplace, and he was getting bored with Toronto's quiet lifestyle. Suddenly he began to worry about his LA lieutenants; he pictured in his mind's eye the faces of the guys that needed to be dealt with.

One final problem remained. April was living with her family and her family was very conservative. Her father was a racist, a passionate Hitlerite. So he considered it most inappropriate for his daughter to associate with a black man. Mafia Frank didn't like April's parents' open hostility, but April insisted on getting their permission. So he launched a gift campaign to buy a change of heart. He bought an expensive Swiss watch for April's mother, a set of American golf clubs for her father and a Japanese computer game console for her younger brother.

Even the most virulent racists relax their attitudes when confronted with a flood of material goods. April's parents gradually had a change of heart. Still, the ideology of a lifetime didn't collapse in a moment. Every day at dinner they exchanged views on Frank. The gift onslaught continued. April's father came to a conclusion about Frank the day he got the 60,000 dollar Cadillac convertible. The verdict was more or less vague but this is the gist of it: *A black man isn't a man at all; a black man is more like an animal. Accordingly I hate blacks. Frank is black. But he's not a black man. He's black all right but he's not a real black man. He's only black on the outside; he's not black inside. His soul is as pure as a white man's soul. Accordingly, he's white. So marrying my daughter does not pose a problem.*

Bit by bit our hopes revived. My husband communicated frequently with Frank in Ottawa and told him to get ready to come back. But something else untoward happened. Someone told April's parents that she and Mafia Frank had been to a nudist beach and smoked marijuana. Once again April's parents began to doubt the reality of Frank's white soul.

About this time too it was revealed that the Cadillac April's father received from Frank was stolen. April's father was summoned to the police station and questioned. The newly burning flame of hope began to flicker in the wind.

One day about three months after my husband had gone to Canada, I got a phone call from my brother. It was time for him to get the scuba diving gear in stock, he said, and he was short of money. When could he hope to get the loan back?

"I'm really sorry," I said, "but I can't promise an exact date at the moment."

I felt myself shrinking into nothing.

"Why not? Originally you said three months, didn't you?" he said testily.

"Yes, I know, I said that at the time, but things got complicated since."

"What's so complicated? You said you were going to import lobsters. Have they not come?"

"That's right," I said. "They haven't come. Frank's still in Toronto. If only Frank would go back to LA!"

"Frank? Who's Frank?"

Who's Frank? My God! Do I have to explain the whole thing from the beginning again?

Two months later my husband came home. It was mid-summer. The soles of my feet had been on fire since morning; my underwear was soaked with sweat again thirty minutes after changing. I was off work that day and took the car to the airport to meet him. He had lost thirty kilos while he was in Canada. At first I hardly knew him. I almost burst into tears when I saw him. He made a face when he saw me; it was hard to know whether he was glad or otherwise. He rolled his big eyes, wishy-washy like a man after torture. He said he was tired and wanted to go home quickly. Every time a horn sounded on the way home, he jumped and looked around.

As soon as we got home he fell on the bed without even washing and went to sleep. Inside two hours he was awake and out in the living room. Too hot, he couldn't sleep, he said. And as if he had suddenly remembered, he looked around and asked where the child was. He nodded blankly when I said he was at cram school. After he had a bath, I got him some of the clothes he wore before he put on weight. Thankfully they fit. The old clothes were faded and smelled of mothballs. He looked ridiculous, like in an old photo. As if he felt strange in his old clothes, he stood in front of the mirror and examined himself carefully. Suddenly he bent his head and began to snivel. I felt bad too, went up to him and put my arms around him. He buried his head in my breast and cried out loud like a child. I patted him on the back as he bawled his head off, tears as big as your fist rolling down. And as he cried he kept saying I'm sorry, I'm sorry. It was almost unintelligible. Suddenly I was crying too. And I found myself repeating the words he used to say to me before he left for Canada. "Not to worry! Everything will be all right."

Two months after my husband came home he got a job. This time it was a company that makes electric stoves. The wages were terrible. But he wasn't in any position to discriminate between hot rice and cold rice so he said nothing disparaging. He was just pleased to get a job in times like these.

That winter, Cousin Frank called. He had opened a shop in Ottawa and had made a life for himself there. He had forgotten about Consuela and had a new woman, he said. A Brazilian woman; like Consuela she was over 100 kilos, but she was younger and prettier, he said with pride. More than twenty years separated them in age.

In addition, Mafia Frank finally returned to LA. My husband asked what had happened. Apparently April's parents had been robbed one night at gunpoint and murdered. April was left on her own. She cried for a few days and then joined Frank in LA. Afterwards folks said that Frank was undoubtedly responsible for the killing of her parents. He was a man to be feared, they said, and they shook their heads. Cousin Frank said he had no problems now, so let's talk about importing lobsters again. My husband thanked him for his consideration but said he was so busy on the job he had no time to think about lobsters. Frank said he understood, and if there was an opportunity in the future, we should both come on a holiday to Canada.

My husband was a different man after the Canada trip. Life's weary shadow draped his fun-loving face; the silly smile was gone and he had a lot less to say. Tales of Frank's derring-do were a thing of the past and I never again saw the Dangle Dance that once entertained me so much. People were living through difficult days.

Time passed. Gradually we paid off our debts. In time we paid my brother everything we owed him. He got the scuba gear into the shop but it didn't sell as well as he anticipated. People are tired of scuba diving already, he said with a sigh. I kept on working in the shopping center. I was jaded, like a footballer who's done first half, second half and extra time. My face became more lined and blotched. I had very little time to look after the child, and I always felt anxious and guilty. I had the feeling we were getting it all wrong. Still the child managed to grow up.

My husband moved to a new job with better wages. To celebrate we went to a lobster house. Nowadays every neighborhood has a couple of lobster houses. We ordered two portions and split them among the three of us. As we ate we talked about Mafia Frank. We hope he's had a happy life with April in LA. And we hope he doesn't hate Koreans any more. And we hope that the Brazilian woman, twenty years younger than Cousin Frank, doesn't leave him. And as we talked we began to giggle and laugh.

Cousin Frank, Mafia Frank, Toronto, Vancouver, Consuela, Chile, the football coach . . . . The stories went on and on and we laughed all the more. Bolivia, Colombia, April, marijuana, the Cadillac . . . . We called out the names that had been our hope and despair, we rolled in our chairs and we grabbed our belly buttons. The other lobster diners stared at us, but we couldn't stop laughing.

Five Poems by Hwang Byeong-Seung

Translated by Chae-Pyong Song
and Darcy L. Brandel

COMING OUT

Perhaps the real me is the back of my head
You become more honest behind me
I, who want to know more about you
Should perhaps walk backwards
After grinding my face on the bare floor

Another real me is my anus
But for you my anus is utterly disgusting
I, who want to know more about you
Should perhaps speak with my anus
Tearing apart my lips, saying please love me

I am ashamed
You carry many shameful animals like me
Inside your pockets and deep in your drawers

Every time you are ashamed
Of hating your shame
You write and erase a postcard

You cut off and attach your wrist

You become a grandfather or a great aunt who died one hundred
years ago

Are you ashamed? Let's shake hands

Your hand is inside the first page you tore off

SIKOKU, THE MAN DRESSED AS WOMAN

Noon spews fire from the sky's hot summit

The lizard writes
He tears it up and writes again

(I want to shake hands, I want to touch you but my hands are in
    the forest)

To the old woman who throws away the parasol and collapses
To the dog that runs away into the fire, dragging its chain

The lizard, whose tail is cut off, writes
He tears it up and writes again
If you bathe in the bathtub, it surely gleams with beauty
If you are eating an apple I will be jealous of it
I am the knife gripped in your hand; it will gladly ruin your heart

At twelve, I was already a great woman who broke out of a man
Sending love letters every day to the boys my age
Who had the habits of rats to foretell the future

(I will not promise until the tail grows back and I can touch your
    hair. The more I try to tell the
truth the stronger my lies become)

There was a time once when someone wrote shit in red on my
    pencil case

(I wonder why the rats cannot walk softly in the moonlight)

So I won't forget the future I endure the stench of the back room

While putting on make-up and taking it off, while putting on a
    skirt and taking off a bra
I feel my stomach rise falsely and suffer morning sickness

The lizard writes
He tears it up and writes again

Your gaze that runs away toward my back whenever we embrace
    each other!

My love, I too have a womb. Is that wrong?
Why in the world do you still question my name?

Sikoku, Sikoku

The lizard with red lips runs

Holding a long letter in his mouth
Following the dog that disappeared into the fire
Climbing over the silence of the collapsed old woman

The lizard runs

At noon when the rose by the window
Is eating fire with dark red teeth

The hands in the forest will receive it
And the tail will read it

(My love, I will tell you once more a strong lie for the last time)

Wait for me, wait for me!

Her Face Is a Battlefield

Like the moment the second hand takes the sixtieth step
Pushing the back of the minute hand that attacks the hour hand

Her face is a battlefield

Like kids at a public cemetery where a festival parade passes by
Who drink ten cups of jostlings and swallow twenty cups of
    wranglings
Whose goal is to knock down

Her face is a battlefield

She is quickly loved and quickly forgotten

Amidst darkness, a woman cries, a second woman cries
A third one rushes outside

Like endless coughs two women spit at each other's face with a
    mirror in between

Two Stillborn Hearts

Like a clown driven into this earth upside down
Twelve years old with too many sweets
Two feet walk on the empty air continuously

Time, like a petty thief, dies in darkness
Little by little, hiccupping
Sparrows enjoy it

Till the thirty-six year-old devil approaches and points at me
(hiccupping)

Till the devil holding a black knife strikes down the twelve-year-
old's neck

Like a clown who shivers in anxiety
(hiccupping, hiccupping)

The child of this earth, whether alive or dead, I don't know!

Twelve years driven into this earth,

The cicada within my ear cannot sleep.

FISH SONG

A fish in the tank listens:
A bird song flows by the window
And the bird greets,
"How are you, Mr. Fish?"

The fish replies
Flexing his gills:
Two water bubbles

The fish in the tank listens:
The bird song flows in through the window
And the bird asks,
"Do you also have a song?"

The fish listens:
The bird bids farewell,
"Take care, Mr. Fish"

The fish replies
Shaking his fins:
Two water bubbles

Images of Seoul:
Choi Ho-Cheol

183

184

187

189

197

SPECIAL FEATURE:

LOVE LYRICS IN LATE MIDDLE KOREAN

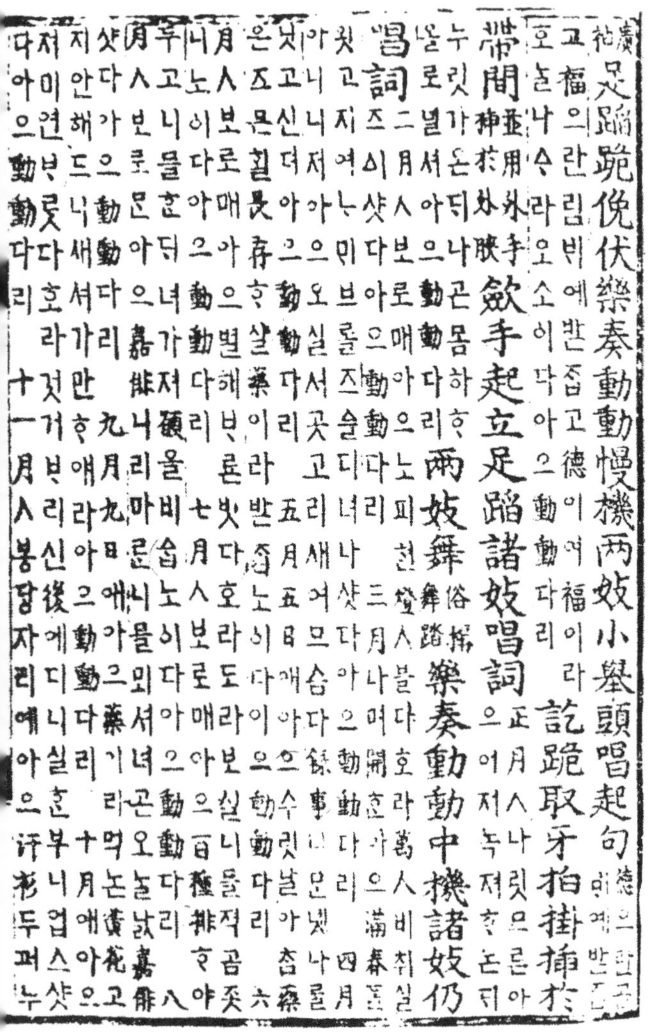

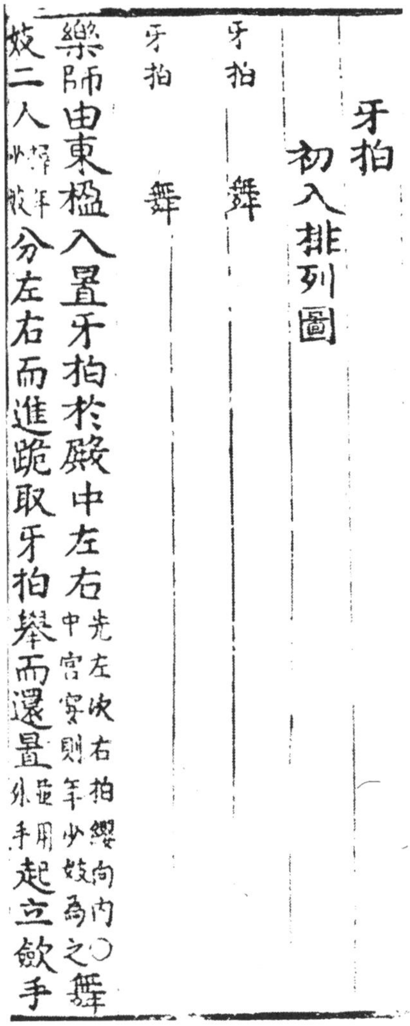

牙拍

初入排列圖

牙拍 舞

牙拍 舞

樂師由東楹入置牙拍於殿中左右 先左次右拍纓向內 中宮宴則年少妓為之○舞

妓二人 分左右而進跪取牙拍舉而還置 起立斂手

Love Lyrics in
Late Middle Korean

by Peter H. Lee

Gesang ist Dasein.
—*Die Sonette an Orpheus*

One of the most intriguing and challenging topics in Korean literary history is the love lyrics in Late Middle Korean. By "lyric" I mean a fictional representation of a personal utterance to be sung.[1] We do not know when the texts and music were composed. The social settings of these anonymous feminine-voiced songs have almost disappeared. Because the predominant

---

* My colleague and friend Professor John B. Duncan was the first reader and offered valuable suggestions. All Korean-language texts were published in Seoul unless indicated otherwise.

Abbreviations

CWS: Kuksa p'yŏnch'an wiwŏnhoe, ed., *Chosŏn wangjo sillok* 朝鮮王朝實錄, 48 vols., 1955-1958.

Hambis: Louis Hambis, "Notes sur l'histoire de Corée à l'époque Mongole," *T'oung Pao* 45 (1957): 151-218.

Kim 1: Kim Myŏngjun, *Koryŏ sogyo chipsŏng* 고려속요집성 (Taunsaem, 2002).

Kim 2a: Kim Myŏngjun, *Akchang kasa yŏn'gu* 악장가사연구 (Taunsaem, 2004).

Kim 2b: Kim Myŏngjun, *Akchang kasa chuhae* 악장가사주해 (Taunsaem, 2004).

KMC: *Koryŏ myŏnghyŏn chip* 高麗名賢集, 5 vols. (Kyŏngin munhwasa, 1972).

KS: Chŏng Inji et al., eds., *Koryŏ sa* 高麗史, 3 vols. (Yŏnse taehakkyo Tongbanghak yŏnguso, 1955-1961).

KSC: Kim Chongsŏ et al., *Koryŏsa chŏryo* 高麗史節要 (Tongguk munhwasa, 1960).

KSY: Kim Kidŏk, Ch'ae Ŭngsik, and Hŏ Hŭngsik, eds., Koryŏ sidae yŏn'gu 고려시대연구 4 (Hanguk chŏngsin munhwa yŏnguwŏn, 2002).

SG: Kim Pusik, *Samguk sagi* 三國史記, ed. Yi Pyŏngdo 李丙燾, 2 vols. (Ŭryu, 1977).

SY: Iryŏn, *Samguk yusa* 三國遺事, ed. Ch'oe Namsŏn 崔南善 (Minjung sŏgwan, 1954).

TS: *Tanglü suoyi* 唐律疏議 (Peking: Zhonghua, 1983).

1. Jonathan Culler, "Changes in the Study of the Lyric," in Chaviva Hošek and Patricia Parker, eds., *Lyric Poetry: Beyond New Criticism* (Ithaca: Cornell University Press, 1985), 38-39.

Azalea

Love Lyrics

in Late

Middle

Korean by

Peter H. Lee

written language among the learned until the mid-fifteenth century was literary Chinese, the prestige language, no song texts could be written down until Chosŏn officials wrote new texts as *contrafactum*[2] (writing new texts for popular melodies) for well-known Koryŏ songs. Because of the sociolinguistic status of the vernacular, we have memorial (oral) but no written transmission. Moreover, we have no textual history to speak of until the compilation of the *Akhak kwebŏm* 樂學軌範 (Guide to the study of music, 1493) and two anonymous compilations— *Siyong hyangak po* 時用鄉樂譜 (Notations for Korean music in contemporary use; ca. early sixteenth century; made known only in 1954)[3] and *Akchang kasa* 樂章歌詞,[4] an anthology of song texts dating from Koryŏ and early Chosŏn. I consider them diplomatic copies of the songs. These texts must have invited innovation as part of the process of transmission (*mouvance* = fluidity).[5] Thus Koryŏ songs owe their survival to the adoption of their accompanying music for court use in Chosŏn. It is unclear, however, how the texts, dubbed "vulgar and obscene" and expunged by Chosŏn censors as late as 1490,[6] managed to survive. Are what we have the precensored or the censored versions? Perhaps these songs were so popular that no one needed to write them down to remember them. Repetition and recurrent refrains—mimetic in origin—of both verse and music made it easy for the unlearned to remember.

Oral delivery was the mode of transmission in an orally based poetic tradition, and we can identify the speaker's gender from verbal

---

2. Stanley Sadie, ed., *The New Grove Dictionary of Music and Musicians*, 2d ed., 29 vols. (London: Macmillan, 2001), 6:367b-370d.

3. Yi Hyegu, *Sinyŏk Akhak kwebŏm* (Kungnip kugagwŏn, 2000) includes a photocopy of the original.

4. Also called *Kukcho sajang*. There are three copies, for which see Kim 2a.

Three extant copies are in the Hōsa Bunko, Kyoto University (discovered 1967; Kim 2b:3-72); in the Yun Sŏndo family (discovered 1975; Kim 2b:73-146); and in the Changsŏgak (royal library; Kim 2b:147-224).

5. *On mouvance see* Peter H. Lee, "The Road to Ch'unhyang," *Azalea* 3 (2010): 276, n. 29.

6. *Sŏngjong sillok* 240:18b; see also Kim 1 for relevant passages on Koryŏ songs in Chosŏn dynastic history, 429-605.

features and textual markers: woman, the locus of unrequited love. Songs are inseparable from their performance. The music composed for performance, together with song lyrics, invites a communal identification of singer and audience.[7] But the texts do not encode information about the speaker's social status and economic class: was she a propertied woman like the Occitan trobairitz of medieval Europe?[8] The singer re-creates emotions in a specific context and shares those emotions with the audience. Was the song performed before a mixed audience? Did they identify more with the speaker than with the speaker's target, the beloved? It was not considered indecorous in the Koryŏ period for women to compose and perform songs of love and to take part in public entertainment—a challenge to male monopoly on desire and language.

About the same period (eleventh to fourteenth centuries) in the West there flourished Mozarabic *kharjas* ("exit"; the oldest known secular lyrics in any Romance language, the earliest ca. 1000);[9] songs by the troubadours and *trobairitz* (ca. 1100-1300) in Old Occitan (Langue d'Oc; Old Provençal)[10] and by the *trouvères* of northern France (late twelfth to thirteenth centuries);[11] Galician-Portuguese songs (fl. 1200-1350), *cantigas d'amor and cantigas*

---

7. David Lindley, *Lyric* (London: Methuen, 1985), 51.

8. Meg Bogin, *The Women Troubadours* (New York: Norton, 1980), 13; Eglal Doss-Quinby et al., *Songs of the Women* Trouvères (New Haven: Yale University Press, 2001); Matilda Tomaryn Bruckner, "The Trobairitz," in *A Handbook of the Troubadours*, eds., F. R. P. Akehurst and Judith M. Davis (Berkeley: University of California Press, 1995), 201-233.

9. Alois Richard Nykl, *Hispano-Arabic Poetry and Its Relations with the Old Provençal Troubadours* (Baltimore: Johns Hopkins University Press, 1946); Linda Fish Compton, *Andalusian Lyrical Poetry and Old Spanish Love Songs: The Muwashshah and Its Kharja* (New York: New York University Press, 1976); J. A. Abu-Haidar, *Hispano-Arabic Literature and the Early Provençal Lyrics* (Richmond, Surrey: Curzon Press, 2001).

10. R. T. Hill and Thomas G. Bergin, *Anthology of the Provençal Troubadours*, 2 vols. (New Haven: Yale University Press, 1973); Bogin, *The Women Troubadours*; and Matilda Tomaryn Bruckner et al., *The Songs of the Women Troubadours* (New York: Garland, 1995); Frederick Goldin, *Lyrics of the Troubadours and Trouvères*: An Anthology and a History (Garden City: Anchor Books, 1973); William D. Paden, *The Voice of the Trobairitz: Perspectives on the Women Troubadours* (Philadelphia: University of Pennsylvania Press, 1989).

11. Doss-Quinby et al., *Songs of the Women* Trouvères.

AZALEA

Love Lyrics
in Late
Middle
Korean by
Peter H. Lee

d'amigo;[12] Minnelieder (twelfth to early fourteenth centuries);[13] Goliardic songs including the *Carmina Burana* (Songs of Beuren);[14] the Cambridge Songs (*Carmina Cantabrigiensia*);[15] and the Harley lyrics (compiled ca. 1314-1325),[16] to mention a few. These Koryŏ songs have come to us from anonymous women who lived and sang from the eleventh to the fourteenth centuries. No contemporary comments survive; the living context for these songs seems lost. Has the twenty-first century reader the means to understand the texts—can we reconstitute the feminine speakers' voices, the first and only voices from that period, the inventors of love lyrics in the vernacular?

Background

The following observations are offered in the hope of better situating our songs in time and space, that is, in their sociopolitical and cultural contexts.[17] My aim is to re-create the time and locality where these songs were sung and to inform the twenty-first-century reader about what certain words meant and what symbolic associations they might have had. In the process of writing this work, I have learned that our criteria should be literary. We should pay attention to these lyrics as song texts, not separating author (even when unknown) from text or text from audience. Given our temporal distance from these works and the paucity of contextual

---

12. Frede Jensen, *Medieval Galician-Portuguese Poetry: An Anthology* (New York: Garland, 1992).

13. Olive Sayce, *The Medieval German Lyric 1150-1300: The Development of Its Themes and Forms in Their European Context* (Oxford: Clarendon, 1982); J. W. Thomas, *Medieval German Lyric Verse: In English Translation* (Chapel Hill: University of North Carolina Press, 1968).

14. P. G. Walsh, tr. and ed., *Love Lyrics from the* Carmina Burana (Chapel Hill: University of North Carolina Press, 1993).

15. Jan M. Ziolkowski, *The Cambridge Songs* (Carmina Cantabrigiensia) (Tempe: Medieval and Renaissance Texts and Studies, 1998).

16. G. L. Brook, *The Harley Lyrics: The Middle English Lyrics of M.S.Harley* 2253 (New York: Barnes and Noble, 1955); Raymond Oliver, *Poems Without Names: The English Lyric, 1200-1500* (Berkeley: University of California Press, 1970).

17. "Everyone knows that the whole context can never be known or represented," says David Perkins in *Is Literary History Possible?* (Baltimore: Johns Hopkins University Press, 1992), 172.

materials, the more information we recover, the better it will illuminate the settings of these oral-derived songs[18] that seem so near and yet so far.

The Mongol Conquest

During its 474 years of history, Koryŏ 高麗 experienced several invasions from the north—Khitans (994-1011), Jurchens (1107-1109), and Mongols (1231-1259), the last being the most traumatic. The Koreans put up stout resistance against the invaders, and on 27 January 1233 Kim Yunhu 金允侯, a Buddhist monk at the Ch'ŏin fortress 處仁城, Yongin 龍仁, killed with a single arrow the Mongol commander Sarta.[19] After six invasions over a 30-year period, the Koreans finally concluded peace with the Mongols in 1259. Adopting a policy of reconciliation, Korea proposed that the Korean crown prince marry a Mongol princess, and Khubilai Khan allowed the prince, later known as King Ch'ungnyŏl, to marry his own daughter (1271).[20] Thereafter Korean princes married Mongol princesses, thus becoming "son-in-law" kings (*kuregen*). Korean princes resided in the Mongol capital as hostages until they became king. At times, the Yuan dynasty determined the succession or punished those unfit to rule; at other times, the Korean ruling class, in collusion with the Mongols, schemed to drive a king from the throne. Korean kings took Mongol names, adopted Mongol hairdos and costumes, and used the Mongolian language. It was not uncommon for Koryŏ aristocrats to take Mongol given names and to adopt Mongol hairdos and customs.

From Ch'ungnyŏl to Kongmin, the succession was as follows:

• Ch'ungnyŏl 忠烈 (1236-1308; r. 1274-1298, 1298-1308, ruled 33 years and 6 months) married Khudulukh-kalmish (d. 1297), a daughter of Khubilai, in 1274. He also had three Korean consorts.[21]

---

18. J. M. Foley, *Immanent Art: From Structure to Meaning in Traditional Oral Epic* (Bloomington: Indiana University Press, 1991), 15.

19. *KS 23:26a-b.*

20. *KS 27:24a.*

21. *KS* 28:1a-32:36a; *KSC* 19:24a-23:16a; Hambis 178-183, 188-189, 192-193. For his Mongol queen see *KS* 89:1a-13a.

Azalea

Love Lyrics

in Late

Middle

Korean by

Peter H. Lee

• Ch'ungsŏn 忠宣 (Ijirbukha; 1275-1325; r. 1298/1-8, 1308-1313, ruled 5 years and 3 months), the oldest son of Ch'ungnyŏl, married (1296) Botashirin (d. 1315), daughter of Kammala, Prince of Jin, and Yesujin (d. 1334). He also had six Korean consorts.[22]

• Ch'ungsuk 忠肅 (Aratnashiri; 1294-1339; r. 1313-1330, 1332-1339, ruled 24 years), the second son of Ch'ungsŏn, whose mother was Yesujin, married (1316) Irinjinbala (d. 1319), the daughter of Asan Temür, Prince of Ying; Ki(ŭ)mdong (married 1324, d. 1325), daughter of Amuge, Prince of Wei; and Bayan Khuldu (married 1333; Princess Kyŏnghwa, sister of Kimdong; d. 1344). He also had three Korean consorts, including Queen Myŏngdŏk (d. 1380; née Hong).[23]

• Ch'unghye 忠惠 (Putashiri; 1315-1334; r. 1330-1332, 1339-1344, ruled 6 years and 10 months), the eldest son of Ch'ungsuk, married (1330) Irinjinbal (Princess Tŏngnyŏng, d. 1375), the daughter of Josbal, Prince of Zhenxi Wujing (Guanxi), great-grandson of Khubilai. He also had three Korean consorts.[24]

• Ch'ungmok 忠穆 (Batmadorji, 1337-1348; r. 1344-1348), son of Ch'unghye, born of Princess Tŏngnyŏng, died at eleven.[25]

• Ch'ungjŏng 忠定 (Chosgamdorji; 1337-1352; r. 1348-1351), Ch'unghye's secondary son, born of the daughter of Yun Kyejong, died at fifteen.[26]

• Kongmin 恭愍 (Bayan Temür; 1330-1374; r. 1351-1374), born of Queen Myŏngdŏk (d. 1380, née Hong), married Putashiri (d. 1365), the daughter of Bolod Temür, Prince of Wei, in 1349.[27] When his beloved queen died of complications from a difficult labor, he drew her likeness, sat before it day and night, wept, and refrained

---

22. *KS* 33:1a-34:9a; *KSC* 23:16a-33b; Hambis 183-94. For his Mongol queen see KS 89:13a-17a.

23. *KS* 34:9a-35:37a; *KSC* 24:1a-25: 2b-12b; Hambis 194-202, 203-204. For his Mongol queen see *KS* 89:17a-24b.

24. *KS* 36:1a-33a; *KSC* 25:1a-2b, 18b-40b; Hambis 202-205. For his Mongol queen see *KS* 89 24b-26b.

25. *KS* 37:1a-16a; *KSC* 25:40b-53a; Hambis 205-207.

26. *KS* 37:16a-25a; *KSC* 26:1a-7b; Hambis 207-208.

27. *KS* 38:1a-44:34b; *KSC* 26:7b-31b; Hambis 208-212. For his Mongol queen see *KS* 89:26b-33a.

from meat for three years.[28] In 1352 he banned Mongol hairdos and costumes, and he stopped using the Mongol reign title in 1356. When the Ming announced the fall of the Yuan, he adopted the Ming reign title in 1370.[29] Already in 1368 he had sent an envoy to the King of Wu (later the founder of the Ming). After a reign of twenty-three years, he was murdered by his own eunuchs.[30] Thus Koryŏ-Mongol marriage relations lasted almost a century.

A glance at the official history of Koryŏ reveals some anomalies in the behavior of Koryŏ kings and Mongol queens (perhaps because they transgressed the taboo). Similar events cannot be found before or after the Mongol domination. Ch'ungnyŏl's fascination with the hunt and falconry, for example, broke all records, and from 1276 onward he was out chasing birds and beasts several times a month, almost every month, throughout the year.[31] In 1282 he went on a hunt in Ch'ungch'ŏng province and crossed the Imjin River. His queen angrily tongue-lashed him, "Hunting is not an urgent business. Why have you brought me here?"[32] The king had no answer. In 1287, Ch'ungnyŏl and his queen went on a hunting trip with fifteen hundred horses.[33] She had admonished him before, in 1280, for consorting with underlings and chasing animals,[34] but he refused to give up the pleasures of hunting and hawking in the farmlands of the people. In 1275 she wanted to pulverize the golden stupa at Hŭngwang Temple, but the king was powerless to stop her and could only weep.[35] She herself had myriad lanterns lit at the palace and had musicians

---

28. *KS* 41:1b; *KSC* 28:8b. For Koryŏ-Mongol marriage relations, see George Qingzhi Zhao, *Marriage as Political Strategy and Cultural Expression: Mongolian Royal Marriages from World Empire to Yuan Dynasty* (New York: Peter Lang, 2008), 61 and 204-205; Morihira Masahiko, "Kōrai ōke to Mongoru kōzoku no tsūkon kankei ni kansuru kakusho" (Notes on the marital relations between the royal house of Koryŏ and the Mongol imperial family), *Tōyōshi kenkyū* 67.3 (2008): 363-401.

29. *KSC* 29:5b.

30. *KS* 44:4a; *KSC* 29:28b.

31. *KS* 28:13a, 14b, 17a-b, 18b.

32. *KS* 89:7b.

33. *KS* 30:8a.

34. *KS* 89:7b.

35. *KS* 89:3b.

Azalea

Love Lyrics

in Late

Middle

Korean by

Peter H. Lee

perform till dawn (1279).[36] In 1277 Ch'ungnyŏl moved to Ch'ŏnhyo Monastery because of an ailment. His queen beat him with a heavy stick (*chang* 杖) to punish him for the small number of attendants following her; when the king entered the monastery before her, she beat him again.[37] Perhaps she recalled her father Khubilai beating his ministers when displeased (*tingzhang*, court beating).[38]

Because Ch'ungsŏn favored his Korean consort Cho (married 1292), daughter of Cho Ingyu 趙仁規, his Mongol queen Botashirin accused Cho of practicing sorcery and Cho's mother of placing a curse on her. She imprisoned Cho Ingyu and his family (his wife and their three sons), subjected his wife to harsh interrogations and torture, and finally sent them to Dadu (Khambalikh, Peking) (1298). Ch'ungsŏn himself, falsely charged, was sent into custody.[39] Cho Ingyu was banished to Anxi (1299) and released only in 1305. The Mongol empress dowager sent five Buddhist and two Daoist monks to remove the curse. The khan asked the visiting Koryŏ scholar An Hyang 安珦 (1243-1306) why Ch'ungsŏn did not love his queen.[40] Indeed, affairs of the heart gave rise to a political and diplomatic crisis. History portrays the Mongol queen as a woman of loose conduct who failed to perform her duties.[41] On her return trip to Korea, Botashirin rode in a carriage decorated with silk, silver, and gold, followed by fifty similar carriages.[42]

The early death of Ch'ungsuk's queen Irinjinbala was investigated, and her court lady and a Korean cook were taken to the Yuan authorities.[43] Annoyed by her jealousy of the Korean consort Tŏk 德妃 (née Hong), Ch'ungsuk slapped Irinjinbala

---

36. *KS* 89:7a.

37. *KS* 89: 4b, 5a.

38. John D. Langlois Jr., ed., *China Under Mongol Rule* (Princeton: Princeton University Press, 1981), 19 (for court beatings of ministers when the khan was displeased).

39. *KS* 89:13b-14b.

40. *KS* 105:29a-b.

41. *KS* 89:15a.

42. *KS* 89:15a.

43. *KS* 34:23a; 89:17b.

twice causing a bloody nose.[44] As princesses of the victorious nation, with vast military power behind them, they broadened their political power at the Korean court and arrogated the right to meddle, make demands, and report the events taking place at court to Peking. Their presence generated widespread tensions. Khudulukh-kalmish's wet nurse was a Korean captive taken first to Peking and then to Korea. Personal attendants (*C. qieliankou*; M. gerin k'eiu)[45] of the queens (Uighurs, Tanguts, and Mongols), and *darughachi* ("one who presses [an official seal]"),[46] the Mongols' surveillance apparatus, indulged in every extravagance-extorted money, accumulated wealth, built mansions for themselves, and had their children intermarry with the Korean upper class, including royal kin. They had come to Korea to enrich themselves. Queens seized land and slaves at will and drove farmers off their land. Ruthless and rapacious, their followers carried out the Mongol policy and served as the queens' spies and secret messengers to Peking, and helped them to amass wealth. Queens—Ch'ungnyŏl's, for example—had vast economic power; accumulated gold, silver, and precious stones; and engaged in trade of pine nuts and ginseng in southern China.

Ch'ungsŏn raped 蒸 his stepmother (1309), consort Sukch'ang 淑昌院妃 (d. 1367), Kim Munyŏn's 金文衍 sister,[47] and recruited beautiful virgins. A victim of intrigue and slander at the Mongol court, he was banished to Turfan (Tibet) in 1320, then recalled (1323),[48] but died in Dadu (1325).[49] Another pathological sexual

---

44. *KS* 89:17b.

45. *KS* 27b3 and 33b6.

46. Elizabeth Endicott-West, *Mongolian Rule in China: Local Administration in the Yuan Dynasty* (Cambridge: Harvard University Press, 1989), 16-19.

47. *KS* 33:21a.

48. *KS* 34:8a, 35:3b-4a; *KSC* 24:15b.

49. *KS* 35:17a. King Ch'ungsŏn was well received by Jenzong (Ayurbarwada, r. 1311-1320) and the empress dowager, but under Yingzong (Shidebala, r. 1320-1323), his erstwhile ungrateful eunuch/slave came to harbor grievances against his master (the king had him flogged for his misdeeds and avarice), bribed Yingzong's close official, and slandered him. With the enthronement of emperor T'ai-ting (Yenzong, Yesun Temur, r. 1324-1328), Ch'ungsŏn was released and returned to Dadu. Chang Tongik, in *Wŏndae Yŏsa charyo chimnok* (A collection of materials related to Koryŏ history in Yuan sources [Seoul taehakkyo

AZALEA

Love Lyrics

in Late

Middle

Korean by

Peter H. Lee

predator, Ch'unghye, described as "debauched and wicked," raped (1339) his stepmothers (consort Su 壽妃, née Kwŏn and Bayan Khuldu)[50] and recruited some hundred beautiful women, high and low, for his pleasure. History records at least five more rapes by him. He roamed the streets incognito, beat anyone he met, and in turn was beaten by hoodlums.[51] Finally six Mongol officials bound him into custody and took him to Dadu;[52] Shundi (Toghōn Temür) accused him of exploiting the people. He was banished to Guangdong and died in Yuezhou, Hunan, at the age of thirty (1344; he may have been poisoned).[53] Did the Korean kings misinterpret the Mongol leviratic custom that sons could marry their deceased fathers' wives and concubines, their own mothers excepted?[54] They might have considered themselves eligible, but they did not marry the women they raped.

Frequent visits of Korean kings to the Mongol capital Dadu and to Shangdu ("Xanadu" of Coleridge's poem "Kubla Khan"), the alternative capital near Zhenglan, some 200 miles north in the steppes of Inner Mongolia, were costly and extravagant. In his 1284 visit, Ch'ungnyŏl's retinue included 1,200 followers, 630 *jin* of silver (350 kg), 2,440 bolts (*p'il* 匹) of hemp, and 1,800 sheets (*ting* 錠) of paper money;[55] his 1296 visit involved some 243 officials, 590 servants, and 990 horses.[56] Expenses of Ch'ungsŏn's 10-year stay in Peking (1298-1308), for example, included 100,000 bolts of cotton

---

ch'ulp'anbu, 1999]) cites 29 materials related to the king in Yuan sources such as poems; prefaces to a collection of royal poems by Wang Yun, Yao Sui, and Zhao Mengfu; letters; an inscription to a stupa; and funeral oration (126-167).

50. *KS* 36:11b; *KSC* 25:13b.

51. *KS* 34:29b, 36:11b.

52. *KS* 36:16a-b, 30a, 31b, 32a; *KSC* 25:29b, 32a.

53. *KS* 36:31b, 32a.

54. Herbert Franke, "Women Under the Dynasties of Conquest," in *China Under Mongol Rule* (Aldershot, Hampshire: Variorum, 1994), 25-31, 38-43; for Korean leviratic custom see Peter H. Lee, ed., *Sourcebook of Korean Civilization*, 2 vols. (New York: Columbia University Press, 1993-1996), 1:53-55. See also Bettine Birge, *Women, Property, and Confucian Reaction in Sung and Yüan China* (Cambridge: Cambridge University Press, 2002), 204, 244.

55. *KSC* 20:41a-b.

56. *KSC* 31:13b-14a.

and 400 bags of rice.[57] The tributes to the Yuan included virgins (the first order for 140 girls came in 1274);[58] shamans and conjurers (1292);[59] eunuchs and monk copyists for the Buddhist scriptures (1290);[60] ginseng (1293);[61] Cheju horses (1298) and white horses (1296);[62] and sparrow hawks (1288).[63] The Koreans received, in return, actors and singing girls (1283);[64] grape wine (1285, 1296, 1297, 1298);[65] silver (1294) and books (1314);[66] bows, arrows, and swords (1353);[67] and rice from southern China (1291).[68]

Life under the Mongols

Words of Mongolian origin entered the Korean lexicon at this time. Some scholars and diplomats appear to have been proficient in Mongolian—for example, Wŏn Kyŏng 元卿 (d. 1302), who accompanied Ch'ungnyŏl and his Mongol queen to the Yuan court and won favor from Khubilai. Summoned by Ch'ungsŏn in Peking, Yi Chehyŏn (1287-1367) exchanged views on the Confucian classics with scholars there, including Yao Sui (1238-1313) and Zhao Mengfu (1254-1322). Cho Ingyu (1227-1308), fluent in Mongolian, served as envoy to the Yuan court some thirty times and was enfeoffed as Lord of P'yŏngyang. It appears, however, that the words of Mongolian origin current at the time are confined to those connected to horses, falcons, and military affairs, words unique to the lifestyle of nomadic people. We can trace twelve words to the horse—for example, *kara mal* (black horse); seven words to falconry—for example, *kalchige* (*gaccighai* = yellowish falcon); and five words to military matters—for example, *kodori*

---

57. *KSC* 23:28b.
58. *KS* 27:46a.
59. *KS* 30:32b and 30a. Only an example, not a complete list, is given.
60. *KS* 30:21a.
61. *KS* 30:39b.
62. *KS* 30:14b; 29:43a-b; *KSC* 45:45b.
63. *KS* 30:14b.
64. *KS* 29:43a-b.
65. *KS* 30:30b; 31:16b, 23b.
66. *KS* 31:3a; 34:20b.
67. *KS* 38:8a; *KSC* 26:13a.
68. *KS* 30:27b.

AZALEA

Love Lyrics

in Late

Middle

Korean by

Peter H. Lee

from *ghodoli* (arrowhead) and *ba'atur* (brave warrior). In addition, the word used only at the Korean court for food, *sura*, may have its origin in *sullen*.[69] This is in sharp contrast to the Norman influence on England for two centuries: "Traces of Norman occupation still survive in the English language today: sixty percent of the modern English vocabulary derives from Romance languages; forty percent from Anglo-Saxon."[70] Korea faced grave challenges to its society and culture, but there was little acculturation to speak of. Mongols had little ideological control over the Koreans as a people. No Korean writer wrote a poem in Mongolian (nor did a Mongol write in Korean), and Uighurs, Turks, Persians, and Syrians under Mongol rule wrote poems in Chinese.[71]

"Severe indeed is the calamity caused by the Tartars," reads Kojong's 高宗 prayer on the occasion of the production of the Buddhist canon. "The nature of their cruelty and vindictiveness is beyond description. With foolishness and stupidity greater than that of beasts, how could they know what is respected in this world and what is called the Buddhadharma? Because of this ignorance there was not a Buddhist image or Buddhist writing that they did not entirely destroy."[72] Mongols burned the woodblocks for the Buddhist scriptures stored at Puin Monastery 符仁寺 (1232) and the stupa at Hwangnyong Monastery 皇龍寺 (1238). In 1254, the Mongol army under Jalayirtai took 206,800 men and women as captives[73]—"Mongols regarded captive peoples as booty, as mere property."[74] Were there any witnesses to this mass abduction? How was this figure arrived

---

69. *Hanguk sa* 21 (1996): 244-250.

70. Laurie A. Finke, *Women's Writing in English: Medieval England* (London: Longman, 1999), 31.

71. Herbert Franke, "Tibetans in Yüan China," in *China Under Mongol Rule*, ed. John D. Langlois Jr., 326.

72. Peter H. Lee and Wm Theodore de Bary, eds., *Sources of Korean Tradition*, vol. 1 (New York: Columbia University Press, 1997), 239.

73. *KS* 24:20a-b.

74. Herbert Franke and Denis Twitchett, eds., *The Cambridge History of China 6: Alien Regimes and Border States*, 907-1368 (Cambridge: Cambridge University Press, 1994), 629.

at—by reports from towns and villages or by a census taken later? Why is there no song in the vernacular or in Chinese? Perhaps because a singer choked in the middle of her utterance, trying to express that which cannot be expressed or considered barbaric the composition of a song after such a holocaust. As many as a quarter million Koreans may have been settled throughout the Yuan empire as slaves, concubines, or farmers.[75] A recent study suggests that Korean "clothing styles became fashionable in elite circles in Dadu," and "the acquisition of Korean concubines became a fad"[76]—for example, the second empress of Toghōn Temür (Shundi, 1320-1370) was Korean.

Used as a "resource base"[77] to support unsuccessful Mongol conquests, Korea during Khubilai's failed attempts to invade Japan (1274, 1281) was reduced to utter despair. He ordered 300 warships built (1274), and Korea conscripted 30,500 men for the purpose and mobilized 6,700 navigators to man the ships, with provisions of 34,312 bags of rice.[78] Another order to build 900 warships came (1279-1280).[79] Mountains and forests were denuded of trees and fields abandoned, and people suffered unspeakable misery. In August 1281, from among 9,960 Korean soldiers and 17,029 helmsmen and crew, only 19,397 returned alive.[80] (Some 3,500 warships and 100,000 soldiers from southern China were destroyed in one night by a typhoon that struck the Kyushu coast on 15 August 1281.)[81] In 1283 Khubilai decided to abandon his plans to invade Japan. But the unprecedented ravage wrought by the Mongol army may be compared to the Black Death that swept Europe between 1347 and 1351.

75. David M. Robinson, *Empire's Twilight: Northeast Asia Under the Mongols* (Cambridge: Harvard University Press, 2009), 50.

76. Robinson, *Empire's Twilight*, 52.

77. Endicott-West, *Mongolian Rule in China*, 112.

78. *KS* 27:43b-44b.

79. *KS* 29:5a.

80. *KS* 29:36a.

81. *KS* 29:34a and Franke and Twichett, eds., *Cambridge History of China* 6: 482-484, and *Cambridge History of Japan*, ed. Kozo Yamamura 3 (1990): 411-423.

AZALEA

Love Lyrics
in Late
Middle
Korean by
Peter H. Lee

Woodblock Printing

Koryǒ's contributions to the woodblock printing of the Buddhist canon and the creation of the graceful beauty of celadon ware exemplify its cultural and artistic achievements. Korea's possession of rare books was, for example, known to Song China, whose scholars occasionally requested certain works unavailable there (as in 960). The first use of cast-metal type to print *Sangjǒng kogǔm ye[mun]* 詳定古今禮文 (Detailed ritual texts of the past and present, ca. 1155-1162), a record indicates, took place in 1234— probably the earliest use in the history of the world. With the discovery of a copy of *dharani* scripture dating from before 751, Silla claims the oldest extant example of woodblock printing in the world. The printing of the first edition of the Buddhist canon began around 1010 in the midst of Khitan attacks. With the Song text as its basis, this edition comprised 5,924 chapters. In 1083 a more complete edition of the canon came to Korea. Based on this and other texts he had obtained in China (1085-1086) and elsewhere, National Preceptor Taegak 大覺國師 (Ŭich'ǒn 義天; 1055-1101), the fourth son of King Munjong, compiled a new catalog of the scriptures and treatises, including works by East Asian exegetes and authors, titled *Sinp'yǒn chejong kyojang ch'ongnok* 新編諸宗 教藏 總錄 (New catalog of the teachings of all the schools, 1090). It listed 1,010 titles in 4,740 chapters (*kwǒn*). Ŭich'ǒn also had blocks carved for supplemental materials he had acquired (*Sok changgyǒng* 續藏 經). Thus by the end of the eleventh century, Korea had one of the most complete collections of Buddhist texts in the world.[82]

Because the woodblocks for the first edition were destroyed by the Mongols (1232), work on a second edition began in 1236 and was completed in 1251. It includes 1,514 titles in 6,791 chapters—a total of 81,258 blocks, each measuring 10 by 27 inches around and one inch thick, and weighing over 8 pounds. The varnished, insect-proofed blocks were carved from the hard and durable wood of

---

82. Lee and de Bary, eds., *Sources of Korean Tradition* 1: 237-239.

214

the *paktal* (*Betula schitii regal*) tree. The four corners of each block were copper-plated to protect it from cracking. Each block was carved on both sides with 23 lines of 14 graphs each. After over a hundred years' storage on Kanghwa Island 江華島, the blocks were first moved to Chijǔng Monastery 智證寺near Seoul, then to Haein Monastery 海印寺 on Mount Kaya (1399), where they have been preserved down to the present (Korean National Treasure no. 32). This is one of the oldest and most complete collections of the Buddhist canon in Chinese. Xylographs from these blocks have served as the basis for three versions published in Japan (1880-1885, 1902-1905, 1924-1934).[83] As the purpose of the first edition was to pray to all the buddhas and bodhisattvas for divine protection of the country from attacks of Khitans, so that of the second, as King Kojong's prayer amply indicates, was to guarantee the nation's safety from Mongol invasions ("to cause the stubborn and vile barbarians to flee far away, and never again let them enter [our] territory").[84] In addition, there were numerous prayer meetings, lantern festivals, harvest festivals, and provision of meager feasts for monks and nuns to accumulate merits and invoke the protection of the Buddha.[85]

Monastic Life

There was probably no double monastery—double communities of men and women governed by an abbess, as in the West—in Koryǒ.[86] The number of nuns in Koryǒ was probably smaller than that during the high Silla, because women, mostly

83. See an introduction in Lewis R. Lancaster with Sung-bae Park, *The Korean Buddhist Canon: A Descriptive Catalogue* (Berkeley: University of California Press, 1979).

84. Lee and de Bary, eds., *Sources of Korean Tradition* 1:238. Gutenberg's invention of the printing press was ca. 1400, and William Caxton set up the British press in Westminster in 1476 (Finke, *Women's Writing in English*, 79).

85. In 1225 and 1228, for example, Kojong granted such a feast for 30,000 monks at the polo field (*KS* 22:28b, 35a); in 1279, Ch'ungnyǒl for 500 monks (*KS* 28:13b); in 1308, Ch'ungsǒn for 2,200 monks and nuns and in 1311, for 10,000 monks and nuns (*KS* 33:18b, 30a) and in 1347, Ch'ungmok for 4,100 monks (*KS* 37:12a).

86. Penny Schine Gold, *The Lady and the Virgin: Image, Attitude, and Experience in Twelfth-Century France* (Chicago: University of Chicago Press, 1985), 78-115.

AZALEA

Love Lyrics
in Late
Middle
Korean by
Peter H. Lee

from the royal family and upper class, became nuns when widowed
or old. They withdrew not to specific nunneries but to their own
hermitages built for them. Pŏbwang Monastery 法王寺 was the
largest, where the reigning king attended the P'algwan festival, and
at Pongŭn Monastery 奉恩寺 the founder's portrait was enshrined
in the memorial hall. For the size and scale of the buildings as
well as the number of monks residing permanently, impressive
were Hŭngwang Monastery 興王寺 with 9,270 square meters of
floor space (completed in 1067) and Hoeam Monastery 檜岩寺
(after Sin U). The percentage of literate monks in Koryŏ was not
high, probably the same as the proportion of intelligentsia in the
capital. The number of professionals (physicians, mathematicians,
geographers, musicians) in the capital was higher than the number
of clergy. Monasteries and temples were used to shelter the
afflicted during the invasions and engaged in setting up Buddhist
endowments, relief granaries, and roadside inns for travelers;
loaning grain at high interest; making wine; and raising livestock.[87]

The Arts

The fame of Koryŏ ware rests on the invention and use of
the technique of inlay, "the most important single contribution
to ceramic history." The development of this technique is dated to
the first half of the twelfth century, sometime between 1123 and
1159. Such inlaid wares as a wide-mouthed water container with
handles, a melon-shaped eight-lobed wine pot, and the "Thousand

---

87. Information in this paragraph is based on that provided by my colleague
Professor Hŏ Hŭngsik of the Academy of Korean Studies (email dated 10 and 12
October 2009). In about the same period in France, we recall the construction of
the abbey of Cluny (founded 910), whose church was one of the largest in Europe;
the Cistercian abbey of Clairvaux (founded by St. Bernard in 1155); Notre-Dame
de Paris (begun 1163); the cathedral of Notre-Dame at Chartres (mid-thirteenth
cent.); the gothic cathedral at Rheims (1210-1311); and Mont-Saint-Michel, a rocky
island surmounted by a monastery that held out for seventy years against English
attackers in the Hundred Years War. We might add here that the Bayeux Tapestry
was "commissioned sometime between 1066 and 1082 by Odo, half brother to
William the Conqueror and Bishop of Bayeux from 1049/50-1097," for which see
Gerald A. Bond, *The Loving Subject: Desire, Eloquence and Power in Romanesque
France* (Philadelphia: University of Pennsylvania Press, 1995), 18-41.

Crane Vase," decorated with forty-six ascending and twenty-three descending cranes, were not only patronized but demanded by the upper classes. Koryŏ celadons evince distinctively Korean colors, glazes, and shapes, maintaining the native predilection for simplicity and spontaneity. Recurrent design motifs included flowers, cranes, and, rarely, human figures; the flower vase is "one of the noblest of all Korean ceramic forms."[88]

Korean music (*sogak*) 俗樂 was performed on many occasions: when sacrifices were offered at the circular mound altar to heaven; at the altars of soil and grain; to the dynastic founder, the Divine Husbandman (Shennong), at the Confucian temple; and when the queen and crown prince were enfeoffed; at the Yŏndŭnghoe 燃燈會 (lantern festival) and P'algwanhoe 八關會 (harvest festival); at the royal mausoleum; and when spirit tablets were enshrined for three years after the death of a king or queen. The dances and songs performed at court (*chŏngjae* 呈才) comprised both instrumental and vocal pieces; songs were usually accompanied by an orchestra. Ancestral shrine music, for example, was performed by two orchestras and accompanied by ritual dances. The ritual music at the Confucian temple was performed antiphonally by two orchestras—the terrace (*tŭngga* 登架) and the ground (*hŏnga* 軒架)—and used such rare instruments as bronze chimes, a set of stone chimes, a wooden percussion instrument shaped like a tiger (ŏ 敔), a rectangular wooden box with a hole on top that was struck with a thick wooden hammer to produce a resounding thump (*ch'uk* 柷), and a baked clay jar struck at the top with a bamboo rod split into nine sections (*pu* 缶). Banquet and ceremonial music included Korean and Chinese music; Chinese music (*Tangak*) included some imported from the Song music bureau (1103-1120) in 1114 (Dasheng xinyue 大晟新樂) and 1116 (Dasheng yayue 大晟雅樂),[89] as well as

---

88. Chewon Kim and Lena Lee Kim, *Arts of Korea* (Tokyo: Kodansha International, 1974), 109.

89. K. L. Pratt, "Music as a Factor in Sino-Korean Diplomatic Relations 1069-1126," *T'oung Pao* 57:4-5 (1976): 199-218 and "Sung Hui Tsung's Musical Diplomacy and the Korean Response," BSOAS 44:3 (1981): 509-521.

AZALEA

Love Lyrics

in Late

Middle

Korean by

Peter H. Lee

melodies for the ci 詞 songs.[90] Later the forty-three ci texts were no longer sung;[91] a contemporary version is an instrumental piece for orchestra (stone chimes, bronze chimes, Chinese transverse flute, Chinese oboe, large Korean transverse flute). Few Korean poets attempted the ci except for two Koryŏ kings—Sŏnjong 宣宗 in 1089 and Yejong 睿宗 in 1116[92]—primarily because they did not speak Chinese and knew little about the contemporary song culture of China. But some scholar-politicians like Yi Changyong 李藏 用 (1201-1272) knew the ci melodies. In 1264 Yi accompanied King Wŏnjong 元宗 to the Mongol court:

Wang E 王鶚 (1190-1273), Hanlin academician, invited Yi to his residence and entertained him with music. A singer sang two pieces of ci lyrics composed by Wu Yangao 吳彥高. Yi hummed softly song words in tune with the melody. Coming up to Yi and grasping his hand, Wang remarked, "You do not speak Chinese but know these songs so well. You must be versed in music." He praised him and his respect for him grew.[93]

Gaoli tujing 高麗圖經 (An envoy's illustrated account of Koryŏ) lists eleven Korean instruments:[94] waist drum (*yogo* 腰鼓); wooden clapper (*pakp'an* 拍板); mouth organ made of thirteen bamboo pipes (*saeng*; C: *sheng* 笙); large mouth organ with thirty-six pipes (*u*; C: yu); double-reed oboe (*p'iri*); horizontal harp (*konghu* 箜篌); Korean lute (*ohyŏn* 五絃); black zither (*kŭm* 琴); Chinese lute (*p'iri*); lute of Kaya (*chaeng* 箏); and large transverse flute (*chŏk* 笛). The "Monograph on Music" in the *History of Koryŏ* (71:30b-31a) lists thirteen musical instruments of Korea: six-stringed black zither 玄

---

90. Song Pangsong's article on the subject in *Hanguk sa* 21 (1996): 453-492.

91. Ch'a Chuhwan, *Koryŏ Tangak ŭi yŏngu* (Tonghwa ch'ulp'an kongsa, 1983) and Yi Hyegu, "Sung Dynasty Music Preserved in Korea and China," in *Hanguk ŭmak nongo* (Seoul taehakkyo ch'ulp'anbu, 1995), 231-259.

92. *KS* 10:19b and 14:10b. Yi Chehyŏn, *Ikchae nan'go* 10 contains his "changdan'gu" (the long-and-short line ci).

93. *KS* 102:23a-29a, esp. 24a.

94. The full title is *Xuanhe fengshi Gaoli tujing*. I have used the Minjok munhwa ch'ujinhoe edition (Sŏhae munjip, 2005), 40:6b (translation on 288-289).

琴; five-stringed Korean lute 琵琶; twelve-stringed lute of Kaya 伽倻琴; thirteen-holed double-reed oboe 大芩; hourglass drum 杖鼓; six-leaved ivory clappers 牙拍; decorated gourd dipper 無㝵; large barrel drum hung from a frame 舞鼓; two-stringed fiddle 嵆琴 ; seven-holed double-reed oboe (*p'illlyul*); thirteen-holed medium transverse flute 中芩; seven-holed small transverse flute 小芩; and six-leaved wooden clapper (pak 拍).

The same monograph (71:31a-43a) lists thirty-two pieces of Koryŏ songs without musical notation and song texts, of which three are dance music: "Mugo (舞鼓)," "Tongdong (動動)," and "Muae." "Mugo" requires two female dancers who beat the drum with drumsticks and dance to music while the female chorus sings "Song of Chŏngŭp" 井邑詞:[95]

> O moon, rise high,
> And shine far and wide.
> *Ŏgiya ŏgangdyori*
> *Aŭ tarongdiri . . .*

"Tongdong" begins with two dancers prostrating themselves in front of the king. Raising their heads, sitting on their knees, and holding the ivory clappers, they sing the introductory stanza of the song "Tongdong":[96]

> Virtue in a rear cup,
> Happiness in a front cup,
> Come to offer
> Virtue and happiness!
> *Aŭ tongdong tari.*

They then rise and dance, hitting ivory clappers, accompanied by the orchestra and a female chorus. At the end the dancers again prostrate themselves in front of the king and then withdraw. This dance continued to be performed till the end of Chosŏn. "Muae" is attributed to Great Master Wŏnhyo 元曉大師 (617-686) of Silla, who is

---

95. *KS* 71:31a-b; for "Mugo" see Yi Hyegu, *Sinyŏk Akhak kwebŏm*, 227-228, 330-331, 503.

96. KS 71:31b-32a; for "Abak" see Yi Hyegu, *Sinyŏk Akhak kwebŏm*, 228-229, 323-328, 502.

AZALEA

Love Lyrics
in Late
Middle
Korean by
Peter H. Lee

牙拍
初入排列圖

牙拍

牙拍

舞

二一六

"Tongdong," *Akhak kwebŏm.*

said to have sung and danced while striking the small gourd dipper.[97] Later someone added a bell to the dipper and hung colored cloth from it. Two female dancers holding a gourd dipper would dance and sing, and other female entertainers would respond and sing a "Song of Nonhindrance," a *gatha* from the Buddhist scripture. This dance, says the "Monograph on Music," originated in the Western Regions, and the text reveals Buddhist diction. It was performed at court and in the monasteries until 1829.

Festivals

Two important state functions were the harvest festival and the lantern festival. The first was originally a Buddhist ceremony in which a layperson received eight prohibitions that he vowed to observe for one day and one night. With its emphasis on abstinence and discipline, the ceremony has religious significance. In Koryŏ, the ceremony gradually became secularized. In his "Ten Injunctions" (943) the dynastic founder outlined the importance of both ceremonies. The sixth injunction deals with the nature and function of the harvest festival, which was to worship "the five sacred and other mountains and rivers, the spirit of heaven, and the dragon god." He concluded the article with a stern admonition: "Villainous courtiers may propose the abandonment or modification of these festivals. No change should be allowed."[98] A two-day ceremony on the fourteenth and fifteenth of the eleventh lunar month consisted mainly of a memorial service in honor of the dynastic founder at Ŭibong Tower 儀鳳樓; royal acknowledgment of congratulatory messages presented by officials from the central administration and the provinces; royal attendance at the dharma assembly held at Pŏbwang Monastery northeast of the palace to pray for peace within and without the state; and presentation of shows and games. On the fifteenth,

97. *KS* 71:32b-33a; for "Muae" see *P'ahan chip* (*KMC* 2), 3:11b-12a; Yi Hyegu, *Sinyŏk Akhak kwebŏm*, 229.

98. Lee, ed., *Sourcebook of Korean Civilization* 1:264 and Lee and de Bary, eds., *Sources of Korean Tradition* 1:155.

Azalea

Love Lyrics
in Late
Middle
Korean by
Peter H. Lee

merchants from Song, Jurchen, and T'amna presented a list of gifts, and there was a royal banquet at which the king would bestow wine, fruits, flowers, and food on the participants, including musicians and actors. It was a festival in which the sovereign and subjects found pleasure all the while observing order and measure. "Music of the four transcendents" dating from Silla accompanied the games, and performers were called *sŏllang*. In Silla members of the *hwarang* 花郎 performed it in order to worship the sacred mountains and rivers as well as dragon kings. In 1168 King Ŭijong 毅宗 lamented the decline of the *hwarang* institution, "which pleased both heaven and the dragon king and brought harmony among the people," and suggested that the sons of noble and wealthy families be recruited to revive it.[99] It appears that the descendants of *hwarang* ceased to participate in the ceremony in the eleventh century, and the assembly, which had been religious in nature in Silla and early Koryŏ, became secularized thereafter.

Lighting the lantern is among the most important ceremonies of Buddhist origin. By lighting the lantern, devotees seek not only to enlighten themselves and put an end to their ignorance but also to praise the boundless compassion of the Buddha, whose mind is as bright as the lighted lantern. This illumination ceremony probably came to Silla with the introduction of Buddhism. *Samguk sagi* 三國史記 (Historical record of the three kingdoms; 1146) mentions lighted lanterns as part of Buddhist ceremonies in 866 and 880.[100] In the Lotus Cloister 法華院 on Mount Chi 赤山 in Shandong, China, whose large Korean community was called "a bit of Korea transplanted to the shores of China," the Koreans celebrated New Year's Eve by lighting the lanterns "as offerings at the Buddha Hall and the scripture storehouse of the cloister."[101] Silla belief was influential in the development of the lantern festival—for example, the mother dragon and her son were thought

99. *KS* 18:36b–37a. See also *KS* 69:12a–33b for a fuller description of the festival.
100. *SG* 11:116 and 118.
101. Edwin O. Reischauer, *Ennin's Travels in T'ang China* (New York: Ronald Press, 155), 282.

to visit the country in the first or second lunar month to foretell a rich or poor harvest. This idea is then closely connected to the folk beliefs of an agricultural society, and in Silla it became a composite incorporating the ceremony for the dragon king and the Buddhist ceremony of lantern offerings. Finally established as a national function in 551, in Silla the lantern festival was generally held at Hwangnyong Monastery.

In Koryŏ the lantern festival was held regularly on the day of the first full moon until 987; in 1010 it was revived during the Khitan invasion by King Hyŏnjong 顯宗, in a temporary palace in Ch'ŏngju 清州 on the fifteenth day of the second lunar month.[102] The festival was held on this day throughout the rest of Koryŏ. After receiving salutations from subjects and viewing shows and games, the king would visit Pongŭn Monastery 奉恩寺 to offer sacrifices to the dynastic founder. In the evening at the royal banquet, both Chinese and Korean music would be performed, and the king and subjects would view the lighted lanterns and exchange impromptu poems. The curfew would be lifted so that the citizens could enjoy the festival late at night. The lantern festival was also held on the eighth day of the fourth month, the Buddha's birthday, and to celebrate the construction of a monastery, for example, Hŭngwang Monastery in 1067.

At both festivals in 1073, female dancers presented Song dances and music. At the lantern festival in 1077, a troupe of fifty-five dancers performed a song and dance forming two four-sinographs phrases each: "*kunwang manse*" (Long live the king) and "*ch'ŏnha t'aep'yŏng*" (Great peace under heaven). In these festivals (and at royal banquets), then, Korean music and dance alternated with Song music and dance. There are three differences between them: first, in Song dances two pole bearers (*chukkanja* 竹竿子) leading the dance troupe proceed to the king, accompanied by the orchestra; second, the beginning (*ch'iŏ* 致語)

---

102. *KS* 69:33a and 1a–11b for a fuller description of the festival.

and end (*kuho* 口號) of the Song dance consist of songs of uneven lines in literary Chinese; and third, the texts of the Song ci sung during the dance are also in Chinese.[103]

AZALEA

Love Lyrics
in Late
Middle
Korean by
Peter H. Lee

In the exorcism rite held at court, masked dancers holding a spear in the right hand and a shield in the left chanted a spell and went through the motion of driving away evil spirits. The ceremony consisted of music, song, and dance, performed by seventy-eight members of the troupe, including twenty-four boys from ages twelve to sixteen wearing masks and red gowns (*chinja* 侲子).[104] The ritual included a demon impersonator called Pangsang-ssi (C: Fagngxiang shi 方相氏, "he who searches for evil spirits in many directions"). About this figure the *Institutes of Zhou comments*: "In his official function, he wears [over his head] a bearskin having four eyes of gold, and is clad in a black upper garment and a red lower garment. Grasping his lance and brandishing his shield, he leads the many officials to perform the seasonal exorcism (*No* 儺), searching through houses and driving out pestilences."[105] Ch'ŏyong 處容 dance and song were part of this ritual and had a religious function. The ceremony was followed by various shows—a lion dance, actors swallowing a knife or spewing fire, masked dancers, and acrobats walking on a bamboo pole. *Sandae* 山臺 plays presented sundry shows and games not only at the harvest and lantern festivals but also at royal outings, upon a king's return from the Yuan, and at court banquets, including those held for victorious generals.[106]

There were also impromptu plays with witty talk and jokes. The Ha Kongjin 河拱辰 play memorialized Ha, who negotiated the withdrawal of the Khitan army in 1010 but was taken prisoner and killed after refusing to serve the enemy.[107] One actor may

---

103. Song Pangsong in *Hanguk sa* 21 (1996): 477.
104. *KS* 64:38a; for Pangsang ssi, see *KS* 64:38a-40a.
105. Derk Bodde, *Festivals in Classical China: New Year and Other Annual Observations During the Han Dynasty 206 B.C.-A.D. 220* (Princeton: Princeton University Press, 1975), 75-81.
106. *KS* 19:7b, 94:11a, and 126:38a.
107. *KS* 94:28a-30a. See Yi Tuhyŏn's article on dance and drama in *Hanguk sa*

have played a double role, or perhaps more than two actors were involved. Under King Kongmin, actors staged how the slaves of the villainous retainer Yŏm Hŭngbang 廉興邦 (d. 1388) exacted taxes from the people.[108] Actors could praise the martyrdom of a patriot or satirize the abuse of power by a corrupt official. Another show depicted traders from the Song, Jurchen, T'amna (Cheju), Japan, and Arabia offering their native products. Some individuals were skilled in Ch'ŏyong dance (Song Kyŏngin 宋景仁 under King Kojong),[109] or in a certain game (General Kan Hong 簡弘)[110] or dance (Im Chae 林宰),[111] or in a kind of mime mimicking a midget (Chŏng Ingyŏng 鄭仁卿).[112] In 1387 Sin U 辛禑 assembled actors from six wards of the capital and had them present shows on the eastern river.[113] Yi Kyubo 李奎報 (1168-1214) viewed a puppet play 弄幻 popular in the streets of the capital;[114] Yi Saek 李穡 viewed an exorcism rite (and mentioned masked actors depicting the people from the Western Regions and China, Ch'ŏyong dance, and a puppet play)[115] and a *sandae* play.[116] Literati enjoyed the lute of Kaya (Yi Kyubo) and the black zither (Ch'oe Cha 崔滋 [1188-1260], Yi Chehyŏn 李齊賢, and Chŏng Mongju 鄭夢周 [1337-1392]) in a song accompanied by the zither or as a solo performance. Female entertainers favored the double-reed oboe; monks, the medium transverse flute; and the literati, the large transverse flute.[117]

When, in 1117, Yejong visited the southern capital (Yangju 楊州), the Khitan refugees there presented Khitan shows.[118] Khitans and Jurchens who sought refuge in Korea and later became

---

21 (1996): 493-511.

108. *KS* 126:28b-29a.

109. *KS* 23:31a.

110. *KS* 30:15b.

111. *KS* 129:41b.

112. *KS* 30:15b.

113. *KS* 136:27a.

114. *Tongguk Yi-sangguk chip, hujip* (*KMC* 1) 3:3b.

115. Yi Hyegu, "Mogŭn sŏnsaeng ŭi 'Kunahaeng,'" in *Pojŏng Hanguk ŭmak yŏngu* (Minsogwŏn, 1996), 294-315 with a corrigenda on 59-61. For the poem see *Mogŭn sigo* (*KMC* 3) 21:9a-b; 33:27a.

116. *Mogŭn sigo* 33:27a.

117. Song Pangsong, *Koryŏ ŭmaksa yŏngu* (Ilchisa, 1992), 116-134.

118. *KS* 14:23b-24a.

AZALEA

Love Lyrics

in Late

Middle

Korean by

Peter H. Lee

naturalized probably brought their popular shows and games. After Ch'ungnyŏl became the son-in-law of the khan, male and female actors arrived (1283).[119] During the king's procession, his honor guards performed music of Bokhara, Turfan, and Indian origin. When the king visited the western or southern capital, musicians and actors performed the Bokhara show.[120]

It appears that Koryŏ kings during the Mongol period loved to sing, dance, and clap hands. At a party honoring the Mongol queen at the Yuan capital, princes and ministers danced (1279);[121] in 1288 at a banquet hosted by the ministers, Ch'ungnyŏl rose and danced several times despite the queen asking him to stop.[122] In the same year, when his generals performed dances and other shows, Ch'ungnyŏl clapped hands, rose, sang, and danced.[123] At the birthday celebration of his son, Ch'ungnyŏl clapped hands and danced. In 1292 at a party honoring the elders, Ch'ungsŏn rose and danced pleasing his parents.[124] At a banquet hosted by the Prince of Chin at the Mongol capital in 1297, Ch'ungnyŏl danced and his queen sang.[125] At Shangdu, at the order of Emperor Chengzong (1294-1307), Ch'ungnyŏl had two Korean attendants sing a Korean song, himself danced, and offered a toast for his long life (1300).[126] At one point, his Mongol queen admonished him for his excessive love of music, adding, "I've never heard of ruling a state with music!"[127] In 1333 Ch'ungsuk's barge floated down the Taedong River 大同江 from the Floating Emerald Tower, and music and song were heard within ten tricents.[128] In 1343 Ch'unghye went to the new palace, had an exorcism performed, and when ministers offered him wine,

---

119. *KS* 29:43b.
120. Song Pangsong, *Koryŏ ŭmaksa yŏngu*, 272-273.
121. *KS* 29:1a; *KSC* 20:15a.
122. *KS* 30:12a; *KSC* 21:7b.
123. *KS* 30:13a.
124. *KS* 30:31b.
125. *KS* 31:16a; *KSC* 21:42a.
126. *KS* 31:30a; *KSC* 22:16a.
127. *KS* 76:8a-b.
128. *KS* 33:31a and 89:8b.

he rose, danced, and ordered others to do the same.[129] Whether sitting before the likeness of his deceased Mongol queen or visiting her grave, Kongmin would have Mongol music performed when offering wine and recall his happy days with her.[130]

Koryŏ Society

According to Martina Deuchler's study on Koryŏ upper-class women (almost nothing is known about the kin structure of commoners and slaves), succession was flexible and nonlinear and primogeniture was absent, daughters receiving an equal allotment of the patrimony, both land and slaves. The majority of households included legally adult sons and married daughters with their husbands. Children growing up in their mother's house developed close emotional ties to their maternal kin. Consanguineous marriage was practiced among the upper class, and union with patrilateral and matrilateral cousins was frequent (as pointed out by a Mongol emperor[131]). Marriage was performed in the house of the bride, and the bridegroom moved in—uxorilocal residence. Women had favorable economic status from their right of inheritance shared with male siblings. Married women enjoyed a strong economic position, retaining their rights as heirs in their natal family. Women did not suffer from separation or the threat of expulsion. After her husband's death, a wife could remarry. There were no secondary wives, and concubines of lower class were not customary. Men and women enjoyed free and easy contact, which caught the eye of Chinese observers such as Xu Jing 徐兢 (1091-1153), who stayed in the Koryŏ capital for about a month in 1123.[132] This situation stands in sharp contrast to what happened to the status of women in the Chosŏn dynasty, as neo-Confucian scholar-officials slowly restructured the social order by institutionalizing, for

---

129. *KS* 36:26a.
130. *KS* 89:29a.
131. *KS* 28:10b-11a; *KSC* 19:33a.
132. Martina Deuchler, *The Confucian Transformation of Korea: A Study of Society and Ideology* (Cambridge: Harvard University Press, 1992), 29-87.

AZALEA

Love Lyrics

in Late

Middle

Korean by

Peter H. Lee

example, primogeniture, patrilineal succession, ancestor worship, and virilocal residence.

Those who are curious about the social and cultural context from which Middle Korean love songs emerged might wish to know more about the status of women—for example, the percentage of women in the population (there were more women than men),[133] life expectancy, and average number of births per woman. Women must have played a vital role in a family's economic structure and household management. Are there such documents as wills, property transactions, seals, bills, civic records, letters, and literary texts? How many women owned books (and what kinds)? Did peasant girls marry later than upper-class women, as in the medieval West? Who were those on the fringes—did they dabble in theft, violence, and sorcery? Were women beaten? In Europe the law allowed "the right of men of all classes to beat their wives, so long as they did not kill them or do excessive damages."[134] Extant Koryŏ sources do not allude to such practices in Koryŏ, but two trouvères of northern France managed to smuggle endemic wife beating into their songs: Moniot d'Arras (ca. 1213-1239) in "Amor mi fait renvoisier et chanter" (Love makes me rejoice and sing)—

Quant pluz me bat et destraint ci jalous,

Tant ai je pluz en amours ma pensee. (lines 8-9)[135]

(The more my jealous husband beats and hounds me, / the more my mind is fixed on love.)

—and Monier de Paris in "Je chevauchoie l'autrier" (I was out riding the other day):

Tot errant me commencoit a raconteur

---

133. *KS* 106:40b.

134. Margaret Wade Labarge, *Women in Medieval Life: A Small Sound of the Trumpet* (London: Hamish Hamilton, 1986), 26; Eileen Power, *Medieval Women* (Cambridge: Cambridge University Press, 1995), 8.

135. Samuel N. Rosenberg, Margaret Switten, and Gerard Le Vot, eds., *Songs of the Troubadours and Trouvères : An Anthology of Poems and Melodies* (New York: Garland, 1998), 296.

Comme ses maris la bat por bien amer. (2:7-8)[136]

(Right away she began to tell me / how her husband beat her for being in love.)

How did Koryŏ society conceptualize sexuality, together with such other categories of identity as gender, race, and religion? Was there sexual contact between members of the same sex? What about the particulars that shaped gender inequity (class and culture included); the status of the uterus; treatment of sterility; policy regarding contraception and abortion; gynecology and obstetrics; and the disorder of pollutions such as nocturnal emissions[137]—all topics treated by medieval Latin writers and physicians (Constantin the Africanus, Hildegard of Bingen, William of Conches, Avicenna, Gerard of Cremona, and Jean Gerson)?[138] No age can be sufficiently understood until the status and contributions of women are made evident.[139]

How did the Koryŏ penal code protect women from sexual violence?

The first article under "Illicit Coitus" (*kanbi* 姦非) concerns supervisory and custodial officials:

• When they commit illicit coitus with an unmarried woman within their area of jurisdiction, the punishment is two years of penal servitude (*to*); if with a married woman, two and one-half years of penal servitude; if by force, three years. When a coitus is by consent, the woman is punished with reduction of one degree.[140]

136. Rosenberg et al., eds., *Songs of the Troubadours and Trouvères*, 348.

137. Dyan Elliott, "Pollution, Illusion, and Masculine Disarray: Nocturnal Emissions and the Sexuality of the Clergy," in *Constructing Medieval Sexuality*, ed. Karma Lochrie et al. (Minneapolis: University of Minnesota Press, 1997), 1-23; Étienne Lamotte, *History of Indian Buddhism: From the Origins to the Śaka Era* (Louvain: Institut Orientaliste, 1988), 274; I. B. Horner, *The Book of the Discipline* (Vinaya-Pitaka) (London: Routledge and Kegan Paul, 1982),192-97. I owe the above two references to my colleague and friend Professor Gregory Schopen of UCLA.

138. Joan Cadden, *Meanings of Sex Differences in the Middle Ages: Medicine, Science and Culture* (Cambridge: Cambridge University Press, 1993), 27, 142, 218.

139. Susan Mosher Stuard, ed., *Women in Medieval Society* (Philadelphia: University of Pennsylvania Press, 1976), 11.

140. *KS* 84:38b; *KSY* 185-186; cf. TS 26:416 (easy to locate translation in Wallace Johnson, *The T'ang Code*, 2 vols. [Princeton: Princeton University Press, 1979-1997.]).

Azalea

Love Lyrics
in Late
Middle
Korean by
Peter H. Lee

The next article concerns illicit coitus by male slaves with commoners:

- Between a lowborn (inhabitant of the forced labor area [*pugok*] or a slave) and his master or his first-degree mourning relatives by consent, the punishment is strangulation; if by force, decapitation. When by consent, the woman's punishment is reduced one degree. When with his relatives of above fifth-degree mourning, their punishment is reduced one degree.[141]

Other articles of this section deal with the following illicit coitus:

- With a secondary wife (ch'ŏp) of father or paternal grandfather, wives of paternal uncles and aunts on the paternal side, sisters, wives of sons and grandsons in the male line, and daughters of brothers—if by consent, the punishment is death by strangulation.[142]

- With a favorite female slave of father or paternal grandfather, the punishment is reduced two degrees.[143]

- A laymen with a Buddhist or Daoist nun, by consent, the punishment is penal servitude of one and one-half years; if by force, two years. When a Buddhist or Daoist nun commits it, the punishment is two and one-half years of penal servitude; if by force, no punishment.[144]

Articles under the "Household and Marriage" (*hohon* 戶婚) section specifically concern the married woman:

- When a wife leaves willfully, the punishment is two years of penal servitude. If she remarries, two and one-half years of penal servitude. One who accepts such a woman as wife will be punished the same, but if he did not know that the woman had a husband, no punishment.[145]

---

141. KS 84:30b-39a; KSY 186-88; cf. TS 26:414. For *pugok* see John B. Duncan, *The Origins of the Chosŏn Dynasty* (Seattle: University of Washington Press, 2000), 33-34; Pak Chonggi, *Koryŏ sidae pugokche yŏngu* (Seoul taehakkyo ch'unlp'anbu, 1990) and *Chibae wa chayul ŭi konggan: Koryŏ ŭi chibang sahoe* (P'ŭrŭn yŏksa, 2002), 130-145 and 516-518.

142. *KS 84:39a; KSY 188-189; cf. TS 26:413.*

143. *KS 84:39a; KSY 188-189; cf. TS 26:413.*

144. *KS 84:39a; KSY 189; cf. TS 26:413.*

145. *KS 84:41a; KSY 205-206; cf. TS 14:190.*

- When a husband leaves his wife without consulting his parents, he will be suspended from office and life exile without added labor.[146]
- When she behaves licentiously, she will be entered in the registry of such women and assigned to the needlework artisan group.[147]

"Great Abominations" (*taeak* 大惡) includes legal codifications of the ethical norms prevalent in Koryŏ society:

- When a wife plots to kill her husband, the punishment is decapitation. When one plots to kill the second-degree mourning relatives of a higher generation, one's maternal grandparents, or one's husband's parents, even when the relative has not been wounded, the punishment is decapitation.[148]
- When a wife or secondary wife curses with bad language the husband's grandparents and parents, the punishment is penal servitude for two years. When she beats them, death by strangulation; when she causes a wound, decapitation. When she causes a wound by mistake, penal servitude for two and one-half years. When she kills by mistake, penal servitude for three years.[149]

The law also specifies the punishment for husband and wife:

- When a husband beats or wounds a wife, he is beaten eighty blows with the heavy stick. When he breaks a tooth or more, ninety blows; when he breaks two teeth or more, one hundred blows. When he breaks a tendon and more, penal servitude of one year; when he breaks hands or feet and more, penal servitude of two years; when he injures more than two items, three years of penal servitude. When he causes her death, strangulation; when he intentionally kills her, decapitation. When cranial hair is pulled out and more, sixty blows of the heavy stick. When it is an accidental death, no punishment.
- When a wife beats a secondary wife, the same punishment

---

146. *KS* 84:42a; *KSY* 212-213.
147. *KS* 84:41b; *KSY* 210.
148. *KS* 84:43a; *KSY* 221-222; cf. *TS* 6:55.
149. *KS* 84:44b; *KSY* 229-230; cf. *TS* 22:330.

AZALEA

Love Lyrics

in Late

Middle

Korean by

Peter H. Lee

as above. (This is contrary to the medieval West where beating of a wife by a husband was sanctioned.)[150]

The "Household and Marriage" section includes articles against human trafficking—selling one's kin, both patrilateral and matrilateral, as slaves by misleading or kidnapping. And under "Great Abominations," there are punishments for those falsely accusing to the court the second-degree mourning relatives of a higher generation (or of the same generation but older), the maternal grandparents, the husband, the husband's paternal grandparents, the third-degree mourning relatives of a higher generation (or of the same generation but older), and the fourth- and fifth-degree mourning relatives—even if the accusation is true, they are punished by penal servitude or life exile.[151]

Koryŏ law acknowledges the brutality of feminine victimization by officials, clerks, professionals, soldiers, and monks, but there must have been a discrepancy between law codes and reality. The law appears to protect women's bodies and patriarchal family honor,[152] but how many marriages, for example, were based on mutual affection rather than political, economic, and familial expediency? How many women were unhappily married, without free consent, and how many men, victims of unfulfilled love and repressed desire? Many such victims found expression in extraconjugal or adulterous love. Who defended women of the lower classes and slaves—the nameless, mute, and rejected; sexual and legal victims of male-defined crimes tried by men?[153] Women's experiences, depending upon their class, education, and occupation, could not have been homogeneous. Can we retrieve what Koryŏ society repressed and marginalized?

Women's experience may not have been homogeneous in education either, and their expectations in life depended on the class they were born into—whether they were propertied elite

---

150. *KS* 84:44b-45a; *KSY* 230-231; cf. *TS* 20:294, 295.
151. *KSY* 202-204, 232-235; cf. *TS* 20:294, 295; 24:346.
152. Kathryn Gravdal, *Ravishing Maidens: Writing Rape in Medieval French Literature and Law* (Philadelphia: University of Pennsylvania Press, 1991), 7.
153. Gravdal, *Ravishing Maidens*, 131.

women, those who married (or were compelled to marry) Mongol soldiers, or were taken to the north to be used as slaves. Estimates of the extent of literacy during the Koryŏ tend to vary among historians. The minority who knew literary Chinese includes members of the royal family and the nobility, administrators, Buddhist monks, scholars, and writers. The portion of adults including women who could read may have been small. In the absence of surviving vernacular manuscripts in *hyangch'al* 鄉札 orthography, *idu* 吏讀, or Chinese—spoken Korean was not the literary language until the mid-fifteenth century—we have little evidence about literacy among women; but writers of literary miscellanies provide intriguing information. Some female entertainers wrote poems in literary Chinese because of their proximity to power and influence, that is analogous to European women writing Latin poems, such as Hrotsvit (fl. tenth century), a Benedictine abbess of Gandersheim in Saxony who wrote Latin poems and plays.[154] Yi Illo (1152-1220), for example, says he wrote a poem for a famous female entertainer known as Wŏnok 原玉, alias Uhu 牛後 (1:22).[155] Ch'oe Cha (1188-1260) praises the poetic talent of Tonginhong 動人紅, an entertainer from P'aengwŏn (3:47), and an entertainer known as Udol 于咄 of Yongsŏng who wrote a quatrain for her guest Song Kukch'ŏm 宋國瞻 (d. 1250), a well-known writer and minister (3:48).[156] Yi Chehyŏn says a poem by a famous entertainer in P'ungju is equal in quality to that composed by Chŏng Sŭmmyŏng (d. 1151), a high state minister (2B:6).[157] Some might have been tutored at home by their learned fathers or brothers or at the convent by learned nuns. Some aristocratic

---

154. Katharina M. Wilson, "The Saxon Canoness: Hrotsvit of Gandersheim," in *Medieval Women Writers*, ed. Katharina M. Wilson (Athens: University of Georgia Press, 1984), 30-63, and *Hrotsvit of Gandersheim: The Ethics of Authorial Stance* (Leiden: Brill, 1988). Joan M. Ferrante, "Public Postures and Private Maneuvers: Roles Medieval Women Play," in *Women and Power in Medieval Ages*, ed. Mary Erler and Maryanne Kowaleski (Athens: University of Georgia Press, 1988), 221-224.

155. *P'ahan chip* (*KMC* 2) 1:10a-b.

156. *Pohan chip* (*KMC* 2) 3:26a-b.

157. *Yŏgong p'aesŏl* (*KMC* 2) 2B: 2b-3a.

Azalea

Love Lyrics
in Late
Middle
Korean by
Peter H. Lee

nuns may have patronized the production of certain devotional or didactic texts; some convents might have had libraries of similar texts to be read to the people. We do not know whether most people remained essentially within oral-aural culture.

Laurie A. Finke's suggestion in Women's Writing in English: Medieval England (1999) bears quoting:

> A literary "artifact" might be written to be read by a single reader. However, it might also be written to be read to a large or small audience, by one individual to another, to be performed, or it might not be written at all. It might be orally composed. In defining reading and writing in the Middle Ages, we must consider all these possibilities . . . . It is possible to have a highly developed culture, including a high level of education, in the absence of written documents . . . . [R]eading was much more likely to be organized as a communal activity than as a private and individual experience. Even women who owned books but could not actually read them could have those books read aloud to a group of women . . . . The practice of collective reading has important implications for how we understand literacy; it may require a radical shift in what we mean by "reading" and "writing." Communal reading . . . constitutes a "textuality of the spoken as well as the written word" . . . , in which literacy relies less on technical mastery of letters than on memory and learning, spreads less through individual acts of reading on the part of single women than by word of mouth among groups of women who may be connected by family ties, by residing in the same convent, or by geographical ties. To understand women's literary activity, then, we must understand more fully their family and social networks and relationships. Whatever writing medieval women produced must have grown out of the kinds of reading communities to which they belonged.[158]

---

158. Finke, *Women's Writings in English*, 64, 71.

Finke's suggestions can help us understand how the lyrics of Middle Korean love songs came into being and were transmitted for centuries. The practice of communal reading existed throughout the Chosŏn period and up to the early decades of the twentieth century in Korea. We should clarify, then, what we mean by literacy, illiteracy, the role of writing, and an interdependence of oral and written modes of communication.

In addition to descriptions of certain women known for their virtue, especially chastity, in the works of male authors of Koryŏ, we have fifty-four tomb epitaphs (*myojimyŏng* 墓誌銘), buried in the graves of Koryŏ women, written between 1110 and 1381. A typical epitaph mentions the rank and title of a woman's husband and son, and her daughter's status (virgin, married, widowed). Images are filtered through the writer's own ideology, biases, and concerns. Every woman is presented as a positive character— helped husband and sons to achieve a successful official career, rendered filial devotion to her parents and in-laws, maintained harmony and order in the large extended family under matrilocal postmarital residence. That her husband became a renowned minister is attributable to her virtue—as is even such a minor episode as refusing a request for a favor lest it compromise the husband's probity. Also highlighted is fidelity after the husband's death (twenty-five out of forty widows did not remarry). All were members of the upper class and invested with titles (3a-6b) commensurate with their husbands'; images of them tell us of male attitudes toward women but are devoid of hostility. Every epitaph mentions weaving and needlework: even the wife, née Kwŏn, of Yi Chehyŏn, a high minister and renowned writer, wove cloth during the day and did needlework at night, perhaps to suggest her diligence and support of the household economy. We recognize the similarities but not the differences among them—indeed, they do not transgress conventional class and gender expectations.[159]

159. Kim Pyŏngin and Yi Hyŏnjŏng, "Myojimyŏng ŭl t'onghaebon Koryŏ sidae yŏin," *Yŏksahak yŏngu* 38 (2010): 37-66.

Azalea

Love Lyrics

in Late

Middle

Korean by

Peter H. Lee

We cannot find women poets who left works comparable, for example, to those of Li Qingzhao (1084-ca.1151) of the Song and Guan Daosheng (1262-1319), the wife of Zhao Mengfu (1254-1322), of the Yuan.[160] The only nun honored with the title "Great Master" by the Koryŏ king is Chinhye 眞慧 (1255-1324). Married in 1268 at age fourteen and later widowed with four sons and three daughters (1301), she attended lectures on Buddhist teachings by such eminent monks as Mugŭk 無極 (1302) and Ch'ŏlsan Sogyŏng 鐵山紹瓊 (1311), went forth from her family with the Buddhist name Sŏnghyo 性曉 (1315), and had a hermitage built for her on Mount South in Kaegyŏng (1320), following the examples of her sisters of the royal and noble families who tended to embrace Buddhism. Her second daughter was one of the virgins offered to the Mongol court.[161]

At least three eminent women in the medieval West whose counterparts are hard to find in East Asia deserve mention. Known for her intellect and contacts with popes, kings, noblemen, and bishops as well as her religious, scientific, and medical writings (Hildegardis causae et curae) in Latin, Hildegard of Bingen (1098-1179) founded a new convent (later elevated to abbey) at Rupertsberg near Bingen, Germany, where she remained as prioress until her death. She knew Latin, scripture, the liturgy, some biblical exegesis, music, natural science, and medicine and was praised as "one of the more original medical writers of the Latin west in the twelfth century."[162] Renowned among her contemporaries for her learning and overwhelming reputation for wisdom as an abbess of

160. Kang-I Sun Chang and Haun Saussy, eds., *Women Writers of Traditional China: An Anthology of Poetry and Criticism* (Stanford: Stanford University Press, 1999) cites six women poets of the Song and some ten of the Yuan. For Li Qingzhao see 89-99 and Guan Daosheng, 126-131.

161. Hŏ Hŭngsik, "Chosŏn ŭi Chŏngyu wa Chinhye: tu sidae yŏsa ŭi pigyo," *Chŏngsin munhwa yŏngu* 97 (2004): 175-198.

162. Barbara Newman, *Sister of Wisdom: St. Hildegard's Theology of the Feminine* (Berkeley: University of California Press, 1987) and Cadden, *Meanings of Sex Difference in the Middle Ages*, 70-88; Joan M. Ferrante, "The Education of Women in the Middle Ages in Theory, Fact, and Fantasy," in *Beyond Their Sex: Learned Women of the European Past*, ed. Patricia H. Labalme (New York: New York University Press, 1980), 16-17, 22-27; Ken Kraft, "The German Visionary: Hildegard of Bingen," in *Medieval Women Writers*, ed. Katharina M. Wilson (Athens: University of Georgia Press, 1984), 109-130.

the Paraclete, Heloise (1101-1164) was expert in Latin, Greek, and Hebrew; wrote in Latin; and frequently cited both the Old and New Testament, the Church Fathers, and such classical authors as Cicero, Seneca, Ovid, Lucan, Persius, and Macrobius. She also studied Plato and logic.[163] The third example is Alienor (Eleanor) of Aquitaine (1122-1204), granddaughter of Guilhem (William), VII Count of Poitiers and IX Duke of Aquitaine (1071-1127), the first troubadour poet of eleven extant songs in Old Occitan.[164] She married Louis VII of France and, after annulment of this marriage (1152), Henry Plantagenet of Anjou (later Henry II of England). She accompanied Louis for the Second Crusade (1147-1149) and led her own troops. The richest heiress of her time and one of the greatest patrons of twelfth-century Europe, she spread the ideology of courtly love, *fin'amor*, throughout Europe and the development of courtly poetry in Poitiers. She remains the medieval West's great— if not the greatest—queen.[165]

The Lyrics

The "Monograph on Music" of the *History of Koryŏ* (71:30b-43b) lists thirty-two titles of Koryŏ songs, most without the original texts, but some with translations by Yi Chehyŏn into heptasyllabic quatrains in literary Chinese (such as "Ogwansan" 五冠山); some are accompanied by the text in Chinese ("P'ungipsong" 風入松), and one by Chang Chin'gong 張晋公 ("Hansongjŏng" 寒松亭) is translated into a pentasyllabic quatrain. From the contextual clues provided in our source, eleven appear to be folk songs; each of eight

---

163. Etienne Gilson, *Heloise and Abelard* (Ann Arbor: University of Michigan Press, 1972); Betty Radice, "The French Scholar-Lover: Heloise," in *Medieval Women Writers*, 90-108; Ferrante, "The Education of Women in the Middle Ages," 13-15 and 19-22; Eileen Kearney, "Heloise: Inquiry and the Sacra Pagina," in *Ambiguous Realities: Women in the Middle Ages and Renaissance*, ed. Carol Levin and Jeannie Watson (Detroit: Wayne State University Press, 1987), 66-79.

164. Gerald A. Bond, *The Poetry of William VII, Count of Poitiers, IX Duke of Aquitaine* (New York: Garland, 1982).

165. Amy Kelly, *Eleanor of Aquitaine and the Four Kings* (Cambridge: Harvard University Press, 1963); and Finke, *Women's Writings in English*, 77. Khubilai's mother, Sorghaghtani Beki (d. 1252), whose four sons became rulers is compared to Eleanor of Aquitaine in Franke and Twichett, eds., *Cambridge History of China* 6:414.

AZALEA

Love Lyrics
in Late
Middle
Korean by
Peter H. Lee

other songs may have been composed by an unknown individual; and four have the composer identified (such as "Pŏlgokcho" 伐谷鳥 by King Yejong). Eleven are praise songs ("Changdan" 長湍); eight are satires ("Sarihwa" 沙里花); five concern women's fidelity ("Wŏnhŭng" 元興); and one treats filial piety ("Ogwansan"). In terms of geographical origin, more than half the titles are from the Koryŏ capital and its vicinity.

Kaegyŏng 開京, the Koryŏ capital, was an international metropolis. Situated beneath Songak 松嶽 (Pine Mountain; also called Puso 扶蘇), with the Yesŏng River 禮成江 to the southwest and the Imjin River 臨津江 to the southeast, both emptying into the Han River 漢江, the city was surrounded by three walls: the outer wall 羅城, built 1020-1029, was 14.3 miles long along the ridge line of the mountain, with 25 gates; the imperial city 皇城 wall's circumference was about 2.9 miles with 20 gates; and the palace city 宮城 wall's circumference was about 1.3 miles with 4 gates. About 7.5 miles west is Pyŏngnan Ferry 碧瀾渡, the port for ships bound for coastal cities on the Yellow Sea and for China. The Song envoy Xu Jing, for example, landed there in 1123. The outer wall became the subject of a folk song, "Kŭmgangsŏng," 金剛城 popular after the return of the king from Kanghwa Island 江華島 to the capital to escape the Mongols. Administratively the city consisted of 5 districts (pu), 35 wards (pang), and 4 suburbs (kyo). The street from east to west—from Sungin 崇仁門 to Sŏnŭi 宣義門 Gates—and Great South Street 南大街, starting from Kwanghwa Gate 光化門, met at the central crossroads (sipchaga 十字街). The official complex was in the northeast of the city, and a commercial district was north of the crossroads with markets for oil, stationery, textiles, tea, and cosmetics, frequented by foreign merchants.[166]

We can visualize this city as it might have been in the thirteenth and fourteenth centuries. "The Turkish Bakery" (ca.

---

166. Pak Yongun, *Koryŏ sidae Kaegyŏng yŏn'gu* (Ilchisa, 1996), esp. pp. 147-165; Kim Ch'anghyŏn, *Koryŏ Kaegyŏng ŭi kujo wa kŭ inyŏm* (Sinsŏwŏn, 2001); Hanguk yŏksa yŏn'guhoe, ed. *Koryŏ ŭi hwangdo Kaegyŏng* (Ch'angjak kwa pip'yŏngsa, 2002).

1296-1303) mentions Muslim bakeries or pastry shops. We do not know whether Muslim astronomers, Nestorian physicians, Mohammedan engineers, Western Asian ortogh ("partners") merchants,[167] Uighurs, and Persians crowded the broad avenues of the city; we do know, however, that at least four Mongols and four Western Asians rose to high civil and military posts and rendered the country important services as royal messengers to Dadu or as military commanders.[168] Indeed, the magistrate of the western capital, P'yŏngyang, Min Po 閔甫, was a Muslim.[169] Kaegyŏng's population was half a million—almost the same size as that of Dadu, with 100,000 households, a figure given by Yu Sŭngdan 俞升旦 (1168-1232) before the transfer of the capital to Kanghwa Island in 1232.[170] In the mid-seventh century, the total population of the Three Kingdoms was 2.58 million, and at its height the Silla capital Kyŏngju 慶州 had 178,936 households.[171] *The History of the Song* estimates Koryŏ's total population at 2.1 million (no source or time given).[172] At the zenith of prosperity, the population of the country was estimated at 2.5 to 3 million. In the early fifteenth century, according to the "Monograph on Geography" of the *Sejong Annals*, Hansŏng, the capital of Chosŏn, had half a million inhabitants, probably omitting women and slaves.[173] In his report of 1471, Yang Sŏngji 梁誠之 (1415-1482), historian, cartographer, and compiler of a gazetteer, gives 700,000 households with 4 million persons for the country.[174]

The meanings of a number of Late Middle Korean words and phrases are still not settled; hence my reading is tentative until a more plausible deciphering of those words becomes available. This is not because the poets were loading every syllable with

---

167. Franke and Twichett, eds., *Cambridge History of China* 6: 6, 388, 499, 546, 658.
168. Peter Yun, "Mongols and Western Asians in the Late Koryŏ Ruling System," *International Journal of Korean History* 3 (2002): 51-69.
169. *KS* 33:39a.
170. *KS* 102:6b.
171. *SY* 1:42
172. *Songshi* 487:14053.
173. *Sejong sillok* 127:3b-4b, esp. 4b.
174. *Sejo sillok* 40:11a.

AZALEA

Love Lyrics
in Late
Middle
Korean by
Peter H. Lee

ore or trying to exploit the ambiguity of words. Certain words appear only in these texts and nowhere else, so critics have been obliged to offer alternative readings and we have to decide which meanings are most suitable in a given context. Moreover, the lyrics appear without punctuation in the original, and we need to read them aloud to hear their rhythm. Late Middle Korean was a tonal language, and King Sejong's writing system "provided a way to record pitches": one dot added to the left of the syllable indicates the going tone (a high pitch); two dots indicate the rising tone (long and rising—a low tone plus a high tone); no dot means it is the even tone.[175] The balance of sounds and pauses—the sound experience of each song—enables us to grasp its sound value.

Late Middle Korean love lyrics, oral-derived texts ("works that reveal oral traditional features but have reached us only in written form"), are without textual and contextual material that might help us reconstruct traditional referentiality, including inherent meaning accrued over two or more centuries. Extratextual information on history, tradition, and genre in oral tradition is lacking, but a close look at the structure of these songs tells us their provenance. A typical line consists of two or three, rarely four or five, metric segments. These songs are stanzaic, but generally the metrical structure of the first stanza is not repeated identically in subsequent ones—that is, the structure is heterometric rather than isometric. The songs are primarily aural, not visual. They do not explore the possibility of homophony, or wordplay, but their consonantal density, intensification of ideas by the accumulation of sounds and key words, reinforces the theme. We do not know whether the texts explore the synesthetic associations peculiar to different categories of vowels (open/closed) and consonants.

A basic unifying device in all poetry, repetition of sounds, words, phrases, lines, and refrains, indicates the structural principle in most of these song lyrics. Patterns of

---

175. Iksop Lee and Robert S. Ramsay, *The Korean Language* (Albany: State University of New York Press, 2000), 288-289.

formal and thematic recurrence set up "expectations which are strengthened while being fulfilled with each successive instance."[176] Repetition, sound patterns running in parallel with syntactic units, the constant presence of meter—these elements distinguish our texts as songs. Again and again we encounter the repetition of phrases and lines:

- "The Turkish Bakery": "*Imalsami . . . namyŏng tŭlmyŏng/ chogomakkan . . . ne marira horira*" (I-IV:3-4) repeated in four stanzas. "*Kŭi charie nado chara karira/ kŭi chandae kat'i tŏpkŏch'ŭni ŏpta*" (I-IV:6, 8)
- "Song of Green Mountain": "*sarori ratta*" (I:1) repeated in I:2-3; "*kadŏnsae ponda*" (III:1) repeated in III:2, 4; "*urŏra saeyo*" (II:1, 2) and "*kadaga tŭrora*" (VII:1, 2:) repeated twice.
- "Treading Frost": "*irich'ŏ tyŏrich'ŏ*" (III:1) and "*kiyakiikka*" (III:1,3) repeated; "*chongjong pyŏngnyok a seangham t'amugan/ kodaesyŏ sŭiyŏdil naemomi*" (II:1-2) repeated.
- "Spring Overflows the Pavilion": I:1-2, 5; II:3; III:1-2, 5; IV:1 and 5; V:1-2, 3-4, 5 repeated.

Time is central to the power of repetition. In the *Confessions* (ca. 397-400) of St. Augustine, what really exists is "the present of things past" (memory), "the present of things present" (sight), and "the present of things future" (expectation). The temporal act of measuring the duration of a syllable is referable only to retrospective evaluation. Only when the syllables have all passed into "the present of things past" (memory), when the repetition and variations have all been enacted within the framework of time, can the real experience of meter be apprehended. Thus it is memory that allows the experience to become fixed, that is, susceptible to valuation through retrospective comparison. St. Augustine uses the enigma of poetic meter—the repetitive feature underlying verse—as a metaphor for the human perception of time.

---

176. Alex Preminger and T.V.F. Brogan, eds., *The New Princeton Encyclopedia of Poetry and Poetics* (Princeton: Princeton University Press, 1993), 1036a.

Azalea

Love Lyrics
in Late
Middle
Korean by
Peter H. Lee

Poetic repetition . . . exists . . . for the enhancement
of one's sense of the passage of time in the poem . . . .
Our experience of the structure of the poem is like our
experience of the perception of time. The structure of
the poem is controlled by repetitive devices which lend
themselves to memory—to the Augustinian sense of
"presentness" of that which has been recited before us. [R]
epetition makes explicit, in the very act of interpreting the
poem, the relation between the shape of the whole and the
enunciation of the part. Thus it is poetic repetition which
allows the reading process to become one of integration
and, finally, of understanding.[177]

Refrains—the repeated verbatim unit of one or more
phrases and lines in the middle or at the end of successive stanzas,
always forming part of a given stanza[178]—are either sung as the
accompaniment to a dance ("Ode to the Seasons") or used to evoke
the sounds of specific musical instruments;[179] usually they are
nonsense phrases that allow the song to carry a tune.

• "Ode to the Seasons": "*aŭ tongdong tari*" (line 5) repeated
thirteen times at the end of each stanza, said to imitate the sounds
of the drum.

• "The Turkish Bakery": "*tarorŏ kŏdiro*" (line 4); "*tŏrŏdungsyŏng
tarirŏdirŏ*," "*tarorŏ kŏdiro tarorŏ*" (line 5); "*wi wi tarorŏ kŏdirŏ
tarorŏ*" (line 7).

• "Song of P'yŏngyang": "*ajŭlkka*" (line 1) and "*wi tuŏrŏngsyŏng
tuŏrŏngsyŏng taringdiri*" repeated fourteen times.

• "Song of Green Mountain": "*yalli yalli yallasyŏng yallari
yalla*" at the end of eight stanzas.

---

177. Laury Magnus, *The Track of the Repetend: Syntactic and Lexical Repetition
in Modern Poetry* (New York: AMS Press, 1989), quotations from pp. 2, 4, 9-10.
178. Preminger and Brogan, eds., *The New Princeton Encyclopedia of Poetry
and Poetics*, 1018b.
179. Chŏng Pyŏnguk, "Akki ŭi kuŭm ŭrobon pyŏlgok ŭi yŏŭmgu," *Kwanak
ŏmun yŏngu* 2 (1977): 1-26, esp. 33.

- "Treading Frost": "*tarong tiusyŏ madŭksari madunŏjŭse nŏuji*" (I:3).
- "Will You Go?": "*nanŭn*" (I:1, II-III:2, IV:1-2), "*wi chŭngjulka t'aep'yŏng sŏngdae*" (I-IV:3) repeated four times.

The density of repetitions and refrains and the constant presence of meter are a reliable index of traditional song in the oral tradition.

In the *Cambridge Song* 49 (copied ca.1050), "Veni dilectissime," one of the four songs that a prude sought to destroy, the refrains go, "et a et o, / et a et o et a et o!" (lines 2 and 4).[180] In "The Cuckoo Song" (first half of the thirteenth century) accompanied by music and Latin instructions for singing it, "cuccu" is uttered ten times in the fourteen-line song, ending with a refrain: "sing, cuccu nu, sing cuccu / sing cuccu, sing cuccu nu!" (sing cuckoo, now sing cuckoo).[181] In a woman's song by an anonymous *trouvère*, "Lasse, pour quoi refusai," five stanzas end with a three-line refrain (lines 10-12):

G'en ferai	I will do
Droit a son plesir,	justice to his wishes,
S'il m'en daigne oir.	If he deigns to hear me.[182]

In "Ballade des Dames du Temps jadis" (Ballad of the Ladies of Time Past) by François Villon (1431-1489), the refrain, "Mais où sont les neiges d'antan!" (line 8: But where shall last year's snow be found?) ends three stanzas.[183] In "Prothalamion" by Edmund Spenser (ca. 1552-1599), "Sweete Themmes, runne softly, till I end my Song" (line 18) occurs as refrain at the end of ten stanzas.[184] The

---

180. Ziolkowski, *The Cambridge Songs*, 49 and 309-311.

181. Mark W. Booth, *The Experience of Songs* (New Haven: Yale University Press, 1981), 30-41.

182. Rosenberg et al., eds. *Songs of the Troubadours and Trouvères*, 213.

183. From André Gide, ed., *Anthologie de la Poésie française* (Paris: Gallimard, 1949), 20; English translation is by Richard Wilbur in Katharine Washburn and John C. Major, eds., *World Poetry: An Anthology of Verse from Antiquity to Our Time* (New York: Norton, 1998), 389.

184. William A. Oram et al., eds., *Edmund Spenser* (New Haven: Yale University Press, 1989), 761-769.

AZALEA

Love Lyrics
in Late
Middle
Korean by
Peter H. Lee

refrain (Spenser called it "undersong"),[185] the most common generic repetend in poetry, easy to track in its ability to add progressively to the poem's meaning, unfolds in time and presupposes a poetic context; it is the unique property of poetry, bound by the poetic line, from which alone it gets its form. As the largest consecutive arrangement of repeated words, a refrain may disrupt and retard the song's development. These Koryŏ refrains offer a foregrounding symmetry, phonic role dominating, devoid of syntax, that functions as a "caesura song" or a "rhythmic intermezzo."[186]

We do not know the approximate time, place, or circumstances of most of these songs. Middle Korean oral poets were all anonymous—we do not know whether they wrote both the texts and melodies or indeed performed their own songs. They drew their material from a common source of reference—a rhetorical tradition developed over the centuries (like the British ballad tradition), the poetic heritage. Performance was relevant to a specific occasion, and the function of performance was entertainment. The songs could be performed by trained singers or ordinary people—preliterate or literate—and are intended to be heard rather than read and hence are inseparable from their performance. The rhetorical devices used are different from those found in a poem designed for reading.[187] A reaction to singing is immediate, ephemeral, and unique.

Meaning is made inherent from associations accruing over generations—what is less said than implied, less textualized than immanent.[188] Audiences participated actively in the actualization of meaning arising from the interplay of text and imagination. To achieve affective meaning requires the listener's participation, to locate the text within the appropriate horizon of expectations,

---

185. John Hollander, *Melodious Guile: Fictive Pattern in Poetic Language* (New Haven: Yale University Press, 1988), 154-159.

186. Magnus, *The Track of the Repetend*, 45-61, esp. 51 and 57-58.

187. Alain Renoir, A Key to Old Poems: *The Oral-Formulaic Approach to the Interpretation of West-Germanic Verse* (University Park: Pennsylvania State University Press, 1988), 160.

188. Foley, *Immanent Art*, 139.

a context for interpretation.[189] But these songs operate within such a universal frame of reference that they can be easily understood and appreciated.

The literary and musical climate wherein these songs were first recorded may tell much about their vicissitudes. After the establishment of the new dynasty of Chosŏn in 1392, officials versed in the rites and music tried to collect and evaluate the musical legacy of the previous dynasty. Musicians and singers associated with the music bureau of Koryŏ were then recruited and ordered to compile the melodies and song texts popular until the beginning of the fifteenth century for use on ceremonial and festive occasions at court. But until the use of the mensural notations and the invention of the Korean alphabet in 1443-1444, the melodies and texts could not be written down. The earliest date these songs could have been recorded in the vernacular was at least sixty years after the founding of Chosŏn.

Some fifty musical pieces to be tested in the process of selecting 518 musicians (akkong 樂工) for the Chosŏn music bureau (changagwŏn 掌樂院) include those of six Koryŏ songs (Kyŏngguk taejŏn 經國大典 3:245-46).[190] The major reason for their survival is the practice known as contrafactum—writing new texts for well-known popular melodies. For example, Chŏng Tojŏn 鄭道傳 (d. 1398) wrote "Napssi ka" 納氏歌 (Song of Naghacu) as contrafactum to the tune of "Song of Green Mountain"; "Sindo ka" 新都歌 (Song of the new capital) to that of "Ode to the Seasons"; and "Chŏng tongbang kok" 靖東方曲 (Pacification of the east) to that of "Song of P'yŏngyang." Yun Hoe 尹淮 (1380-1436) wrote "Ponghwang ŭm" 鳳凰吟 (Song of the Phoenix) to the tune of "Spring Overflows the Pavilion."[191]

189. Foley, *Immanent Art*, 40-43. See Hans Robert Jauss, "Literary History as a Challenge to Literary Theory," in *Toward an Aesthetic of Reception* (Minneapolis: University of Minnesota Press, 1982), 24; and Robert Holub, *Reception Theory* (London: Methuen, 1984), 60.

190. Han Ugŭn et al., trs., *Kyŏngguk taejŏn* (Hanguk chŏngsin munhwa yŏnguwŏn, 1992) 1:245-246 and 2:443-245. Five hundred eighteen are from the lower class and 397 aksaeng from the commoners, a total of 915 musicians.

191. Peter H. Lee, ed., *A History of Korean Literature* (Cambridge: Cambridge University Press, 2003), 148-150.

Azalea

Love Lyrics
in Late
Middle
Korean by
Peter H. Lee

Thus although the song texts might have been dubbed "vulgar and obscene," their melodies, probably together with the texts, were able to be preserved for almost six centuries despite occasional criticism of their diction. Song lyrics and musical notations for other songs discussed here are preserved in the *Notation for Korean Music in Contemporary Use* (early sixteenth century) and *Akchang kasa*, an anthology of eulogies and song texts (date unknown).

There is no one right way to translate the songs of Silla (*hyangga* 鄉歌) and Koryŏ (*sogyo*). Indeed it is advisable to retranslate those songs, because they have the capacity to disclose previously unseen dimensions and new aspects with each reading as one takes into account the latest philological and literary research. Since the publication of *The Columbia Anthology of Traditional Korean Poetry* (New York, 2002), I have incorporated in this reading the latest linguistic and literary research.

"Ode to the Seasons"

We have seen that the Tongdong dance was performed at court during the Chosŏn dynasty, and existed from the time of Koguryŏ.[192] The annual events according to the lunar calendar include: the lantern festival; the Double Five, when women play on a swing; the fifteenth of the sixth month (*yudu* 流頭), when people wash their hair in the east-flowing river and farmers pray to the dragon god for a good harvest; the festival of the dead, on the fifteenth of the seventh month (*paekchung* 百中); the fifteenth of the eighth month (*kawi*); the mid-autumn festival; and the Double Nine (*chungyang* 重陽), when people collect yellow chrysanthemums and make glutinous rice cakes.

The first stanza of "Ode to the Seasons" serves as an introduction—dance and song as an offering to the king. "*Nasara osyoida*" (line 4), usually read as "come to offer" or "have come to offer," can also be read as an appeal to gods and spirits to appear

---

192. *Sŏngjong sillok* 132:4a.

and offer blessings to the king. Here the lyric speaker is a woman—she refers to herself as "an abandoned comb" (st. 7) and "a sliced berry" (*chomiyŏn parat*; st. 11) and addresses her beloved as "my clerk" (*noksa* 錄事)–a member of the literate class (st. 5)—who throughout the twelve lunar months registers her communications to her beloved. In stanza 2, "river water" (*narit mul*) now freezes and now melts—winter and spring seem to coexist. There is a change in nature, but none in her status. Although she wishes for a new life, no movement or change seems to arrive. Then she likens her beloved to a "lofty lantern" (st. 3), herself to plums (or azaleas, st. 4);—he is presented here as an admirable person ("your magnificent figure") who "shines upon the world," an object of adoration by the people. Like a lantern and plum blossoms, they are separated—she can admire him from a distance and he is not hers alone. In stanza 5 the speaker's attention changes from sight to sound—the song of the orioles makes her heart ache. They come "without forgetting," but unlike the revolving seasons, he is "forgetting bygone days." In stanza 8 on the feast of the dead, she prays that she may be with him even after death—one reading, but not a contextually correct one, proposes that he is dead. Her abandoned self is compared to a "comb cast from a cliff," but at least he looks back at her (*torabosil nim*), if not "after her." In stanza 12 the speaker finds herself on a dirt floor with only a sheet to cover her and laments: "O lonely life, more sorrowful than anything else," or "I've burnt my sorrow like fuel."[193] Night seems related to the feminine, the passive, and the unconscious. In stanza 13 she offers him chopsticks carved from pepperwood (*punji namu*), used as eating utensils in Korea, but "an unknown guest" holds them: her beloved is a permanent absence.

"The Turkish Bakery"

"The Turkish Bakery" is ascribed to O Cham 吳潛 (fl. 1296-

---

193. Kim Wanjin, *Hyangga wa Koryŏ kayo* (Seouldae ch'unlp'anbu, 2000), 195.

AZALEA

Love Lyrics

in Late

Middle

Korean by

Peter H. Lee

1345), a crafty sycophant and traitor who tried to flatter and further corrupt King Ch'ungnyŏl—who is described as "intimate with small men," and reportedly indulged in dance, music, and parties.[194] O worked with Kim Wŏnsang 金元祥 (d. 1339) and Sŏk Ch'ŏnbo 石天輔, another traitor. He succeeded in alienating the king from his heir (later Ch'ungsŏn). Later O was sent in custody to the Yuan court and exiled to Anxi (1304), but he was recalled and served two more kings—Ch'ungsŏn and Ch'ungsuk. In collusion with the Simyang prince Ko (d. 1345), Ch'ungnyŏl's grandson, O attempted to dethrone Ch'ungsuk and steal the throne for Ko, even proposing that Koryŏ be made a province of the Mongol empire.

After describing the background of the song, the "Monograph on Music" (71:41a) cites two pentasyllabic quatrains in Chinese titled "Samjang" 三藏 and "Saryong" 蛇龍 respectively:

I went to Samjang Temple to light the lamp,
A monk grasps me by the wrist.
    If this story goes out of the temple,
    You're a talebearer, little altar boy! ["Samjang"]

                    *

I heard a snake bit a dragon's tail
And crossed the top of Mount Tai.
    Even when myriad people say a word,
    Using discretion depends on two minds. ["Saryong"][195]

The first quatrain translates the first four lines of the song in the *Akchang kasa*, but we do not know the author and translator of the two quatrains. On the basis of the statement in the history that O and others recruited beautiful female entertainers, slaves, and shamans from all over the country and taught them to sing the

194. Pak Nojun, *Koryŏ kayo ŭi yŏngu* (Saemunsa, 1990), 182–191. For O Cham see *KSC* 22:13b-14a; *KS* 71:42a-b; 125: 17a-21a.

195. For the motif of "a groundless rumor" in the *sasŏl sijo*, see Peter H. Lee, ed., *The Columbia Anthology of Traditional Korean Poetry* (New York: Columbia University Press, 2002), 153.

雙花店

솽
화
뎜
에
솽
화

雙花店에 雙花 사라 가고신된 回回아비 내 손모글

주여이다 이 말ᄉᆞ미 이 뎜店 밧긔 나명들명 다로러거

디러 죠고맛감 삿기광대 네마리라호리라 더러

셩 다리러디러 다리러디러 다로러거디러 다로러

긔 자리예 나도 자라 가리라 위위 다로러거디러 나

로러 긔 잔ᄃᆡ ᄀᆞ티 덦거츠니 업다 ○ 三藏寺애 블

혀라 가고신된 그 뎔社主ㅣ 내 손모글 주여이다 이

맔ᄉᆞ미 이 뎔밧긔 나명들명 다로러거디러죠고맛

간삿기 上座ㅣ 네 마리라 호리라 더러둥셩 다리러

디러다 다리러디러 다로러거디러 다로러 긔 자리예

나도 자라 가리라 위위 다로러거디러 다로러 긔 잔

ᄃᆡᄀᆞ티 덦거츠니업다 ○ 드레우므레 므를 길라 가

고신된 우믌 龍이 내 손모글 주여이다 이 말ᄉᆞ미 이

우믈 밧긔 나명들명 다로러거디러 둥셩 다리러

바가 네마리라 호리라 더러둥셩 다리러디러

러디러다 다로러 긔 자리예 나도 자라

츠니업다 ○ 술풀지븨 수를 사라 가고신된 그 짓

아비 내 손모글 주여이다 이 말ᄉᆞ미 이 집 밧긔 나명

들명 다로러거디러죠고맛 갓 싀구비가 네마리라

호리라 더러둥셩 다리러디러 다리러디러 다로러거

디러다 다로러 긔 자리예 나도 자라 가리라 위위 다로러

러거디러다 다로러 긔 잔ᄃᆡ ᄀᆞ티 덦거츠니 업다

"Bakery" (Ssanghwajŏm), *Akchang kasa*.

AZALEA

Love Lyrics
in Late
Middle
Korean by
Peter H. Lee

song, it is possible that they or their subordinates collected popular folk songs that might appeal to the king's taste and compiled them into a "new song." In the fifth month of 1299, when this song was introduced, the king, aged sixty-three, reveled with nubile women some forty years his junior, handpicked by his fawning underlings, at a hunting lodge near Sugang Palace on Mount Maje.[196] So 1299 must be the terminus a quo for the performance of the song. The date of the song, then, is between 1296 and 1303, the terminus ad quem when O was sent into custody.

The first female speaker narrates her adventures at four different places: a Muslim bakery, Samjang Temple, a well, and a tavern. She allows the Muslim baker (*Hoehoe* 回回 *abi*), who has a shop in the capital, to grasp her wrist. She has either tempted him or vice versa and asks the actor to keep the secret. From what the second speaker says, it appears that the actor has failed to keep his mouth shut. Hence "I too will go to his bed"! The second speaker is presented as more active than the first and describes the room as "a narrow place, sultry and dark" (*tŏmgŏch'ida*), whose range of meaning includes "stifling, stuffy, messy, dirty, and packed with things." Unlike the usual lyric, which is monologic (only one voice speaks), this song is said to be dialogic—perhaps the first woman sang the first part and the second woman the rest of the song beginning "I too will go to his bed." But lines 6-8 could equally have been uttered by the first woman. She is speechless with surprise at the old Turk's audacity; but his touch sensualizes and disinhibits her. Then she recalls what her friend has told her about her experience and says to herself, "I too will go to his bed, / A narrow place, sultry and dark," which was her friend's description and seems to have added more spice and temptation. The well and the dragon in stanza 3 are read by one critic as alluding to the palace and the king. Nonsense sounds consisting mainly of a liquid (*r/l*) and open-throated vowels whose values are not certain are mimetic in

---

196. Pak Nojun, *Koryŏ kayo ŭi yŏngu*, 277.

origin, their rhythmic pulsations perhaps evoking erotic sensations. "*Tarirŏdirŏ*" imitates the sound of the large transverse flute; "*tŏrŏ*" again the large transverse flute; "*tungsyŏng*" the drum and large gong; "*kŏdiryŏ*" the two-stringed fiddle—the mouth sounds (kusŏng 口聲)[197] of several musical instruments. Because she does manual chores such as drawing water, buying a bun, and purchasing wine, the first speaker is of low origin according to the same reader, who sees this as a satire on the morally corrupt life of the king and his court rather than the sexual openness of Koryŏ society.

Who could have been the speaker, especially the first speaker? Is she a sexually voracious female—an invention of male desire and the source of fascination, mystery, and sexual power? Or does she possess physical perfection—a requisite attribute of the gorgeous heroine in romance? She must have been utterly alluring—free-spirited, adventurous, and sirenic.

"Song of P'yŏngyang"

Consisting of fourteen stanzas with a nonsense word (*ajŭlkka*) and refrains, stanzas 5-8 repeat stanzas 10-11 of "Song of the Gong and Chimes." "*Takkondae*" (repaired) refers to the city of Sŏgyŏng 西京, the western capital—that is, P'yŏngyang, also called the "small capital" 小京. Another reading proposes "where we nurtured our love," but the word "repaired" in fact modifies "small capital." "*Koesirandae*" (line 4) is read, "the place you love, if you love that place, because you love that place." The speaker declares that she will stop spinning and leave with him. Although she has a lingering attachment to the city and her means of livelihood, which contributes to her support, she will transcend time and space to follow her beloved.[198] "Even a heartless person would not abandon me after I gave up my hometown and livelihood." She stakes her life and death. Stanzas. 5-8 (the second stanza in our translation omitting the refrains) recur in "Song of the Gong and Chimes," a

---

197. Walter Kaufmann, *Musical Notations of the Orient: Notational Systems of Continental East, South, and Central Asia* (Bloomington: Indiana University Press, 1967), 169-170.

198. Pak Nojun, *Koryŏ kayo ŭi yŏngu*, 278.

251

Love Lyrics

in Late

Middle

Korean by

Peter H. Lee

"Song of P'yŏngyang," *Siyong hyangak po.*

pledge couched in impossibilities. The thread is fidelity, but what about the pearls that shatter, the wound inflicted, the agony of separation?[199]

In part 3 (stanzas 9-12 in the original), the speaker, alienated and deceived, turns her grudge to a boatman on the Taedong River, the river standing for the distance between her and her beloved. The boatman, the third party, becomes her target of scorn, an abetter who has allowed her love to leave, hence a detestable person. The boatman's job is a mean one, and his wife must be a loose (*rŏmnandi*) woman. How does our speaker know about her promiscuous conduct? Here, as in Troubadour songs and "The Turkish Bakery," we have a gossip, or scandalmonger, one of "those who murmur in unadorned speech."[200] She is a cousin of the Western *lauzengier*. The line has also been read, "Not knowing she too will cross the river" (as you let my beloved cross it, so she too will cross it to follow him)—a forced reading. Or "Stop being a boatman and take care of your own wife!" or "Don't be so impudent! You will know how I feel only when your wife has crossed the river and left you"—an equally forced paraphrase. "He will pluck another flower" (*kŏkkoriida*) has been read as "*kŏkkol ida*," the boat will turn over—an unlikely curse. Another reading offers, "I will pluck a flower" (comparing herself to a plant that cannot move or a blossom about to wither that she will pluck out)—contextually implausible. Is it gibberish bewailing her lot? On the basis of the recurring motifs and imagery in extant folk songs, "Song of P'yŏngyang" seems firmly rooted in them.[201] In the refrain "*wi tuŏrŏngsyŏng taringdiri*," "*tuŏrŏng*" is the mouth sound of the six-stringed black zither; "*syŏng*" refers to phonomimes of a large gong or cymbal; "*tarangdirŏri*" is the sound of the large transverse flute.[202]

199. Pak Nojun, *Koryŏ kayo ŭi yŏngu*, 283.

200. Mariann Sanders Regan, *Love Words: The Self and the Text in Medieval and Renaissance Poetry* (Ithaca: Cornell University Press, 1982), 100.

201. Yang T'aesun, *Hanguk siga ŭi chonghapchŏk koch'al* (Minsogwŏn, 2003), 188-227; repeats the same in Yun Yŏgo et al., eds., *Hanguk siga nŏlp'yŏ ilkki* (Munch'angsa, 2006), 11-45; Pak Nojun, *Koryŏ kayo ŭi yŏngu*, 187-197.

202. Two Galician-Portuguese songs evoke the stormy sea, waves, and

"Song of Green Mountain"

Azalea

Love Lyrics

in Late

Middle

Korean by

Peter H. Lee

The eight-stanza song (ca. 1232-1259) is riddled with textual cruxes. Its historical background may provide a clue to its genesis. At the second invasion of Sarta in 1232, Ch'oe U 崔瑀 (d. 1249), a military strongman, ordered a forced evacuation of the people to mountains and islands; this was considered the best way to avoid the ravages of the Mongol hordes.[203] In the same year the court moved to Kanghwa Island, but the commoners and farmers could not all follow. The song may have been composed between 1232 and 1257 when there was a cease-fire.[204] The two spaces mentioned are green mountain and sea, the first taking up four stanzas but the second only three. Hence, in order to restore a structural balance, some propose that stanzas 5 and 6 should be reversed, the extant version being a copyist's error.

"*Sarori ratta*" (line 1) is read "I'd like to live, must, will, live." In stanza 2, "cry" (*urŏra*) is repeated three times plus "is crying" (*uniroda*). It may be a command, "cry!"—the bird should share the speaker's sorrow.[205] In stanza 2, "I've more sorrow than you"—as a displaced person he has to survive on tree bark and grass roots; however, he does not mention the plain that was reduced to ashes. "The passing bird" (*kadŏnsae*; st. 3: the bird that has passed) is also read as "the land allowed a tenant for his service, dry or wet fields allowed him" (*kaldŏn sarae*). The speaker sees not the bird but a patch of land beyond the river with "a mossy plow" (*ingmudŭn changŭl*), a "mossy woman's encased ornamental knife, usually hung at the waist," a "rusted weapon," or "a red flower."[206] If a

---

boatman. From Martin Codax we have "Ondas do mar de Vigo" (st. 2): "Waves of the bay of Vigo, / Tell me whether you have seen my friend? / And, oh God, whether he will come soon?" And there is Mendinho's song, "Sedia-m'eu na ermida de San Simion": "I have no boatman, and I cannot row, / I, beautiful girl, shall die in the stormy sea: / while waiting for my friend, / while waiting for my friend" (st. 6). See Fred Jensen, ed. and tr,. *Medieval Galician-Portuguese Poetry: An Anthology* (New York: Garland, 1992), 207 and 235.

203. *KS* 23:14a-b.
204. Pak Nojun, *Koryŏ kayo ŭi yŏngu*, 96-99.
205. Pak Nojun, *Koryŏ kayo ŭi yŏngu*, 109.
206. Kim 1:140.

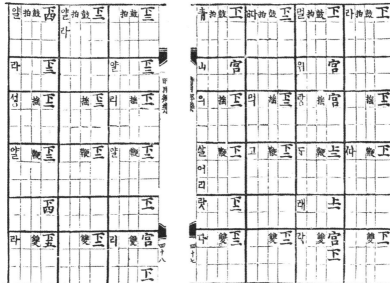

"Green mountain," *Siyong hyangak po.*

AZALEA

Love Lyrics
in Late
Middle
Korean by
Peter H. Lee

person with a mossy plow is not the speaker, then the line says, "Have you seen a man with a mossy plow?"

In stanza 4 the speaker appeals to the listeners, "Where no man comes or goes, / How am I to pass the night?" The stone in stanza 5 has been the subject of lively discussion. Do the refugees watch out for an intruder and throw stones at a man who looks like a beggar? Or is it a symbolic statement that his pain is like being hit by stones? "No one to hate or love"—he is expressionless; at his gloomy prospects he gives up hope; he is plunged into despair. If stanzas 5 and 6 are reversed, the number of stanzas devoted to the sea equals that devoted to the mountain. Stanza 5 then begins, as in stanza 1, with a declaration: "Let's live, let's live, / Let's live by the sea." Stanza 6 introduces another crux, "*aejŏngji*" or "*chŏngji*," read as an "isolated kitchen," "small kitchen," or "forked road."[207] "*Namajagi*," according to a report, is found to be greens growing on Kanghwa Island, not "seaweed."[208] "The stag fiddling / perched on a bamboo pole" is one of the acrobatic acts performed by a professional entertainer. The wine mentioned in stanza 8 ("I have brewed strong wine") should be consumed by someone else, perhaps referring to a group of roving actors.

The song ends with "What shall I do now?" (*ŏtti hariikko*), which recalls "What shall be done?" (*ŏtti harikko*) in "Song of Ch'ŏyong" (ca. 875-886). The speaker has not reached the sea, but registers resignation.[209] Note the repetition of "r" and "o" and enumerative particles repeated (*rang/ ran*) to fit the text to music reminiscent of the typical sound patterns of folk song: *mŏrwirang taraerang* (with wild grapes and thyme); *irigong tyŏrigong* (this way and that); *orido karido* (no man comes or goes); *najŭran pamŭran* (day . . . night); *mŭirido koerido* (to love or hate). The refrain, *yalliyalli yallasyŏng yallari yalla*, may represent the mouth sound of the conical oboe, and *syŏng*, the cymbal or large gong.

207. Sŏng Hogyŏng, *Koryŏ sidae siga yŏngu* (T'aehaksa, 2006), 357-377 and 379-387.
208. Pak Nojun, *Koryŏ kayo ŭi yŏngu*, 115.
209. Kim Wanjin thinks that the speaker is a woman, esp. in sts. 7-8 (Hyangga wa Koryŏ kayo, 217).

"Treading Frost"

Some think this song is not of folk origin but a composition by a member of the intelligentsia, such as Ch'ae Hongch'ŏl 蔡洪哲 (1262-1340).[210] In stanza 1 the female speaker is questioning her beloved, who has made her sleepless ("awake half the night"), a symptom of lovesickness everywhere. Following an awful path, it is he who comes to sleep with her, not she going to his place. The dreadful path associated with death cannot be a simile for the speaker (one construes that she is a young widow who is debating remarriage).[211] One reader thinks that the changeable weather—rain followed by snow—is compared to her betrayal; hence in stanza 2 she invokes the Avici hell, "the last of the eight hot hells, in which punishment, pain, form, birth, and death continue without intermission."[212] The sound of footsteps down a frost-laden path is perhaps evoked by the alliteration of "s" in "sŏrin sŏsŏksari."[213] In addition to a narrow winding path, the awful path translates "yŏlmyŏngkil," where ten kings preside over the ten departments of purgatory.[214] We do not know why the speaker thinks she deserves such a punishment. Was she not faithful? Does her "different mountain path" resemble "a pass in a tangled wood, an awful path"? Their pledge in the past was "let's do this, let's do that"—which can be as easily broken as easily made. In the final line she makes another pledge: let's go together to the same place, let's live together. As ice comes after frost, and frost and ice betoken severe cold, let's not bring calamity upon ourselves and keep out of harm's way.

The latest attempt at textual exegesis, especially the middle stanza where two lines are repeated in the original, suggests that the first line consisting of seven sinographs—"*pyŏngnyŏk*

---

210. *KS* 108: 11b-13b. Yi Hyŏngsang (1653-1733), in *Pyŏngwa sŏnsaeng munjip* 8:150, suggests this attribution, Pak, *Koryŏ kayo ŭi yŏngu*, 187-197.

211. Yun Sŏnghyŏn, *Sogyo ŭi arŭmdaum* (T'aehaksa, 2007), 118.

212. William E. Soothill and Lewis Hodous, *A Dictionary of Chinese Buddhist Terms* (London: Kegan Paul, Trench, Trubner, 1937), 383a.

213. Kim Sangch'ŏl reads "*sŏrin*" as "beset with grief and hope" and "*sŏksŏksari*" as "dull life" in *Koryŏ sidae ŭi siga ŭi t'amsaek* (Kyŏngin munhwasa, 2004), 302-308.

214. Soothill and Hodous, *A Dictionary of Chinese Buddhist Terms*, 51b.

AZALEA

Love Lyrics
in Late
Middle
Korean by
Peter H. Lee

saengham t'amugan" 霹靂生陷墮無間—is something akin to
hyangch'al orthography. (No extant Koryŏ songs have a line in
seven-sinograph phrasing.) The critic reads "*saengham*" as a "living
pit" (vagina), "*mugan*" as "without pause," and "*yŏlmyŏngkil*" (the
awful path) as "the path to ecstasy." The lines, he proposes, conceal
the speaker's erotic desire behind a highly coded phrase—almost
an argot, a kind of underworld jargon: "*Tchŏng tchŏng* ceaseless
thunderbolts on my vagina, / Cause me to die on and on, / Ah,
would I let another penis enter my body?" She tries to express an
emotion so intense, pleasure so rapturous, that it is akin to the
experience of death—she compares her orgasm to thunderbolts
striking her sexual organ.[215] This reading is calculated to shock by
its unexpected and capricious deciphering. But the translator does
not assemble philological evidence in support of his reading, thus
casting aspersions on the reliability of his proposal. The same lines
were hitherto read: "At times thunderbolts, ah, / My body will fall
into the Avici hell / And perish at once." We now understand why
this song, especially the middle stanza, was dubbed "licentious" by
Chosŏn Confucian moralists.

Let us return to stanza 2. I think it likely that this stanza is
a later interpolation by someone who knew snippets of Buddhist
texts, especially because the line in question does not harmonize
with the diction and mood of the song as a whole. It is a soliloquy
by the speaker, who thinks she might find herself soon in infernal
flames. Were there forces that conspired against her, such as spies
that pry into others' love affairs, callous mockers (*lauzengier*)? She
would rather see herself than her beloved in Avici hell, contrary to an
anonymous motet for three voices by a trouvère: "But I see someone
else here / Who, I think—/ May he burn in hell—/ jealously guards

---

215. Cho Yongho, "'Isang kok' ŭi ŭimi wa ŭmsajŏk sŏngkkyŏk," *Tongbang
hakchi* 148 (Dec. 2009): 141-177. See Ulf Malm, *Dolssor Conina: Lust, the Bawdy,
and Obscenity in Medieval Occitan and Galician-Portuguese Troubadou Poetry
and Latin Secular Love Song* (Uppsala University Library, 2001) on nudity and
explicit genital references (e.g., "con," "fur," "forte").

me."[216] We do not know whether the speaker associates love with death. In our texts no woman wishes to plunge a dagger in her breast or down a cup of poison. The speaker does not believe in revenge, and so great is her genuine contrition that we wish her well.

"Spring Overflows the Pavilion"

Yun Hoe (1380-1436) wrote "Ponghwangŭm" (Song of the Phoenix), a revised version of "Song of Ch'ŏyong," as *contrafactum* to the tune of this song.[217] The anonymous compiler of the Akchang kasa added the term "*pyŏlsa*" 別詞 (separate text) to indicate what follows. What he called "another text" is in fact the original, and Yun's new words are another text used as court/ritual music. This tune was also used, with minor changes, for other early Chosŏn eulogies.

The song opens with startling imagery. The speaker declares that even if she were to die of cold (-*ŭlmangjŏng*) on a bed made of bamboo leaves, were she to freeze to death with him on the ice, she would wish their night of love to "run slow, run slow," perhaps because the arrival of dawn will separate them, as in the *alba*. "*Kyŏnggyŏng*" in "*Kyŏnggyŏng koch'imsang*," a five-word phrase in literary Chinese, means "uneasy, restless, and alone in bed." How did this phrase sound to the listener, and what were its associations? "Peach blossoms have no worry" is a trope of personification (prosopopoeia). Peach blossoms "laugh at" (*piutta*) or "scorn" the spring breeze for its transience. This may, one translator suggests, allude to her beloved's affair with another woman and hence be expressing jealousy. Such a reading, however, is far-fetched and not supported by the text.[218]

"May my soul be with yours," followed by "*pŏ.gi.si.dŏ.ni nwi. si.si.ni.ika*," implying "insists," yields the sense of "Who persuaded me this was true?" She has learned that a man's deep-sworn vow is false, but she does not upbraid him. Now she knows firsthand that such promises of fidelity are meaningless in the reality of an affair.[219]

---

216. Doss-Quinby et al., *Songs of the Women* Trouvères, 236 (no. 69, motet, line 12).
217. For the text and melodies see *Sejong sillok* 146:1a-27b.
218. Pak Nojun, *Koryŏ kayo ŭi yŏngu*, 256.
219. Kim Sangch'ŏl thinks sts. 2-3 are interpolations (278).

AZALEA

Love Lyrics
in Late
Middle
Korean by
Peter H. Lee

The "duck" in stanza 4, which is in dialogue form, is her beloved, represented here as a playboy; the shoal (*yŏhŭl*) is another woman; the swamp (*so*) is the speaker. One reading addresses the duck, "Why do you come to me who has her own man?" The duck answers, "If the swamp freezes, the shoal will do." While the duck is free to move around, both the swamp and the shoal are passive; water in its many forms stands for the feminine. Mount South is read by one translator as "the warmest place on the floor nearest the fireplace,"[220] with a jade pillow and a damask quilt. "*Sahyang kaksi*" (literally "a musk lady") is a woman festooned with a pouch filled with musk, which is a cure for lovesickness. Stanza 5 spoken by her lover, which connects with stanza 1, represents the acme of the speaker's imagination, and we respond powerfully to her dream of fulfilled love in perfect harmony. The last one-line stanza begins "*Aso nimha*," meaning both "O" and "Know this," recalling the same in the last line of "Treading Frost" (III:3) and in "Regret" ("Chŏng Kwajŏng" 鄭瓜亭, line 11). The song ends with a desire to "live forever together."

"Will You Go?"

In stanza 1 of 'Will You Go?' (*kasiri*), consisting of four three-line stanzas, "Will you go?" is repeated three times. "*Nanŭn*" (literally "I") ending line 2 throughout the song is generally read as a meaningless word inserted to keep the rhythm. It is also read as the sound of the double-reed oboe (*p'iri*). The first part of the refrain in line 3 is meaningless, too, followed by a four-syllable phrase in Chinese (O age of great peace and plenty), a later addition of a cliché in eulogies. Stanza 3 says, "I could hold and keep you," and the range of meanings suggested for "*sŏnhada*" includes: candid, displeasing, reluctant, look at each other, by mistake. What it says is, "If what I do is displeasing to you—trying to stop him physically from leaving." "*Sŏrŏn nim*" in stanza 4 means "lamentable, distressing." The speaker, able to suppress sorrow, resigns herself to the situation.

---

220. Pak Nojun, *Koryŏ kayo ŭi yŏngu*, 262.

"Song of Chŏngŭp"

In this song consisting of eleven lines without division, of which five are refrains, a woman speaker addresses the moon. "*Kom*" in "*nop'i kom*" (high) and "*miri kom*" (far) is a suffix for emphasis. "*Chŏjae*" (line 6) is "market," or the place name Chŏnju 全州. "*Chŭndae*" (line 6) is read as "mud, muddy road, disgrace, and stain" by extension. The whole line goes, "Don't cause injury to others, or suffer injury." "*Ŏnŭida*" (line 8) means "everywhere, whichever, anyone"; "*nok'osira*," "leave and come, leave everything and come." "*Nae kanondae*" (line 9) is suggested to mean "where I go, I go out to meet, where I live," "may darkness not overtake him or me." Our source provides the following gloss: administratively, Chŏngŭp belonged to Chŏnju. A traveling salesman from Chŏngŭp went on a peddling tour but did not return for a long time. His wife climbed atop a rock on a mountain and awaited him. Apprehensive lest he should get hurt on his night journey, she compared the imagined danger to the filth of muddy water. Tradition says that there is a rock where wives looked out for husbands.

"Song of the Gong and Chimes"

This song begins with a three-line introduction and continues in ten three-line stanzas. After offering a series of impossibilities, the song declares that only if these ever occur shall "we part from the virtuous lord" as the refrain in the third, fourth, and fifth stanzas states. The use of *adynata* (impossibilities) as a rhetorical device in the poetry of praise and vow is a commonplace. Stanzas 10 and 11 must have been popular as an independent song, as they occur in stanzas 5-8 of "Song of P'yŏngyang." The "virtuous lord" (*yudŏkhasin nim*) is usually construed as referring to a king, but in a song of pledges between two lovers, it is more likely to refer to a beloved.

Understanding the Songs

These songs are known by the titles given by the compilers, not the authors of the texts. Situated to be read first, the title's

AZALEA

Love Lyrics
in Late
Middle
Korean by
Peter H. Lee

presence presupposes a reader. So it is obvious that the titles were given after the texts were written and before they were presented to the reader by someone other than the author. The title *"Tongdong"* ("Ode to the Seasons") for a song accompanying a court dance was given probably by the compilers of the *Guide to the Study of Music* (1493).[221] Another song whose title was given by the same source is *"Chŏngŭp sa"* 井邑詞 ("Song of Chŏngŭp").[222] Chŏngŭp is an old name of Chŏngju in North Chŏlla province; this is said to be the only song dating from Paekche. Several titles come from the first word of the text: *"Ssanghwajŏm"* 雙花店 ("The Turkish Bakery"), *"Sŏgyŏng pyŏlgok"* 西京別曲 ("Song of P'yŏngyang"), and *"Kasiri"* 가시리 ("Will You Go?"). Although *"ch'ŏngsan"* (green mountain) occurs twice in the first two lines, the current title, *"Ch'ŏngsan pyŏlgok,"* 青山別曲 is not really apt, because the speaker also wishes to go to the sea. The title of *"Isang kok"* 履霜曲 ("Treading Frost") may have been inspired by the content of the first two lines; *"Manjŏnch'un"* 滿殿春 ("Spring Overflows the Pavilion") does not appear to be the original title, but may be inspired by a *ci* tune title, *"Manting fang"* 滿庭芳 (Courtyard full of fragrance). The title should not intrude on the song's internal space nor impose a perspective on it from outside.[223] We have, then, first word/ line identifiers,[224] as with a sijo or one of Shakespeare's sonnets: *"Ch'ŏngsalli pyŏkkyesuya"* is the first two metric segments of a famous *sijo* by Hwang Chini 黃眞伊 (ca. 1506-1544), for example, and "My mistress' eyes are nothing like the sun" identifies sonnet 130.

Unlike women troubadours (*trobairitz*), who were "all aristocratic and propertied women from the valley of the Rhone,"[225] the speakers of these songs do not encode information about their social status or economic class. The bare minimal

221. Yi Hyegu, *Sinyŏk Akhak kwebŏm*, 3:8b-9a; 5:7b-8b.
222. Yi Hyegu, *Sinyŏk Akhak kwebŏm*, 5:10a-b.
223. Anne Ferry, *The Title to the Poem* (Stanford: Stanford University Press, 1996), 263.
224. Ferry, *The Title to the Poem*, 261.
225. Bogin, *The Women Troubadours*, 132.

262

diction leaves out most contextual clues. We can identify the gender of the speaker from distinctive verbal features and tropes. The feminine speaker typically employs repetition and nonsense jingles, which place her voice close to the roots of lyric and make it easy for the unlearned to remember.[226] Her subject is the recurrent universal features of love, especially of separation—"a study in the ambiguities of time . . . .

One of those moments called 'then' contains [her] beloved."[227] Most songs are by abandoned women, the locus of unrequited passion. Love requires physical presence, and it should survive separation, but the male is the agent of separation. Time, the eater of youth, is also a separator. Her song is an exploration of the torments of love with a sense of urgency. Devastated by the end of a relationship, she speaks as love bids her—a forsaken woman suffering from the pangs of love and hate, the typical female voice, for example, in Mozarabic kharjas appended to the Arabic *Muwashshah* (composed 1000-1150).[228]

"Born into this world, I live alone." "I lie on a dirt floor, with only a sheet to cover me." "Lonely life, night without you" ("Ode to the Seasons"). "Do you come, who made me lie awake half the night?" ("Treading Frost"). Riding the swell of anguish, she is sleepless with longing, a symptom of lovesickness, telltale signs of which include darkened vision, sunken eyes, sudden sweating, irregular palpitations of the heart, whirring in the ears, jaundiced color, wasted arms, helplessness, stupor, pallor, anorexia.[229] Sappho's "melter of limbs," Eros, is "sweetbitter" (glukupikron).[230] Our speaker compares herself to a comb cast

226. Doris Earnshaw, *The Female Voice in Medieval Romance Lyric* (New York: Peter Lang, 1988), 135.

227. Anne Carson, *Eros the Bittersweet: An Essay* (Princeton: Princeton University Press, 1986), 117.

228. Compton, *Andalusian Lyrical Poetry and Old Spanish Love Songs.*

229. Donald A. Beecher and Massimo Ciavolella, trs., *Jacques Ferrand, A Treatise on Lovesickness* (Syracuse: Syracuse University Press, 1990), 50; Mary Frances Wack, *Lovesickness in the Middle Ages: The Viaticum and Its Commentaries* (Philadelphia: University of Pennsylvania Press, 1990), 40 passim.

230. Carson, *Eros the Bittersweet*, 3, 38.

Azalea

Love Lyrics

in Late

Middle

Korean by

Peter H. Lee

from a cliff, or a "sliced berry," cruelly mutilated. Her song offers sharp memorable images in plain diction and is able to compress an event into just a few words. Pleasure and pain are inextricable, hence oxymoron is born, such as that of ice that sets the lover on fire ("Spring Overflows the Pavilion").[231] "If only I am with you" ("Ode to the Seasons"); "If you love me, I'll follow you with tears" ("Song of P'yŏngyang"); "O love, let us be forever together" ("Spring Overflows the Pavilion"); "Ah love, living with you is my vow" ("Treading Frost"); "But return as soon as you leave" ("Will You Go?"); "I am, in the end, complete myself only in and because of my relation to you!"[232] The feminine speaker in "Spring Overflows the Pavilion" wishes to build a bamboo mat on the ice and die of cold with her beloved. We cannot help responding to her startling imagery, her fondness for particulars, and her imaginative power. She relates emotion in a specific context and shares that emotion with her audience. In the words of Thomas C. Moser Jr., "Erotic situation invites linguistic manipulation, and erotic energy becomes grammatical energy."[233]

In these anonymous female-voiced songs, wherein the woman is the subject (the lyric "I"), the central concern is meditation on the contours of absence. This anonymity and the genre dictate a feminine speaker and female authorship. In similar songs in the West, such as medieval German women's songs (*Frauenlieder*), and Galician-Portuguese *cantigas d'amigo* (love songs in the female voice) and cantigas d'amor (love songs in the male voice), "most are composed . . . exclusively by men."[234] "The male poet could choose, with equal legitimacy, between a mode that allowed him to speak as a man and a mode that enabled him to appropriate

231. Mariann Sanders Regan, *Love Words: The Self and the Text in Medieval and Renaissance Poetry* (Ithaca: Cornell University Press, 1982), 68.

232. William Waters, *Poetry's Touch: On Lyric Address* (Ithaca: Cornell University Press, 2003), 155.

233. Thomas C. Moser Jr., *A Cosmos of Desire: The Medieval Latin Erotic Lyric in English Manuscripts* (Ann Arbor: University of Michigan Press, 2004), 165.

234. William E. Jackson, "The Woman's Song in Medieval German Poetry," in *Vox Feminae: Studies on Medieval Women's Songs*, ed. John F. Plummer (Kalamazoo: Western Michigan University Press, 1981), 53.

the imaginary feminine, to speak as a woman [as in traditional China and Korea]."[235] "The female voice boasts that a man loves her, whereas the male voice never boasts that a woman loves him."[236] "Thus, whereas for the feminine it is possible to present oneself as both speaking subject and the object of another's desire, for the masculine it is not."[237] If male poets wished to appropriate female discourse in Middle Korean love songs, they might have sought "a kind of poetic justice, compensating for the suffering inflicted by a cruel or indifferent mistress by portraying a woman who had to beg mercy from an insensitive lover."[238] But such was impossible in a culture where one did not believe that only by love could a man become virtuous and noble as in the western *fin'amor / amour courtois*. In Koryŏ's oral vernacular lyric tradition, "a loving woman separated from her beloved might have belonged to the lower popular register";[239] but judging from their diction and imagery, these songs could not have been composed by nonliterate women.

We are likely to focus more on the gender of the text and less on the gender of the author and identify with the poetic speaker more than with the speaker's beloved.[240] Our speaker dares to talk of love, to compose, to perform her song. The gender of the song's target audience is male, but it is also a mixed audience. Of course the singer in the here and now is not the speaker, and though a song may be addressed to her single male recipient, it is always meant to be overheard by other people.[241] Audiences knew the

235. Julian Weiss, "On the Conventionality of the CANTIGAS d'AMOR," in *Medieval Lyric: Genres in Historical Context*, ed. William D. Paden (Urbana: University of Illinois Press, 2000), 132. Earl Miner says, "In cultures with affective-expressive poetics, the poet tends to be identified with the speaker of the poem, and the reader is presumed also to be stirred so much as to be likely to turn to lyric expression," and "Chinese in particular have identified—in the absence of proof to the contrary—the speaker of a lyric with the biographical poet," *Comparative Poetics: An Intercultural Essay on Theories of Literature* (Princeton: Princeton University Press, 1990), 120 and 233.

236. William D. Paden, "Introduction," in *Medieval Lyric*, ed. William D. Paden, 7.

237. Weiss, "On the Conventionality of the CANTIGAS d'AMOR," 133.

238. Doss-Quinby et al., *Songs of the Women* Trouvères, 13.

239. Doss-Quinby et al., *Songs of the Women* Trouvères, 8.

240. Waters, *Poetry's Touch*, 2.

241. Waters, *Poetry's Touch*, 19.

AZALEA

Love Lyrics
in Late
Middle
Korean by
Peter H. Lee

text by heart and might be expected to join the soloist in singing the refrain. Thus a song invites a communal identification of singer and audience.[242] Inseparable from performance, songs are transferable—to be sung by others.[243] They are a call for fellowship. The lyric's inability to belong fully to its personal addressee is universal;[244] these songs outlived their authors. Aware of the importance of language to subjectivity and empowerment,[245] aware too of the poetic sense of self, a typical author enjoyed the freedom of her linguistic utterance as desirous feminine subject. But a real woman's experience would have been very different and should be seen "within the context of institutional structures shaped largely by men, reflecting male concerns."[246] Woman's sexual activity was perhaps less controlled in medieval Korea than in later times by a plethora of fierce prohibitions.

Does this reading help us who no longer speak Late Middle Korean vernacular to draw nearer to the medieval Korean literary experience? How can we educate ourselves to read these songs as a speaker of Middle Korean might have done? The poets may have introduced subtle variations, as did their singers and audiences. But unlike the troubadour *canso* (love song), known to us in many versions, these songs came down in only one version, and we do not know the medieval audiences' expectations and experiences. Because there has been nothing resembling these songs in Korean literary history before or since, only repeated readings will bring us closer to the experience of the medieval audience. Hundreds of students studied these songs and accompanying music for music bureau examinations until the end of the nineteenth century, and many others did so, we hope, on various other occasions. The songs began to be noticed

242. Lindley, *Lyric*, 51.
243. Lindley, *Lyric*, 52.
244. Waters, *Poetry's Touch*, 25.
245. Simon Gaunt, *Gender and Genre in Medieval French Literature* (Cambridge: Cambridge University Press, 1995), 178.
246. Gold, *The Lady and the Virgin*, xviii.

in the 1920s, but we need more in-depth studies of them as love lyrics from medieval Korea. Each should be understood "as it was in the historical moment of its appearance."[247] The undying power of these songs will continue to stimulate literary debate and lead many to discover that they are a watershed—if not a summit—in the tradition of Korean love lyrics.

---

247. Amelia E. Van Vleck, *Memory and Re-Creation in Troubadour Lyric* (Berkeley: University of California Press, 1991), 209.

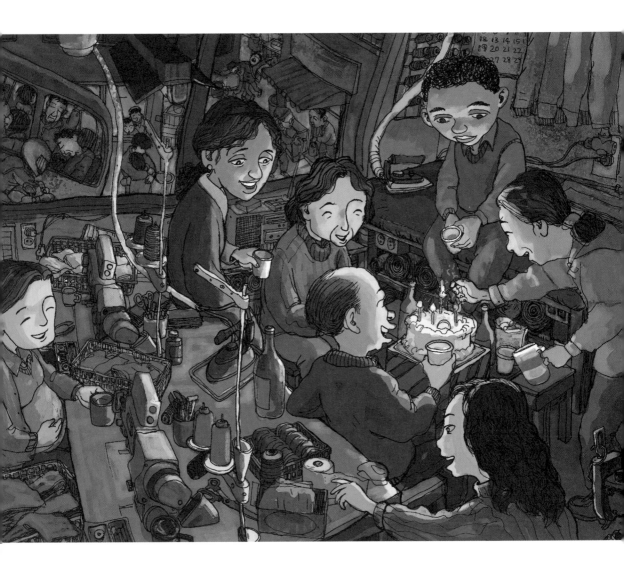

Five Poems by Jin Eun-young

Translated by Jeon Seung-hee

SPRING HAS COME

A guy spills a can of green paint.
I don't have red.
I'll have to chop off my wrist.

My Beautiful Laundrette[1]

To Grandmother who had managed to crawl up to the second floor
    balcony, lean on its railings, and yell at me for leaving her alone,
When I ran away from her curses that sounded like the cawing of a
    raven in a cage,
After handing her a bottle of clear liquor;

To Grandmother who hurled abuses that were flapping
Like blue diapers hung on every rooftop in an alley on a windy day
When I ran away, holding hands with a neighborhood friend;

Although I ran away from her without ever turning around,
"Bitch, is that bitch your secret lover?"
Rang sharply in the street like a broken golden horn.

On that street I was holding your soft hand in mine,
"Maybe I am really in love with her."
To Grandmother who awoke the man in me like Proust, the French
    master of the literature of reminiscence;

To myself who yelled at you, my sister, and opposed you even more
    stubbornly than mom and dad,
When you were crying in front of me, because you wanted to marry a
    young would-be composer who neither had money nor knew tricks;

To my sister, who treasured the completely tattered *Selected*
    American Short Stories
That I read and put aside:
"You're the worst snob in the world. Why did you give me 'The Gift
    of the Magi,' if you were going to be like this?"[2]

---

1. This is the title of a 1985 film based on the screenplay by Hanif Kureishi.
2. "The Gift of the Magi" is a well-known short story written by O. Henry

"I may, but you shouldn't."

The words I couldn't utter pricked my index finger in the pocket
    of my orange baseball jacket like a safety pin left there and
    forgotten long ago.

Although I wrote a dissertation on the solemn principle of strict
    emptiness,
The only thing I remember now is
The stain on cotton cloth in the remarks by Monk Nagarjuna.[3]
The stain was . . . multi-colored.
Like in the poem by Kim Yi-dŭm,[4]
Perhaps it was a star-shaped stain? To all those who are wondering
    only about their shapes and colors;

I show you my beautiful laundrette.

To my first love and ex-boyfriend, who smiled—perhaps he was
    sneering at me or maybe just envious of me—and said, "You're
    still living like a student who's boarding herself," the first time
    he visited my house in ten years;

You, harmless bastard! Aren't you living with a woman with a coy
    mouth in an apartment in a newly developed suburban city?
In fact, I loved that stupidity of yours, those dreams like
    Bachelard's clouds, which you blew into my room and which
    floated in it.

The Haengdang-dong moon village district office, in which I
    worked as a grade nine civil servant for six months after I

---

about a poor young couple who are dealing with the challenges of buying a secret
Christmas gift for each other with very little money.

    3. Nagarjuna (ca. 150-250 CE) is an important Buddhist teacher and
philosopher. Along with his disciple Aryadeva, he is credited with founding the
Madhyamaka school of Mahayana Buddhism.

    4. Kim Yi-dŭm is a contemporary poet. The title of one of her books of poetry
is *A Star-shaped Stain*.

graduated from high school.[5]

I can't even go back to that labyrinthine place, because it became a

large apartment complex.

In that scrawny alley, spiders must have been dying alone, crying

out to all the gods of the world.

"If you hadn't quit your job then, what pay grade would you be

by now?" Father still tries to calculate like a parent who keeps

toting up the age of his stillborn child.

To Father who's still nagging me like a child, "How nice it would be

if you stopped being a poet and teacher and made some money!

We could move to Bundang";[6]

I show you my beautiful laundrette-

A place in which, once you bury your face in the heaps of hanging

clothes, you can't see any mysterious expressions,

Confessions that are neither my clothes nor yours,

Confessions hanging way up high only in here, because they can't

be worn outside.

I show you this natural dirt of mine-

What you, hygiene freaks, reach out to and love.

The harder you iron the clothes, the more they stick to your skin.

All that was written in the old credit ledger was *In Search of Lost Time*,

Selected American Short Stories, *Madhayamaka*, old bibliography,[7]

Water and dream.

Hello, clothes,

Hurry up and go find those who left you here. In my life's

midsummer, hens are laying warm yellow eggs on a poultry farm;

Everyone, holding only white flowers like dried-up forsythias,

reeking of bleach near the stream,

Sneaked away, taking only their bodies.

5. A "moon village" is slang for a poor urban area, usually located on a slope
or hillside. The ninth is the lowest grade in the Korean civil service system.

6. Bundang is the name of one of the newly developed suburban areas near Seoul.

7. *Madhyamaka* is a book by Nagarjuna.

THERE'S NO FORGETTING

The person who hated me the most died.
He was reborn to be my body.

The person whom I loved the most died.
And he became a river.

   He is my noon and my midnight.
   His soft hair
   Flowed into four rivers, sprinkling the fragrances of fruits and
   stars in all seasons.

When I was young, I read a story in *A Thousand and One Nights*,
   in which
All the people of a kingdom became fish.
They swam with the flow of the river as they pleased, and then

There was a king who hated the river the most.
He died.
He was reborn to become a politician.

There was a king who hated the river the most.
I died and was reborn.
And I turned him into a politician.

I am someone who hates the most
What I loved the most.

The river's my noon and my midnight
My honey, my bile, my down there.

In *A Thousand and One Nights* of my childhood, all residents of a city
Became fish; the river that dies

Will soon be reborn as my body
With mysterious diseases and unfamiliar stench like the nimble
    arms and legs of a relay runner.

There was a time when all the residents of a city
Were fish; once, they flowed as they pleased
Into a vacant territory, like water.

OPHELIA

All love has the memory of drowning.
I learned it
While flowing on the red water
Like a white paper boat.

Hearts that have been carried down to the beach
Sprout up as soft braille from the hot sand
For the wet fingers of a blind person.

People who have been hanging around the empty bottom of the river
Come to me and buy food-
Bread made of an even mixture of ground glass and wheat flour.

A soap bubble might be infinitely swelling up with transparent joy.
I might be able to take you to the city where there is a rosy palace.
It's unlikely that I will forget that dizzying kiss, mixed with brown fur,
Between winter and evening.
It feels as if we can hide everything under the vast velvet of love.
It feels as if all of these are lies.
It looks as if a hungry seagull is sucking the dry nipple of the sky so hard
That its white bite marks are flying across the water.

This city is like a child who writes down the same single sentence
    forever and ever.
Shanties that fell out like baby teeth were thrown over the red moon.
A blood- and soot-stained liquor bottle is rolling down the white slope.
I feel like inserting an unchangeable line from my first book of
    poetry into my last one.
Youth, well . . . , it feels as if it's gone.
A soft yellow wing, with thousands of gray bells hanging underneath-
It feels as if it's slowly soaring.

It seems that gold puts its hand down the throat of a poor person
    and forces him to vomit everything.
Stars are rolling in the thin green vomit.
God might be a fake traffic accident victim.
He might have never taken the medicine prescribed by angels.
He might be breaking his blue capsules in half and pouring out
    all the granules.

Bye, bye, it's snowing on the broken gray of a slate roof.

All the things I saw might be lies.

It looks as if the wings of the silver bats, hanging onto the moon,
    are breaking off.

ON CINEMA:

A Day in the Life of Kubo the Film Critic

A Day in the Life of Kubo
the Film Critic
(P'yŏngnon'ga Kubo-ssi ŭi iril)[1]

by Josie Sohn

A *Day in the Life of Kubo the Film Critic* (2009) is a serial of unfinished short stories written by a university student and featured in *A Short Love for Film* (P'illŭm e kwanhan tchalbŭn sarang),[2] a not-for-profit film magazine produced by university students and young professionals in Seoul. As the title suggests, these vignettes are an adaptation of *A Day in the Life of Kubo the Novelist* (1934), written by Pak T'aewŏn, which has been adapted many times in literary and other genres.

The new *Kubo* is particularly noteworthy in its parody of the contemporary film culture shared by young cinephiles living in Seoul. I suggest, in fact, that Kubo the film critic, though not a university student himself, is a veritable alter ego of today's young cinephiles. Like the critic in the narrative, who cannot land a stable job, many are fragile neoliberal subjects whose cosmopolitan tastes and knowledge of world cinema do not

* I owe particular thanks to Professors Nancy Abelmann, Christopher Hanscom, Nicholas Harkness, Jiyeon Kang, and Sunyoung Park for their careful reading and insightful comments on an earlier draft of this paper. I also thank Katherine Lee, Franklin Rausch, Michael Sprunger, and James Welker for their helpful suggestions and tireless support.

1. All translations are mine unless otherwise noted.
2. The magazine borrows its title from a 1988 Polish film, *Krótki film o milosci* (A short film about love), directed by Krzysztof Kieslowski. The English title of the magazine is not mine.

AZALEA

A Day in the
Life of Kubo the
Film Critic by
Josie Sohn

translate readily into economic stability. *Kubo the Film Critic*, in short, can be appreciated as a fictional embodiment of young cinephiles of the "88-manwŏn generation"[3] who are economically insecure and burdened by the intense competition of South Korean society today.

This is not to say, however, that the recent adaptation makes no reference to the original. Following the translation, I consider, first, how the text critiques the pedantic culture of cinephiles and education-driven South Korean society by employing film theory in a manner that differs strikingly from how the original *Kubo* employs literary and philosophical discourses. I also address the ways in which *Kubo the Film Critic* signals the emergence of a generation fluent in visual or cinematic language by transforming the writerly text of *Kubo the Novelist* into a cinematic one. In *Kubo the Film Critic*, the reader can experience a cinematic vision and pacing that differ significantly from the original.

In my translation of *Kubo the Film Critic*, I have made every effort to preserve the format, style, and language of the original text because of their significance for the tone and spirit of the narrative.[4] A faithful translation of cryptic words and run-on sentences, for example, reflects how intentionally difficult these stories are to read in the original language. Wherever applicable, I have glossed my translation choices in the footnotes. The following is the first two episodes in the unfinished three-part series published from January to March of 2009.[5]

⌐

---

3. See U Sŏkhun and Pak Kwŏnil, *88-manwŏn sedae: chŏlmang ŭi sidae e ssŭnŭn hŭimang ŭi kyŏngjehak* (88-manwŏn generation: writing economics of hope in days of despair) (Seoul: Redian, 2007).

4. See Walter Benjamin, "The Task of the Translator," in *Illuminations* (New York: Schocken Books, 1968), 69-82.

5. Volumes 18 to 20.

A Day in the Life of Kubo the Film Critic (評論家)[6]

Written by An Sŏngyong (former staff writer)

Episode 1, "Metropolitan 'Ŏ-bu-ŏ-bu'"

As the year 2008 drew to a close, on a morning a few days before the end of December, Kubo, a film critic, awoke from sleep. Despite the different alarm clocks going off simultaneously in three or four households, he felt nostalgic for sounds like those of magpies and temple bells, like those he used to hear on holiday mornings when he stayed at the head house[7] in the countryside. However, as Kubo brushed his teeth he asked, "Have I ever lived in the countryside?" and thought himself strange for longing for such things since he had lived in the city all his life. Those who live in the city have idealized images of rural life, each his or her own.[8] Kubo, too, had his own mental images of rural landscapes that he absorbed from television. Having heard the magpie's call for the first time in a *Rural Diary*[9] episode as a child, he indulged in wishful thinking that a magpie might fly in from a nonexistent hometown. He left home without eating breakfast and was already lighting a cigarette the moment the number on the elevator changed from 2 to 1. Once the elevator doors opened, he puffed hastily at his cigarette and slipped out of the building. As Kubo walked the twenty steps or so from the elevator to the front entrance of the building, three residents saw him but did not bother to take any interest in his illegal smoking. They say you get your nose chopped off if you so much as blink in the city, but he

---

6. The author—or the narrator—often adds *hanja* (Chinese characters) and/ or English words in parentheses. I have incorporated this by retaining *hanja* and replacing English with romanized transliteration of Korean. I do not, however, indicate whether *hanja* or English is added next to or substituted entirely for Korean. While I do not expect every reader to recognize *hanja* cognates, they are meant, in part, to demonstrate the visual impact in the text.

7. The "head house" (*kŭnjip*; 宗家) refers to the household of one's eldest agnatic relative.

8. The original sentence is gender neutral.

9. *Rural Diary* (Chŏnwŏn ilgi) is the longest running South Korean "drama" dating from October 21, 1980 to December 29, 2002 (broadcast by MBC).

considered this urban oppressiveness a plus as long as it did not interfere with his trivial transgressions.

Azalea

A Day in the
Life of Kubo the
Film Critic by
Josie Sohn

Kubo was an expert in overcoming the indifference of his neighbors through metropolitan optimism. He waited for the bus to Chongno so he could catch a movie at an early-bird price. Before long, the number 414 bus that passes by Chongno 2-*ga* arrived. Kubo boarded the bus and was relieved when he spotted an empty seat behind the passengers lining up to get off. When a high school girl who boarded through the back door cut through the crowd and landed safely in that seat, however, he no longer felt so magnanimous. Kubo saw the quorum (定數) of a metropolitan kind in the high school girl who shoved away the passengers on their way out as if she were going through some moving boxes while she spoke into the speaker attached to an electronic device oh-so-coquettishly. Could the binary sound (*bainŏri saundŭ*) synchronized to digital signs be more human than mechanical heaviness (力學的重量感)? Kubo, remembering how he himself had to wake up to the binary signals (二陣信號的) of alarm clocks, was about to critique the dehumanization (沒人格化) of modern subjects but soon realized that he, too, was a lone wolf when he arrived at the conclusion that it is yet another medieval (中世的) paradox (*p'aradoksŭ*) to attribute anything other than protein mass to the mechanical heaviness as he sat among the passengers. Kubo was a man who gradually lost friends because he distanced himself too much from using machines. He knew too well that in this day and age one cannot have meaningful human relationships without a cellular phone and the Internet, but it was his nature to find more pleasure in critiquing such things than in breaking out of solitude. And his thorough professionalism was just about to reveal a new understanding of metropolitan identity from his own sense of isolation. Kubo, not wanting to lose the new ideas that stimulated his scalp as protein compounds agitated in his pituitary gland, got out his notepad and scrawled a few sentences starting with a capital M. He did so, however, only to cross them all out upon realizing how they sounded like a sci-fi cliché. The high school girl who landed in the empty seat next to an old man who snoozed as he rested his head on the window had already hung up the phone and was listening to music through ear buds. She took a black plastic bag out of her bag and started eating a red bean bun that she must have bought from a convenience store rather than a bakery. Kubo felt sorry for something in the figure of the girl who wolfed down the bun without even any milk, and he wondered if his attempt to arrive at a new philosophy of the metropolitan through that high school girl was nothing other than a deformed manifestation of his abject desire to sit in the empty seat. The bus passed by Kwanghwamun in no time at all, and there was a jet-black giant hammering slowly outside the window on the right side. The iron structure that raised and dropped its right hand all year long like Chaplin in *Modern Times* was wearing a red Santa Claus hat, a gift, maybe, from the landlord of the Cinecube building. Kubo, as he witnessed this capitalistic paternalism, was comforted and thought, "He will spend a warm winter this year!" He found room for generosity in his heart once again, enough to feel affinity with a machine-man.

At five minutes to 10 o'clock, Kubo arrived at Sponge House located in the direction of Ch'ŏnggyech'ŏn at Chongno 2-ga. The winter sun that was yet to rise above Dusan Tower in Tongdaemun cast a rectangular shadow on the 4-lane road. Kubo scanned the show times in considerable discomfort because the cold wind that entered his nostrils filled up his respiratory organs with secretions, making it hard to talk.

Theater 1	10:30	*Romantic Island*
Theater 2	11:30	*Waltz with Bashir*
Theater 6	11:00	*I Just Didn't Do It*

He did not have a particular movie that he wanted to watch and was more interested in secondary facts such as what the theater district looks like or what sort of people come to watch

AZALEA

A Day in the
Life of Kubo the
Film Critic by
Josie Sohn

movies early in the morning on a weekday. As he openly expressed his contempt for mechanical devices, cinema for Kubo was not an object of appreciation and love but more often an object of criticism and conquest. As a film critic, his philosophy (觀) of cinema dictated that film, too, was a mere mechanical illusion (幻影), and this made him accept his lot as a lone heretic. The problem of whether cinema is of primary (主) importance and the audience secondary (副次), or whether the audience is primary and cinema secondary in a space that is theater was the very theme of the editorial he was to contribute to an upcoming issue of *Kino21*.

Kubo approached a *hottŏk* stall to observe what was new with moviegoers. The face of the woman who was pressing down the round dough on the hot iron plate lit up as if Kubo was the first customer of the day. His heart warmed up to the woman's smile, which resembled that of Pokkil's (福吉) mother,[10] indeed more so than he did to the sizzling cooking oil. The woman appeared to be deaf. Not wishing to make her envy his eloquence by starting meaningless small talk, he handed her a thousand-*wŏn* bill with a smile. Kubo turned his head in order to look at the box office after receiving his green tea *hottŏk*. Not even a single person was at the box office, probably because the first movie would not start until thirty minutes later. The sugary hotcake that became thinner with the soaring price of flour did not promise more than fifteen minutes of savoring even if he could take all the time in the world. After a minute passed as Kubo waited for his *hottŏk* to cool down, he took a bite as small as one fifteenth and looked around the theater as he gained (得) a sense of satisfying his hunger. He reminisced about the good old CineCore because Sponge House did not feel at all like a theater to him. He recalled Myungbo Plaza and Academy Cinema, too. While Kubo was slowly chewing the last one-fifteenth portion, the first audience member appeared. He was a middle-aged man around Kubo's age. He looked more like

10. Pokkil's mother is a character in *Rural Diary*.

a laid-off person who left home this morning after telling his wife that he was off to work than a provincial salary man on a business trip to Seoul. Kubo was about to exchange nods with the woman after blowing his nose vigorously but instantly resented her after he turned his body to throw away the paper he had held the *hottŏk* with and saw the menu, "Green tea *hottŏk* 700 *wŏn*," realizing that his 300 *wŏn* had been filched. He quickly turned towards the box office feeling heartless once again.

". . . Which movie are you going to see?"

The box office girl who was as cold as in the days of CineCore pressed him. Kubo, however, could not open his mouth so easily. He thought his nose would explode and fire out the mucus that stuffed his respiratory organ if he so much as said one word. Reluctantly, Kubo could do nothing more than mumble, "Ŏ-bu-ŏ-bu," as he wheezed through his mouth. The box office girl, having seen him hanging around the *hottŏk* stall without uttering a single word, decided without giving it a thought that he was deaf and asked,

"*Romantic Island for 10:30?*"

Kubo shook his head up and down and received his ticket on the spot.

The jobless man, the first person in the audience, and Kubo, the second, were the only ones in the theater. Kubo was able to relieve himself and blow his nose during the trailers. It was not that he did not care about the person who sat behind him, but a sense of camaraderie of a certain kind was already growing between them. Kubo, after dropping a bundle of tissues on the floor and wiping around his nose and mouth, realized that he had not spoken a single word that day. He could have talked to the deaf woman ten minutes ago. Before that, if his neighbors were even slightly more ethical, Kubo would have engaged in a petty squabble with them. What if a magpie had really flown in from Yangch'on-ni[11] this morning? Kubo would have jerked

---

11. The setting of *Rural Diary*.

AZALEA

A Day in the
Life of Kubo the
Film Critic by
Josie Sohn

out a meaningless word of greeting. He felt sorry that he missed all those chances when he had so many occasions to talk this morning. He thought his sense of remorse would abate a little if Yujin and Yi Sugyŏng[12] could console the heart of that jobless man, the first person in the audience, as they strolled down the tropical beach in their bikinis.

As Kubo looked at the other member of the audience who would not leave his seat in the back row until the credits ended, he thought it would be nice to get a mobile phone from him if he was indeed a phone salesman on a business trip from the countryside.

Episode 2, "The Freudian Rings the Bell Twice"

The name "Friends" kept getting on Kubo's nerves. "Friends" sounded too close to the adnominal phrase (冠形語) "uri."[13] Kubo was on his way to Insa-dong to meet his high school pal whom he had not seen in a long time and arrived there an hour early, but he decided to make a short stop at Nagwŏn Arcade because he did not want to give the impression to his old friend (知友) that he was a loafer (閑良). The courtyard of Seoul Art Cinema—from where one could get a bird's-eye-view of the Chongno Tower that stands aloft, looking more like a phallus (p'allusŭ) than a pharos—was bustling as if every cinephile in the country had gathered there. Kubo was caught off guard by the unexpectedly large crowd, and only when he turned his head to look for the scientific forecast (豫報) of this unforeseen disaster was he able to discover a poster in which Marilyn Monroe in a red dress stood with her arms wide open. It was the poster of the "Friends Film Festival at the Cinematheque" that Seoul Art Cinema hosts early every year. Kubo, instead of feeling sentimental about how fast the year had gone by (隔世之感), grew anxious that he did not yet belong (束) to the "friends" of the cinematheque.

---

12. The names of the lead actresses in *Romantic Island* (dir. Kang Cheol-woo, 2008).
13. *Uri* can mean we, our, or us, depending on the usage.

January of last year (一年前一月), fresh back from studying abroad in France, Kubo was a young man flush with ambition (功名心) to make a name for himself as a film critic. He had vowed to be invited to the film festival a year later as one of the friends, but now he found his way into the Friends Festival as an outsider, already so aged. Kubo, remembering the prime of his youth when he still had dreams, asks himself what made him so old and worn. He wants to find an actual enemy (敵), but all he can do is resent the world, an abstraction (抽象). Kubo the film critic thus came to understand the meaning of years only after discovering the symptom (徵候) of old age (老年) called *tedium vitae* (厭世感).

He could not watch the opening film directed by Murnau since he had to leave soon, but he nonetheless entered the theater as he fumbled with his wallet that he had taken from his breast pocket for no reason. He knew only too well that he would run into acquaintances (因緣) who, unlike him, are actively working as critics (評論家), but his unconscious had already edged out the ego (*ego*) and was on its way to the darkroom (暗室) from where the motion picture was being projected. Did not a certain theorist (理論家) say that to watch a film is to regress (退行) into the subconscious? If that subconscious turns towards darkness, it would only be right for a film maniac (狂) to obey. Somehow, Kubo finds himself becoming gallant. The superego (超自我) that wanted to keep the appointment with his friend had long since submitted to the unconscious, and, like a neuropathy (神經症), a feeling of certainty budded inside that he would be able to watch the film as artlessly as he would with an old friend. Kubo the neo-Freudian (*neo-p'ŭroidiŏn*) decided to allow (許) more liberty to his unconscious.

Kubo stood in line.

Unwitting audiences led by the subconscious lined up at the box office. As if things that had been repressed for the past year returned (歸還) right at that moment and muddled the critic's consciousness, Kubo's ears were exposed to more ruckus than usual. He caught a throng (一軍) of cinephiles in the middle of a heated discussion about Murnau.

AZALEA

A Day in the
Life of Kubo the
Film Critic by
Josie Sohn

Murnau directed his first feature film *The Blue Boy* in 1919. From that year on until 1926 when the Fox called him to Hollywood. He made 21 features. Unfortunately the majority of the films he made in Germany did not survive except for some broken bits and pieces. A lot of people had a go at studying the Jekyll and Hyde personality and Murnau too made *Nosferatu* with a subtitle *A Symphony of Horror* in 1921. It was a more faithful version of Bram Stoker's *Dracula* than any other films that came after it The acting of Max Schreck who played the hairraising vampire is still believable. Then there is *The Last Laugh* (1924) starring Emil Jannings the acting alone tells the story so flawlessly that it's captionless. The real revolution of this film was the moving camera which Murnau used so deftly The dynamic camera goes anywhere. The audience was mesmerized by the camera that moved up and down the stairs and in and out the doors. It was a revolutionary artistry back then to make such an extravagant picture out of a simple story of a proud doorman demoted to a washroom attendant because of his age. He is also called an impressionist because he produced amazing spectacles and a sense of realism through his technique of the camera movements. et cetera et cetera et cetera[14]

Kubo feels small because of the surrealistic amount of film knowledge the general audience has and imagines, as he shifts (轉嫁) the locus of his self-deprecation (自激之心) to his business card (名銜) in his wallet that says he is a film critic, that the man who poured out this impassioned speech without even remembering to put spaces between words is in fact a debater (論客) out of office (在野), himself yet to be included among the friends. That, however, did not allow him to save face as an academic (學人). As he felt the need to find a way to save himself, he thought of his teacher, Dr. Sigmund Freud (P'ŭroit' ŭ). And he arrived at Jacques-Marie-Émile Lacan (Chak'ŭ Lak'ang), a fellow disciple and an elder brother (同門師兄) much older (年高) than himself. Kubo was thus giving

---

14. In the original, there is no space between the words.

birth to a new idea (思想) through the metonymy of consciousness. *Let the business card have the subjectivity of the film critic; it's only a construction of this abstract world. The subconscious of film critics is not facing the darkroom but only lined up to get connections to directors. My unconscious will be foregrounded (前景化) by getting rid of the business card. Cinema wants to befriend the subconscious, not a film critic.* In Kubo's mind, the three debaters (論者) he ran into were Cerberus guarding the entrance to the "Friends"; he imagined passing them by and arriving at the abyss of myth.

In no time, there was only one college girl waiting to purchase her ticket in front of Kubo. Kubo was a bit rundown as he suffered the last rite of passage (通過儀禮) to the "Friends" and stood even closer behind her as he held his wallet. The student turned around after receiving her precious ticket. Alas, Kubo collided with her as if with Persephone herself in the underworld. Kubo's wallet dropped to the ground and spat out a credit card, a transportation card, and a few beauty salon coupons. The student, all flustered, stooped down hurriedly to gather them and offered a word of apology as she handed him his wallet. Kubo caught a whiff of the sweet scent of shampoo. Right at that moment, Kubo realizes that he had been in the wrong about his unconscious all along. He was hoping secretly for his business card—which he paid fifteen thousand *wŏn* at Ulchi-*ro* 4-*ga* to be inscribed "Kim Kubo, Film Critic" (映畫評論家金仇甫)—to be stuck in there among the beauty salon coupons. His unconscious had not yet disposed of the film critic's business card. It was a moment in which he regained his lost ambition after a long year. He recalls how his unconscious led him to Nagwŏn Arcade an hour ago. The subconscious seemed to remember Kubo the young man who returned home with ambition a year ago. That is why it made him line up behind the girl's head instead of the darkroom. His subconscious had prepared a business card in his wallet and made him stand in line holding it, all to interpellate him as a film critic.

Kubo the film critic handed the student a business card with the warm smile of a middle-aged man and gained (得) a feeling of rejuvenation (回春) as he walked out of Nagwŏn Arcade. His friend of sixteen years was waiting for him in Insa-*dong*.

Azalea

A Day in the
Life of Kubo the
Film Critic by
Josie Sohn

⤸

Intertextuality: Between and Behind the Texts

To have it out or not? that is the question—
Whether 'tis better for the jaws to suffer
The pangs and torments of an aching tooth,
Or to take steel against a host of troubles

—The Dental Soliloquy

A Day in the Life of Kubo the Film Critic, introduced above, borrows its title from *A Day in the Life of Kubo the Novelist* (1934),[15] the colonial-period (1910-1945) novella written by Pak T'aewŏn (1909-1986). A close friend of the ultra-modernist poet Yi Sang (1910-1937) whose literary double also appears in one of Pak's works,[16] Pak himself was a modernist writer of "pure literature" (*sunsu munhak*), of which *Kubo the Novelist* is a good example, that separates literature from politics.[17] In the narrative, that Kubo is an intellectual living under Japanese colonial rule is likewise not the most salient point although it is significant as background that informs the narrative. Pure literature as a concept was opposed to the proletarian literature (*kyegŭp munhak*)[18] of the time, although Pak is equally famous for having turned Left after the liberation from Japan in 1945 and defecting to the North at the onset of

---

15. The serial was featured in *Chosŏn chungang ilbo* (Korean central daily) from August 1 to September 11 of 1934.

16. See Kim Tongsik, "Tosijŏk kamsusŏng kwa modŏnijŭm munhak" (Urban sensibilities and modernist literature), in *Sosŏlga Kubo-ssi ŭi iril: Pak T'aewŏn tanp'yŏnsŏn* (A day in the life of Kubo the novelist: short stories of Pak T'aewŏn), ed. Kim Tongsik (Seoul: Kŭllurim Ch'ulp'ansa, 2008), 486.

17. Pak T'aewŏn joined Kuinhoe ("the league of nine"), a literary society that supported pure literature, in 1933. See Kim Tongsik, "Tosijŏk kamsusŏng," 480.

18. Proletarian literature is also referred to as "tendency literature" (*kyŏnghyang munhak*).

the Korean War in 1950. While the most interesting tidbit from Pak's biography for today's cinephiles must be the fact that he is the maternal grandfather of the star filmmaker Bong Joon-ho, Pak's move to the North is not insignificant for the analysis of intertextuality between *Kubo the Novelist*, a modernist novella, and *Kubo the Film Critic*, a particular type of parody—I will return to this term—written about seventy five years later by a cinephile.

What I would like to suggest here is that An, the cinephile author, was able to adapt Pak's work partly because there were already a great number of precedents of parodies despite the fact that all of Pak's works, branded wholesale as "red," had been officially banned in South Korea until as late as 1988.[19] To put it differently, An did not merely imitate *Kubo the Novelist* but participated in a literary subculture that parodied Pak's beloved fictional persona. This point will be made clearer when I discuss how An borrows motifs and writing structure not only from the original but also from Ch'oe Inhun's *A Day in the Life of Kubo the Novelist* (1969-1972), perhaps the most well-known work among the many adaptations of Pak's work. In fact, Ch'oe Chaebong, a literary columnist, notes that no other modern Korean literary piece has been the object of as many parodies (*p'aerŏdi*) and homage (*omaju*) as *Kubo the Novelist*.[20] He writes,

> Pak T'aewŏn himself must have had no idea how this
> multifaceted and experimental novella would inspire the
> next generation of authors and continue to live as parodies.
> Between 1969 and 1972, a period when Pak's works were
> still banned [in South Korea] because of his repatriation
> to North Korea, Ch'oe Inhun (1936–) wrote as many as

19. Interview with Pak Hyŏnsuk, CEO of a publisher that introduced "defector literature" in the 1980s. See *Minjog21*, September 2003.

20. Ch'oe, Chaebong, "Kŏul nara chakka dŭl, 10: sosŏlga Kubo-ssi ŭi iril" (Authors in the world of mirrors, 10: a day in the life of Kubo the novelist) in *Culture webzine nabi* (Munhwa webjin nabi, October 12, 2009). http://nabeeya .yes24.com/Life/detail_view.aspx?CD_MENU=21&SUB_CD_MENU=21&ID_ CONTENT=1388&TYPE=&NAVIACHIVE=Y

AZALEA

A Day in the
Life of Kubo the
Film Critic by
Josie Sohn

fifteen episodes of *A Day in the Life of Kubo the Novelist* and published the series as a book. In the early 1990s, Chu Insŏk (1963–) produced five installments . . . and Yun Humyŏng (1946–) released two episodes [of the same title] in the 2000s. Although it is not a novel, O Kyuwŏn's (1941-2007) 1987 poetry collection . . . included fourteen pieces of "A Day in the Life of Kubo the Poet."

Kubo's popularity in literature is indeed incredible considering the fact that at least two writers did not fear crossing political boundaries in South Korea where every aspect of life was governed by strong anticommunist military regimes. The South Korean government exercised strict anticommunist censorship under the banner of national security well past the Seoul Olympics in 1988 when the discourse of reunification entered public education and replaced that of anticommunism under the newly elected president Roh Tae-woo (1987-1993). As late as the winter of 1989, the South Korean government continued its surveillance of literary activities and arrested, for example, the editor-in-chief of a prestigious literary magazine, *Ch'angjak kwa pip'yŏng* (Creation and criticism), when he received and published a travelogue to North Korea by Hwang Sŏgyŏng who was staying in West Germany at the time.[21] That the literary life of Kubo-*ssi* continued after the military regimes suggests, moreover, that the writers were not merely interested in making a political statement through their adaptation of a stigmatized novella. Today, references to Kubo proliferate even outside of literature, a few examples of which include an archaeological travelogue that recreates Kubo's day in Kyŏngsŏng;[22] a history of modern photography told from the perspective of the author as Kubo;[23] an English book on eco-

21. *Tong'a ilbo*, November 24, 1989.
22. Cho Idam, *Kubo-ssi wa tŏburŏ Kyŏngsŏng ŭl kada* (Going to Kyŏngsŏng with Kubo) (Seoul: Param Kudu, 2009).
23. Yi Kyŏngmin, *Kubo-ssi, sajin kugyŏng kada*, 1883-1945 (Kubo, gone out to a photo excursion, 1883-1945) (Seoul: Archive Books, 2007).

conscious consumption, which in translation adds the story of a day in the life of Kubo the contemporary consumer in Seoul;[24] and a collection of writings on movies and other episodes such as the Pusan International Film Festival written from the perspective of Kubo the contemporary novelist.[25]

I imagine that the central motivation for parodying Kubo has not been necessarily or exclusively political (either anticolonial or leftist) for many writers even as Pak's move to North Korea has rendered his novel political ironically beyond the text itself. I argue instead that what is useful is the structure of Pak's novella that describes a day in the life of an individual as well as the idiosyncratic character of a *flâneur*[26] who observes the world around him as he loiters in deep self-reflection, making his interiority intimate to readers. Kubo, although an intellectual qua novelist, is in fact not very different from the Parisian *flâneur*[27] whose habitat was the boulevards outside the arcades and who, given a precarious economic situation, excelled in his "trade of not trading."[28] The *flâneur*, in other words, could do nothing but to observe, making social space personal.[29] Kubo the novelist, likewise, dwells in the margins of his own habitat, educated but

24. John C. Ryan and Alan T. Durning, *Noksaek simin Kubo-ssi ŭi haru* (A day in the life of Kubo the green citizen; original title, *Stuff: the Secret Lives of Everyday Things*, trans. Ko Munyŏng (Seoul: Kŭmulk'o, 2002).

25. Chu Insŏk, *Sosŏlga Kubo-ssi ŭi yŏnghwa kugyŏng* (Kubo the novelist's movie excursion) (Seoul: Review and Review, 1997). The PIFF episode in Chu's book is the most analogous to An's work; however, there is no particular evidence that An borrows from Chu.

26. For further discussions on the theme of Kubo as a *flâneur* (*sanch'aekja*) in relation to the modern city, see Kim Tongsik, "Tosijŏk kamsusŏng," 487; and Ch'ŏn Chŏnghwan, "Singminji modŏnijŭm ŭi sŏngch'wi wa unmyŏng" (Fulfillment and fate of colonial modernism), in *Sosŏlga Kubo-ssi ŭi iril: Pak T'aewŏn tanp'yŏnsŏn* (A day in the life of Kubo the novelist: short stories of Pak T'aewŏn), ed. Ch'ŏn Chŏnghwan (Seoul: Munhak kwa Chisŏngsa, 2005), 451.

27. See Walter Benjamin, *The Arcades Project* (Boston: Harvard University Press, 1999 [1982]).

28. Susan Buck-Morss, "The Flâneur, the Sandwichman and the Whore: The Politics of Loitering," in *Walter Benjamin and the Arcades Project*, ed. Beatrice Hanssen (London and New York: Continuum International Publishing Group, 2006), 35.

29. Buck-Morss argues that "flânerie was an ideological attempt to reprivatize social space, and to give assurance that the individual's passive observation was adequate for knowledge of social reality" (36).

AZALEA

A Day in the
Life of Kubo the
Film Critic by
Josie Sohn

disempowered and constantly in search of happiness.[30] That the act of beholding—he observes Kyŏngsŏng in order to take on modernology (modŏnolloji) in the novella—characterizes Kubo is, then, not a haphazard motif but arguably a defining characteristic of the weak who are unable to do nothing but. What I would like to stress here is that the motif of the looking and loitering of Kubo the colonized intellectual, in addition to the plot structure, is what makes the Kubo the Novelist so adaptable. Parody of this kind has been popular in the history of literature. This point will be easier to grasp if I compare Kubo to The Tragedy of Hamlet, Prince of Denmark. Not surprisingly, Hamlet was decidedly the most favored character impersonated by writers in the Victorian era when parody was nearly a "spectator sport" as shown in the epigraph of "Hamlet at the Dentist's."[31] What makes Hamlet such a good character to imitate is, of course, his spirit in agony and indecisiveness embodied in his famous monologue, "To be, or not to be," apart from the particularities of his dire circumstance. It is the signature, so to speak, of this easily adaptable phrase that makes Hamlet the object of so many parodies. It is the same with Kubo. His walks and thoughts are a signature that can be copied.[32]

Kubo the Novelist, however, is not quite the same as the forged signature in "The Purloined Letter" whose form matters more than its content.[33] The way in which I use the term "intertextuality," in fact, looks beyond "the banal sense of 'study of sources.'"[34] It is true that the particular ways in which the original(s) is written provide a ready-made plot structure and character for An, the

---

30. Kubo's search for happiness is a recurring motif in Pak's Kubo.

31. Beate Müller, Parody: Dimensions and Perspectives (Amsterdam; Atlanta, GA: Rodopi, 1997), 131, 141.

32. Cf. Ch'ŏn Chŏnghwan, "Singminji modŏnijŭm," 447-475. Ch'ŏn offers a slightly different but valid argument that the next generation writers wrote the novels with the same title because "Kubo" became a byword for the Korean "novelist" as Kubo the Novelist was considered the modernist novel par excellence (471-2).

33. See Barbara Johnson, "The Frame of Reference: Poe, Lacan, Derrida," Yale French Studies 55/56 (1977): 457-505.

34. Julia Kristeva, Revolution in Poetic Language (New York: Columbia University Press, 1984 [1974]), 60.

cinephile writer. I maintain, however, that the genealogy of *Kubo* demonstrates intertextuality in a narrower sense, which points to the "*transposition . . . of enunciative and denotative positionality.*"[35] In other words, Kubo's socio-discursive position as a speaking subject changes every time he is transposed to a different historical period. On the one hand, he is characterized by his walking and thinking on the margins of society, but because of this "empty" form, on the other hand, each parody can enable Kubo to observe and critique the contemporary era. Pak's *Kubo* (1934), for instance, lampoons the portrait of a passive intellectual of the colonial period; Ch'oe's *Kubo* (1969-1972), on the other hand, is concerned with the division of the Korean peninsula; Chu's *Kubo* (1991-1995), last but not least, grapples with the irreconcilable difference between the memories of the 1980s and the realities of the 1990s.[36]

Kubo the Film Critic similarly offers a portrait of young elites in contemporary South Korea, although, like the originals, An's short stories are not preoccupied exclusively with the politics of the times. I have introduced Kubo the film critic above as the literary or imaginary double of young cinephiles of today for whom, as for the critic, it is not easy to land a stable job even upon graduating from a top-tier university. Their cosmopolitan taste in foreign movies and knowledge of foreign theories neither necessarily become the fruits of nor guarantee economic security. I suggest that Kubo the film critic is arguably a fictional embodiment of the "88-*manwŏn* generation," a now-popular term coined by U Sŏkhun and Pak Kwŏnil, an economist-journalist team, that describes South Korean youth in their twenties. U and Pak came up with 88-*manwŏn*, roughly equivalent to 880 US dollars, to suggest the average monthly wage of youths in their twenties as short-term

35. Ibid., original italics.
36. Ch'oe, Chaebong, "Kŏul nara chakka dŭl, 10: sosŏlga Kubo-ssi ŭi iril" (Authors in the world of mirrors, 10: a day in the life of Kubo the novelist) in *Culture webzine nabi* (Munhwa webjin nabi, October 12, 2009). http://nabeeya .yes24.com/Life/detail_view.aspx?CD_MENU=21&SUB_CD_MENU=21&ID_ CONTENT=1388&TYPE=&NAVIACHIVE=Y

AZALEA

A Day in the
Life of Kubo the
Film Critic by
Josie Sohn

employees.[37] Many youths are highly—perhaps excessively—educated, speak at least one foreign language (English), and accrue certificates of various trades. They are, however, not likely to be able to use their educational assets to the fullest because of the unequal structure of the South Korean economy. At the heart of U and Pak's argument is that these 88-*manwŏn* generation youths not only compete against each other, which is a given in a neoliberal society, but, more significantly, against the "military rule" generation and the "386" generation who are already established in society and are not likely to make way for the next generation.[38] U likens this to a "Battle Royale," a sadistic game of survival.[39] Kubo's predicament speaks to this brutality. Kubo, like today's university graduates in South Korea, is over-educated—in the sense that his degree in cinema studies from France did ensure him sufficient peace of mind to buy a hottŏk for a snack—and under-employed for his very capabilities; yet he nonetheless had to risk becoming over-educated in order to do what he wants to do in life.

Kubo the Film Critic, in this sense, is a "parody" in a couple of ways. The fan adaptation, on the one hand, reproduces the style and form of *Kubo the Novelist* for its own use; but, on the other hand, it transcends the context of the original to critique the present. In both ways, the short stories do not fit the category of a "parody" in the colloquial sense of the term since the stories do not seem to make fun of either the originals or society with witticism and ridicule. *Kubo the Film Critic*, to borrow the words of Linda Hutcheon, "is repetition, but repetition that includes difference

---

37. U and Pak coined this term after the "*mileuristas*" (the thousand euro generation) of Spain.

38. U and Pak, 88-*manwŏn sedae*, 17-19. The military rule or the yushin generation refers to those who came of age during Park Chung Hee's regime (1961-1979). The 386 generation refers to those who were born in the 1960s and attended college in the 1980s; and they were in their thirties, when the term was coined in the 1990s.

39. U and Pak, 88-*manwŏn sedae*, 18. This is a reference to *Battle Royale* (dir. Kinji Fukasaku, 2000). For further discussion on this film, see Frédéric Neyrat, "A Sovereign Game: On Kinji Fukasaku's *Battle Royale* (2001)," in *Translation, Biopolitics, Colonial Difference*, ed. Naoki Sakai and Jon Solomon (Hong Kong: Hong Kong University Press, 2006), 97-108.

(Deleuze 1968)."[40] *Kubo the Film Critic*, a product of intertextual parody, is not solely an outcome of pure textual and formal relations; neither is it a straightforward hermeneutic exercise that depends entirely on the imagination of the reader-writer.[41] Ch'oe Chaebong, the literary columnist, was quite right in saying that the subsequent adaptations of *Kubo the Novelist* have been both parodies (*p'aerŏdi*) and homage (*omaju*).

Parody of Pedantic Cinephiles

It is from this perspective—that youths are fragile neoliberal subjects burdened with self-management under intense economic competition—that we should look at the parody in *Kubo the Film Critic* as a critique of the pedantic culture of cinephiles.[42] That is to say, as will be made clearer in my analysis below, *Kubo the Film Critic* illustrates how the worth of young people can be reduced to nothing without knowledge. This attitude towards knowledge and intellectual life is, in fact, what differentiates *Kubo the Film Critic* from *Kubo the Novelist*. In this section, I will limit my comparative analysis to Pak's *Kubo* (1934) and Ch'oe's *Kubo* (1969-1972) because An's adaptation is largely based on these two.

In both cases of Kubo the novelist, knowledge and intellectual life contribute directly to the realistic depiction of the character, an intellectual. By realism, apart from its historical and theoretical development, I do not mean the representation of truth but only a believable representation.[43] It is beside the point that these works are considered modernist paragons, something conventionally seen as antithetical to realism. As the literary critic Kim Kiu argues,

---

40. Linda Hutcheon, *A Theory of Parody: The Teachings of Twentieth-Century Art Forms* (Urbana: University of Illinois Press, 2000 [1985]), 37.

41. Hutcheon further defines parody as "imitation with critical ironic distance, whose irony can cut both ways. Ironic versions of 'trans-contextualization' and inversion are its major formal operatives, and the range of pragmatic ethos is from scornful ridicule to reverential homage" (37).

42. Chapter 3 of my dissertation investigates the use of Western film theory among young cinephiles.

43. See Pam Morris, *Realism (The New Critical Idiom)* (London; New York: Routledge, 2003) for a more comprehensive overview of this very "slippery" (2) term.

AZALEA

A Day in the
Life of Kubo the
Film Critic by
Josie Sohn

moreover, the discourses based on philosophy and social sciences in *Kubo the Novelist* should not be considered philosophy and social sciences proper; once summoned in a literary work, they become literary discourses.[44] Kubo the novelist, to wit, becomes a realistic character, a believable case, especially because of his intellectual life. Kubo the colonized intellectual, for instance, has literally encyclopedic knowledge of pathologies, philosophizes about modern capitalism, observes the modern city, and discusses Joyce. Kubo the postwar novelist likewise gives a lecture, interacts with other intellectuals, and discusses Beckett, Chekhov, and a host of other writers. *In Kubo the Film Critic*, on the other hand, the man's poor observations of the metropolitan—clearly a parody of modernology—render him a questionable intellectual. The second episode, "The Freudian Rings the Bell Twice," in particular is conspicuously and purposely pseudo-academic with its misuse of psychoanalytic jargon. What I would like to draw attention to here, however, is not the almost comical appropriation and conflation of (some defunct) Freudian terms used by Kubo the *ersatz* neo-Freudian. An interesting and astute psychoanalytic drama instead unfolds at the level of the plot structure as "the bell rings twice."

In order to look at the narrative more meaningfully, we first need to consider yet another thread of intertextuality. The title of the second episode is clearly a twist on *The Postman Always Rings Twice* (dir. Tay Garnett, 1946), based on a 1934 crime novel by James M. Cain. There is, however, "no postman in the book, no doorbell, and no single, dual, or any ring"[45] in either Cain's novel or An's short story. How exactly does the bell ring then? We can start with an account of how Cain came across the title in a conversation. The screenwriter Vincent Lawrence was telling Cain about how anxious he becomes whenever he waits to hear from his producer:

---

44. Kim Kiu, *I[i-i] iron ŭi kujo: Ch'oe Inhun yesullon yŏn'gu* (The structure of I(-i-i) theory: a theoretical study of Ch'oe Inhun's art) (Seoul: JNC, 2009), 127.

45. Gary Dexter, *Why Not Catch-21?: The Stories behind the Titles* (London: Frances Lincoln Ltd., 2008), 168.

Then, he [Lawrence] said, 'I almost went nuts. I'd sit and watch for the postman, and then I'd think, "You got to cut this out," and then when I left the window I'd be listening for his ring. How I'd know it was the postman was that he'd always ring twice."

He went on with more of the harrowing tale, but I [Cain] cut in on him suddenly. I said: 'Vincent, I think you've given me a title for that book.'

"What's that?"

"The Postman Always Rings Twice."

"Say, he rang twice for Chambers, didn't he?"

"That's the idea."

"And on that second ring, Chambers had to answer, didn't he? Couldn't hide out in the backyard any more."

"His number was up, I'd say."

"I like it."

"Then that's it."[46]

The postman is thus a metaphor for the "fate, nemesis, retribution, [and] divine justice"[47] that visits Frank Chambers for the second and last time to announce that his days are finally numbered for murdering the husband of Cora Papadakis, a woman with whom he has an affair.

That the title of An's second episode cites this film while the story does not have any direct references to bells or the film itself is significant because we are left with only one possible answer as to why An used the title. In this episode replete with psychoanalytic discourse, the bell that rings twice undoubtedly points to—not a Freudian but—the Lacanian "letter," which is tantamount to the signifier.[48] What is of particular importance is that the letter/signifier is in itself meaningless and therefore "constantly insists in

46. Ibid.
47. Ibid.
48. Bruce Fink, *Lacan to the Letter: Reading Écrits Closely* (Minneapolis: University of Minnesota Press, 2004), 79.

AZALEA

A Day in the
Life of Kubo the
Film Critic by
Josie Sohn

inscribing itself in the subject's life."[49] It, in other words, delivers fate—this should not be confused with "death" as in the case of Frank Chambers in the film—just as the bell delivers the fate of the listener in the film. The letter returns again and again, to put it in simpler words, because the subject's significance (existence) ceases to be without the signifier that gives meaning.[50] The postman's bell, to put it differently, is the very explicit sign of how a "letter always arrives at its destination."[51] Slavoj Žižek, commenting on *The Postman Always Rings Twice*, notes that the murderer's "fate is sealed" and "events take their inexorable course"[52] because the letter cannot not arrive at its destination. The murderer can no longer fake his identity or believe in his own fabrication.

In "The Freudian Rings the Bell Twice," too, we see a letter finally arriving at its destination and announcing the fate of Kubo the film critic. It is none other than his business card. The first instance in which Kubo remembers his business card is when he encounters a film buff at the Friends Festival (which is, in real life, annually held at the Seoul Art Cinema). Kubo feels small compared to the man whose knowledge about film is surrealistic. Refusing even to save face, however, Kubo rejects his business card as a metonym for a film critic, which he denounces as a mere jobber lined up to get to know directors. Instead, he chooses defiantly to be a true friend of cinema and gets in another line to purchase a ticket to the first screening of the festival. In this psychoanalytical drama, however, Kubo cannot not receive the letter delivering his fate. Kubo, probably sexually deprived as well,[53] stands right behind the girl who is getting her ticket and, alas, collides with her.

---

49. Dylan Evans, *An Introductory Dictionary of Lacanian Psychoanalysis* (London; New York: Routledge, 2001 [1997]), 100.

50. This is my understanding of Lacan.

51. Slavoj Žižek, *Enjoy Your Symptom!: Jacques Lacan in Hollywood and Out* (revised edition) (London and New York: Routledge, 2001), 10. This phrase is originally Lacan's. Whether or not Žižek is right about his critique of Derrida's reading of Lacan—namely, if it is possible for the letter to not arrive at its destination—is beyond the scope of this paper.

52. Slavoj Žižek, *Enjoy Your Symptom!*, 169.

53. Sexual privation is another characteristic of Kubo the novelist in Pak's work.

Because of this accident, Kubo's wallet drops to the ground, spilling out a credit card, a transportation card, and a few beauty salon coupons. Before he is able to think, he wishes for his business card to be stuck among the coupons for the girl to see. Kubo has no way to avoid admitting that he was in the wrong about his identity. He is, and loves being, a film critic. It is no coincidence that the girl is given a grand entrance as Persephone—goddess of underworld. It is as if the girl announces the "death"[54] of Kubo without his identity as a film critic. Kubo must receive the letter since he is worthless without his fate, without the signifier that tells him that he is a film critic. With the letter at its destination, Kubo now walks out of the theater feeling young once again.

This episode, on the one hand, mocks the pedantic culture of cinephiles by showing *in the narrative content* that his education is of no great value; it hardly puts food on the table. Education is certainly one type of capital, but film theory in no way approaches the education capital considered proper for South Koreans who seek stable and well-paying occupations such as medical doctor or civil servant. In this sense, the story is comparable to Pak's *Kubo* in which Kubo is unable to (or refuses to) find a job that pays him a monthly salary even with a university degree from Tokyo. This episode also offers a funny and pitiable spectacle of a typical social "loser" (*lujŏ*), a film snob who has nothing to speak of except the little knowledge that he possesses. What is fundamentally different from the originals, however, is that in *Kubo the Film Critic*, it is a person's worth—apart from his economic capability (remember that a subject is nothing without the signifier)—that is at stake. By embedding a critical theory not only in the narrative content but also *in the plot structure*, the story seems to offer a meta-theoretical or intellectual commentary. Will the 88-*manwŏn* generation be anything without education? Even a film critic whose education does not add up to much has to hold on to this, the sole guarantor of his worth, the

---

54. Again, death is not to be confused with fate; the girl is not the letter but the business card is.

letter that must arrive. To put this in a more mundane light, this episode seems to acknowledge the sad reality that knowledge has become nothing, unless accompanied by a price tag.

A Day in the
Life of Kubo the
Film Critic by
Josie Sohn

Visual Literacy: Turning a Writerly Text into a Cinematic One

In this way, the character of Kubo the film critic resembles the colonized intellectual more than the postwar novelist in that he is a dreamer, spending more time observing than doing anything. The writer of *Pilsa*, however, borrows his formal structure and motifs significantly more from Ch'oe's version of *Kubo the Novelist* written in 1969-1972. Whereas Pak's *Kubo* tells the story of a single day in the life of the novelist (in addition to a brief account of his mother's), like An's, each short episode in Ch'oe's *Kubo* narrates the day of the novelist, with the entire collection of stories taking place over about three years. In addition, motifs such as savoring one fifteenth of a *hottŏk* at a time (a twist on the tobacco in Ch'oe's tale), having a "magnanimous" heart, listening to magpies in the morning, and imagining the countryside are all conspicuous signs of parody in An's fan adaptation. There is, however, one thing that fundamentally differs between the two works. That is to say, An transforms the writerly text of Ch'oe's *Kubo* into a very cinematic one. The first paragraphs of each *Kubo*, in particular, are analogous except that *Kubo the Film Critic* incorporates filmic elements largely absent in *Kubo the Novelist*, as I illustrate below. For the sake of comparison, here is the first paragraph of the first episode in Ch'oe's *Kubo the Novelist*:

> As the year 1969 drew to a close, on a morning a few days before the end of the winter solstice, Kubo, a novelist, woke up from his sleep. As he woke up, something that looked like a scroll unfurled in his head and soon disappeared. Kubo recognized it right away; it was a to-do list for the day. That scroll vanished in a wink of an eye as it was meant for Kubo and him only. Kubo stayed in bed even after waking from

his slumber. A magpie is crying; Kubo pictured the bird that must be bobbing its head every time its vocal chords vibrate as it sits on the end of a leafless branch on one of the few paulownia trees planted in the apartment's lawn outside his window that was only about three or four steps away from his bed. Then, as always, Kubo became melancholy. Although Kubo was an exceptionally scientific novelist, he was very superstitious when it came to the cry of magpies in the morning. Kubo questioned why he had such a folkloric[55] heart when he did not even grow up in the countryside. Then, the sad feelings disappeared. It's always like this, Kubo thought; he felt yet another sort of sadness. That the cry of magpie is sorrowful means this. They say a good thing will happen when a magpie cries.[56]

We encounter many things here but only as a series of mental images that Kubo the novelist pictures in his mind. We see the scroll that delivers a to-do list; we then move on to a magpie that Kubo does not see but nonetheless describes in detail; and we learn even the setting only as he remembers it. In other words, we see everything through his interiority, a distinctive trait of a modernist literary work.[57] The readers of *Kubo the Novelist* experience an *ersatz* first person point of view of Kubo (as if he is the narrator) although he is a third person character because the narrator allows the reader to see exactly what Kubo himself sees without necessarily showing him from the moment he opens his eyes. To rephrase in filmic terms, we do not see Kubo much from the camera's point of view.

This is exactly the difference we experience from our encounter

---

55. *t'osok ŭi*.

56. As of the fall of 2010, there was no English translation available for this novel.

57. See Kōjin Karatani, *Origins of Modern Japanese Literature* (Durham: Duke University Press, 1993); Seiji M. Lippit, *Topographies of Japanese Modernism* (New York: Columbia University Press, 2002); Michael D. Shin, "Interior Landscapes: Yi Kwangsu's The Heartless and the Origins of Modern Literature," in *Colonial Modernity in Korea*, eds. Gi-Wook Shin and Michael Robinson (Cambridge: Harvard University Press, 2004 [1999]), 248-287.

Azalea

A Day in the
Life of Kubo the
Film Critic by
Josie Sohn

with Kubo the film critic. Instead of seeing what the film critic sees, we see him as we listen to his thoughts on alarm clocks, temple bells, and rural life. In other words, *Kubo the Film Critic* produces an effect of seeing from the camera's point of view. Although the camera's point of view is certainly not the only way of experiencing vision in cinema (cf. shot-reverse-shot),[58] a film, generally speaking, cannot exist without the apparatus. *Kubo the Film Critic*, moreover, adds a series of actions missing in the original. Making these actions cinematic is how the narrator uses "elliptical editing," to use another film terminology. An ellipsis, in brief, signifies a temporal transition from a shot (one continuous take) to the next shot, thus presenting the story faster than in the narrative time. This is a temporal jump cut, so to speak. Kubo the film critic, for instance, wakes up and thinks about magpies and temple bells in his bed quite like the novelist. In the next sentence (read "shot"), however, we see him brushing his teeth as he muses about urban and rural lives. In the following shots, we see him moving from place to place: leaving home, lighting a cigarette in the elevator, and in no time out walking in the streets. If we consider this a writerly text, it is perhaps delivered too hurriedly, lacking in intimate descriptions of the protagonist. However, if we consider this a cinematic text, we can appreciate the economical execution of the narrative as we listen to the narrator (An's short stories are also much shorter than Ch'oe's). Thanks to the narrator who functions as voiceover narration, we not only learn that Kubo has not had his breakfast and that a few people spotted him smoking in the building but also experience more dynamic visual movements than in the original. Indeed, the "'vital principle' of the cinema" lies beyond performance or even beauty; it is "the sheer pleasure of watching someone—a specific body—moving on screen."[59]

I imagine that such cinematic qualities beyond the (mere) references to movies in *Kubo the Film Critic* would be what excites

58. A shot-reverse-shot in the simplest form is a construction of three shots that establishes a subject's point of view by showing the subject, the object being looked at, and then the subject. In other words, we know who is looking and at what.

59. Christian Keathley, *Cinephilia and History, or The Wind in the Trees* (Bloomington; Indianapolis: Indiana University Press, 2006), 49.

the cinephile who reads An's adaptation. Moreover, this turning of a writerly text into a cinematic one suggests the (already present) emergence of a generation fluent in visual language. Perhaps this is why An borrowed more from the postwar novelist rather than the colonial intellectual since Pak T'aewŏn is known for a writing style inspired by a cinematic technique of storytelling.[60] Had An used only Pak's work, he would not have been able to write an effective parody, one that repeats but with difference. The ways in which Kubo the Film Critic is narrated imply that visuality is part and parcel of the language of the generation who grew up with visual media. Indeed, in both episodes introduced in this essay, the "last promenade" of Kubo is the theater, the place where the fantasies of the flâneur materialize.[61] This is also probably why the Kubo series ended prematurely after just three episodes although An resigned from the magazine for personal reasons. Solely from the perspective of the narrative, I suggest that the narrator of *Kubo the Film Critic* could no longer recount Kubo's daily life because, in the third episode, the poor critic ends up at a "B" film festival (not of B-movies). Hosted by a Pak Ch'an'guk,[62] the festival happens a few subway stations away from the Pusan International Film Festival. Once the cinephile leaves his "last promenade," to which film festivals certainly belong, there are no more stories left to tell.

---

60. See Kim Yangsŏn, 1930-nyŏndae modŏnijŭm sosŏl ŭi yŏnghwa kippŏp: kŭndaesŏng ŭi ch'ehŏm mit panŭng ŭl chungsimŭro (The cinematic technique of storytelling in the 1930s modernist novels: focusing on the experience of and response to modernity), *Han'guk munhak iron kwa pip'yŏng* 9 (2000): 52-74; and Park Bae-sik, 1930-nyŏndae Pak T'aewŏn sosŏl ŭi yŏnghwa kippŏp (The cinematic technique of storytelling in Pak T'aewŏn's 1930s novels), *Munhak kwa yŏngsang* 9/1 (2008): 83-109.

61. See Walter Benjamin, *The Arcades Project*, 895. The last promenade for the flâneur is the department store, "which makes use of flânerie itself to sell goods" (10); "There his fantasies were materialized" (895).

62. The irony, of course, is that director Park Chan-wook is an avid fan of B-movies.

Five Poems by
Kim Min-Jeong

Translated by Jeon Seung-hee

UNEXPECTED EFFECT

In the dead of winter, children in Kangwŏn Province
Brandish dried pollacks,
Which indeed make a swishing sound quite like swords.
Excited, children brandish them even more.
As the edge is everything to a sword,
The best part of a dried pollack is its body.
Dried pollacks, served in a soup for breakfast —
My younger sister spoons it first,
As if she were the head of our family,
Because she is lactating.

Two women in the warmer part of the *ondol* room

Laugh, slapping each other's back.

Returning from a supermarket thirty minutes away

With a tub of Together,[1] with three spoons stuck in it, they

Laugh, pinching each other's thigh.

One of them abruptly stands up, saying, "It started." On the floor, there's

Blood as if from a nosebleed, what you find after rubbing what felt like a snivel.

"You still do it? You must be fed up, huh!"

One of them, taking off her white socks and wiping the floor with them,

Laughs, rolling her two blood-smeared socks.

Friends.

---

1. "Together" is a name of a brand of ice-cream.

Mom filleted her own hands while filleting halibut.

I took her to the emergency room and laid her on the bed.

Her doctor's name was Kim Kŭn of all names.[2]

Oh, does Kŭn mean 'root'?

Your name is the same as the name of someone I know.

He was busy stitching.

There's a poet named Kim Kŭn . . .

Busy stitching, he didn't say a word.

There is such a word as

No-good-feeling.

---

2. There is a contemporary Korean poet named Kim Kŭn.

Past midnight, in front of a toy stall across the street from the
   Kumkang Shoe Store, a man is picking a stuffed animal for a
   woman. The woman points to an extra-large white bear, almost
   as tall as herself. Since I cannot sleep without you, I'll sleep
   with him in my arms whenever you're away. The vendor briskly
   cleans the white bear wrapped in clear plastic with a duster.
   Knitting her brows, the woman folds her arms. The vendor
   vigorously cleans the white bear wrapped in clear plastic with
   a dry cloth. Don't you have a new one? The white bear became
   a silver bear because of all the dust. The vendor goes to the
   next stall, borrows an extra-large white bear, and comes back,
   carrying it on her back like a grown child. Meanwhile, the man
   and woman go across the street. They are already on the other
   side, as the green light was blinking, as it in fact suited them
   to run away with lightning speed. Damn you, sons of bitches,
   you, fuckers! Once, we asked a vendor who was selling the
   national flags to take them out so we could take a good look.
   We negotiated the price with her as if we were going to buy one,
   but then ran away with lightning speed, after saying it's too
   expensive. Like the man and woman, we probably deserved the
   curse she threw at us with her fist raised, Damn you!
Because we were in love.

A HAPPINESS CALLED HARM

The man who proposed to me on the day we first met
Dumped me exactly a month later.
Announcing the break-up, he said:

What did you say when we were passing by the bus terminal
    one night?
All the buses come back to sleep, as it's getting late.
You pretended to be innocent, didn't you? Because you're a poet?
Is that poetry? I didn't realize.

You didn't laugh at all while we were watching *My Boss, My
    Teacher*, did you?
It's because it wasn't funny at all. I would have laughed if it were.
You put on airs, didn't you? Because you're a poet?
Is that poetry? I didn't realize.

You ate the rose petal decorations on the plate of snapper sashimi,
    didn't you?
It's because I didn't want to waste those fresh petals.
You pretended to be weird, didn't you? Because you're a poet?
Is that poetry? I didn't realize.

You were the true master of poetry.
I didn't realize it then.
I'm sorry. I respectfully offer you
A nom de plume, '개새끼.'[3]

---

3. 개새끼 means "son of a bitch." In the original Korean poem, this word was
written in English.

311

Did you look it up in the dictionary? So that nobody could see it,

The letter was sealed tight with spit.

The man opens it and the son of a bitch rinses it with water.

Only then do I play angel with the devil,

Writing a poem about a moment in this landscape, because I
   am a poet.

ANOTHER PERSPECTIVE ON
YI SANG

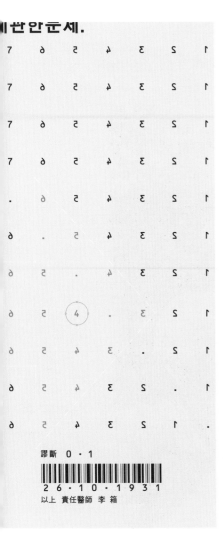

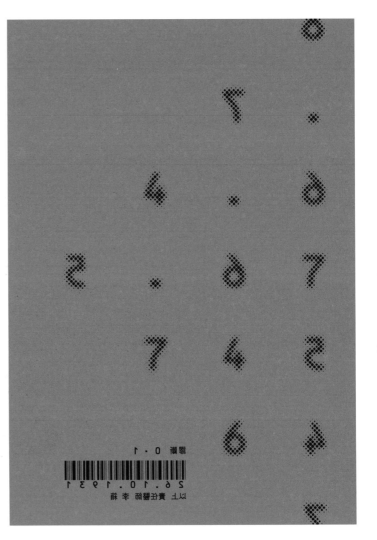

Leveling the Metropole: Awakening and Disillusionment in Yi Sang's "Tokyo"

by John M. Frankl

Introduction

The life and works of the enigmatic artist now best known as Yi Sang are inextricably imbricated with the modern histories of Korea and Japan. Yi came into the world Kim Haegyŏng on September 23, 1910, less than one month after Japan formally annexed Korea. He was born in the capital city of Seoul, then Keijō, where he spent a full twenty-six years of his life. He lived only twenty-six years and seven months, passing away on April 17, 1937 during his first and only stay in Tokyo. Prior to his roughly six months in the empire's capital, his entire experience outside Keijō had consisted of two brief trips to convalesce at local hot springs resorts—one in Inch'ŏn, only a short distance from his home and only for one week, and the other in Sŏngch'ŏn, which was more remote and where he managed to endure three weeks.[1] Thus, prior to his final half year in Tokyo, Yi essentially knew only Keijō, the capital city of Chosen, and an integral part of the growing Japanese empire. He was born into a situation where there was no Korean nation state, came of age in a Keijō that often aspired to mimic Tokyo, and died in a Tokyo that was the undisputed metropole of a

---

1. Actually, he again spent only one week at the actual hot springs—the following two weeks were spent in the nearby town of Sŏngch'ŏn where his friend Wŏn Yongsŏk was working for the colonial government.

burgeoning imperium. Despite the undeniable traction that these ponderous biographical and historical forces exerted upon Yi's life, however, he was never subsumed by either Japan or Korea, Tokyo or Keijō. He finally lived as an idiosyncratic individual, an expert architect, and an acclaimed artist who neither desired nor suffered any national subjecthood.

His striking confidence notwithstanding, Yi was also very much affected by and integrated with his milieu. He lived as an outlier, but not a hermit. He produced unique works, but he also worked well with others. From school literary magazines during his formative years to adult coteries such as the *Kuinhoe*, Yi believed in participation. Due to this, he necessarily underwent comparisons—both external and self-inflicted—to those around him. And while he nearly always triumphed in terms of both raw ability and actual production—both academic and artistic—his record did suffer from one crucial flaw or absence. Unlike so many of his mentors and contemporaries, Yi had never been to Tokyo. His prodigious talents notwithstanding, the halo effect conferred by time in Tokyo cannot be underestimated for a colonial intellectual and artist active in the mid-1930s. Whether this lacuna in his curriculum vitae was held over Yi by others as the one and only criterion by which they could outstrip him, or self-inflicted as a sort of colonial inferiority complex, Yi was keenly aware of it. His first published essay, "Hyŏlsŏ samt'ae (Three forms of writing in blood)," begins with a section subtitled 'Oscar Wilde' in which Yi recounts his passively and poignantly waiting—in a strikingly homoerotic voice—for a dear friend to return from Tokyo.[2]

---

2. I write "strikingly" only because so much attention has been lavished upon Yi's creative genius, his tumultuous relationships with women, and the relationships between the two. Due to the opacity of the literary works themselves, scholars invariably fall back upon biographical criticism to explicate Yi's poetry and fiction. Although beyond the scope of the current study, the overt nod to Wilde opens up many new productive avenues of inquiry into Yi Sang's life and art, particularly the potential role of repressed homosexuality as an engine for creativity and production. On a more general note regarding the connection between these two flamboyant artists, the deeper one delves into Yi's various works, the more prescient appear Wilde's remarks regarding conformity

Uk[3] is not the name I wish to call him. But let us call him Uk for now. As recently as 1930, Uk was as infinitely sincere as his girlish bob, and his attitude and passion in devoting himself to the path of art were sincere as well.

That year, when I was bedridden, nearly taken by severe illness, Uk, having endured no more than a few months of desolate life in Tokyo, with an ineffable love/affection (愛情), sent me postcards, two or three each day, with the pathos of a flower girl scattering petals upon the wedding aisle, how excited he must have been upon the ferry's deck.[4]

Uk does return to Keijō and to Yi Sang, but Tokyo has changed him. This opening subsection of the essay concludes with the following lines, bemoaning this change: "But, Uk, you were also a clever young student who came to possess a calculating side that allowed you deftly to dissect and organize into separate vignettes the flamelike passion arising from *this*." The antecedent for *this* is the description above this final sentence of their lives together, lives in which they shared a single room, "lived a life of free and unfettered creation," and their souls were able to cavort in perfect, undifferentiated harmony.

Yi was a mere twenty years old in 1930, yet as an artist he was already greatly affected by the departures for and the returns from Tokyo of his contemporaries. In addition, long prior to his foray into essay writing, Tokyo loomed large in Yi's world. Having received his professional training as an architect from a Japanese imperial school, and having been employed as an architect by the colonial government general, both physical and cultural extensions of Tokyo in Keijō, Yi's academic and professional

---

or consistency as the last refuge of the unimaginative.

3. In his essay "Please Bury Me Deep in the Mountains," Mun Chonghyŏk, one of Yi Sang's closest friends from high school, recounts that Uk was the nickname Yi used to refer to him. See "*Simsim sanch'ŏn-e mudŏjuo*," in *Yŏwŏn*, April, 1969.

4. Yi Sang, "*Hyŏlsŏ samt'ae* (Three forms of writing in blood)," in *Sinyŏsŏng* (New woman), June, 1934.

fate was intimately tied to the metropole. Unlike so many of his contemporaries, however, Yi lacked the wherewithal to venture to Tokyo for study, work, or pleasure. All of these factors commingled to create a curious combination: Yi simultaneously appears to have suffered from a slight inferiority complex combined with a bold confidence and desire to venture to Tokyo and prove himself at the center. The former appears somewhat more objective and quantitative, based on his actual lack of experience, while the latter is more subjective and qualitative, based on Yi's own very real achievements in Keijō and others' continual recognition of his genius. These others included both Koreans and Japanese, artists and professionals. But Keijō was not Tokyo, and neither Yi nor anyone else could be fully certain of his true place and stature in the empire until he had proven himself at its core.

When Yi did finally make it to Tokyo in 1936, he was already quite famous and also quite ill. Professionally and personally he had little to lose or to gain by embellishing his impressions of the city he had so longed to see and experience. While there he penned a number of works, many of which bear tangible signs of their provenance. As its title implies, however, the essay "Tokyo" is where Yi most saliently and transparently recorded his impressions of the principal city. Perhaps contrary to conventional expectations, and to his own doubts prior to the journey, Yi was not humbled by what and whom he observed and encountered. Certain nationalist critics have viewed the essay as representing a sort of admission of and repentance for a hubris possible only while residing in the periphery.[5] A reading of the text itself, devoid of anachronistic, nation-based needs for clear loyalties and contrition, however, exposes something very different: a deliberate and systematic tour through and leveling of Tokyo's most sacred landmarks, which were also, not coincidentally, precisely what had previously held Yi and many other colonial intellectuals in thrall.

5. See Kim Yunsik, *Yi Sang yŏn'gu* (A study of Yi Sang) (Seoul: Munhak sasangsa, 1987), 338.

Yi takes his readers from the Marunouchi Building to Shinjuku to the Ginza. He even includes a brief aside regarding the Imperial Palace. And at each stop he is careful to express fully just how underwhelmed he is by Tokyo.

The Artist as a Young Man

Yi literally lived and died in Japan, never knowing an independent Korean nation-state. Yet in keeping with the many other enigmatic aspects of his life, and in spite of the sort of tumultuous social circumstances that often accompany mad genius, he appears to have spent many of his days as a rather content and productive colonial subject. At only two years of age he is adopted by his father's elder brother, Kim Yŏnp'il, a man with the social and financial means to ensure that Yi could be properly educated. His uncle works for the Japanese colonial government, and sends Yi to the Sinmyŏng School where, at the age of seven, a student report records his fondness for drawing. At eleven he graduates and enters the Tonggwang School; the next year Tonggwang is annexed by Posŏng Normal High School, the predecessor of Korea University. It is at Posŏng that Yi meets Yi Hŏn'gu, Im Hwa, Wŏn Yongsŏk, and other future intellectual leaders of the colony. It is also there that he begins to pursue art seriously; at the age of fourteen he submits an oil painting, generically titled Landscape, which is accepted for an intramural art exhibition. At the age of sixteen, Yi graduates and enters Keijō Industrial High School, the precursor to Seoul National University's College of Engineering. Yi is now truly among the colonial elite. He joins the Department of Architecture, and in an entering class of sixteen, he is one of only two ethnically Korean students. Being surrounded by Japanese peers, however, does not deter him from becoming the editor-in-chief of the student magazine *Shipwreck* (難破船), in which he also publishes his first works of poetry. In addition to these extracurricular achievements, he obtains impeccable academic marks, graduating first in his class.

His formal education ends here, in March 1929, at the age of eighteen. Somewhat following in his uncle's footsteps, by April, less than one month later, he has secured employment in the Architectural Division of the Japanese Government General's Office of Internal Affairs. While technically a bureaucrat, Yi's passion for expression remains unhindered. While an employee of the colonial government, he wins both first and third places in a contest to design the inaugural cover page of *Chosen to kenchiku* (Korea and architecture), the first professional architectural journal devoted to architecture on the Korean peninsula.[6] Somewhat unexpectedly, in 1931, it is also in this "Korean" "architectural" journal that Yi publishes his first poems; they are written entirely in Japanese.[7] Despite his professional and poetic accomplishments, however, Yi Sang remains elusive. Just as he was an acclaimed painter before ever making his foray into architecture, his first works of prose fiction also defy facile temporal delineation. Even before his poems were published, in early 1930, at the age of nineteen, he begins serializing his first novel, December 12. The original title, written vertically and very concerned with geometrical shapes and repetition, is emblematic of his later work.[8] It was written entirely in Korean, illustrated by Yi himself, and serialized from February 1930 in the monthly journal *Chosŏn*.[9]

---

6. This is tremendously significant. Not only was Yi, as a Korean, allowed to enter multiple designs—we have no way of knowing if he submitted more than two—but his submissions garnered the top and third places in the contest. Just as he was free to compete with and to best his Japanese peers as a student at the predecessor of Seoul National University, so too does his professional career appear to have been based on a meritocracy and not on a hierarchy of race, Japanese over Korean.

7. The poems, also in Japanese, that Yi published in the student magazine Shipwreck were mentioned above. While significant, these were not externally reviewed, nor did they likely go out to a wider audience beyond the walls of the school. As such, the poems in *Chosen to kenchiku* may be seen as his first true publications.

8. The title, albeit vertically in the original, reads "十二月十二日". Much of Yi's later works also revolve as much or more around architectural constructions of words on the page than semantics or prosody.

9. Another testament to Yi's wide-ranging talents and interests was that he often provided the illustrations for his own works and those of other renowned writers during the 1930s. His illustrations of Pak T'aewŏn's novel *Sosŏl-ga Kubo-ssi ŭi ilil* (A day in the life of the novelist Kubo) are perhaps the best known example.

In an enigmatic fashion that was quite natural for him but that confounds later nationalist critics, Yi seamlessly integrates a career as a high-level Japanese government bureaucrat, a Korean-language novelist, and a Japanese-language poet.

From his graduation and nearly immediate employment, Yi's professional and literary careers move forward apace. He continues to publish innovative poetry and fiction in both Korean and Japanese. He also continues to paint, having his work Chisang selected for the 1931 Chosen Fine Art Exhibition, the single largest and most important event of its kind on the peninsula.[10] Even while pursuing a career as an architect, Yi is no dilettante. Rather, he masterfully balances several somewhat disparate pursuits, producing, and winning awards for, literature and art at the highest levels. His momentum, however, is interrupted by death and declining health. In 1932 Yi's uncle, now adoptive father, passes. He returns to live with his birth parents for the first time in over 20 years. The following year, in 1933, his declining health, evidenced by increasing bouts of hemoptysis, forces him to leave Keijō for the first time in his life.

In March of 1933, Yi tenders his resignation from the Government General, and retires to Paekch'ŏn Hot Springs near Inch'ŏn in order to convalesce. Intensely bored, he is able to endure less than two weeks before returning to Keijō. Even while there, rather than resting, he meets the *kisaeng* Kŭmhong. They return to Keijō together and, with the inheritance left to him by his late uncle, open the café *Chebi* (The Swallow). Yi proves a better artist than entrepreneur; the café soon fails. A series of similar attempts in the near future meets with similar ends. Mirroring these failures, his health also continues to decline.

---

10. I have been unable to find the Chinese characters for the work's title: "*Chisang*." Like the name Yi Sang, without the Chinese, there are several possible meanings, including but not limited to "Supremacy," "The Earth's Surface," "The Lay of the Land," "Terrestrial Phenomena," and "On Paper." This exhibition (*Chosen bijitsu tenrankai* 朝鮮美術展覽會) ran from 1922 to 1944, was based on the Imperial Art Institute Exhibition in Japan, and served as a sort of absolute official criterion for the judgment of art. Selection for inclusion here was no small affair, and Yi was no mere dilettante.

In contrast to his businesses and health, however, Yi's literary/artistic career soars. Over the next three years (1933-1936) he publishes the majority of his poetry, prose fiction, and essays. In contrast to his early forays into painting, fiction, and poetry, Yi does not publish his first essays until 1934. Essays such as "Three Forms of Writing in Blood (*Hyŏlsŏ samt'ae*)," published in the June issue of *Sinyŏsŏng*, and "Autumn of the Promenades (*Sanch'aek ŭi kaŭl*)," which appeared in the October issue of Sindonga, clearly display that Yi is already a practiced and confident flâneur.[11] Earlier iterations of department stores, cafes, and people he will later catalog in Tokyo all appear in his essays documenting his various promenades about Keijō.

It is also during his literary prime, however, that Yi is compelled to leave Keijō for the second time. In fall of 1935, again for tuberculosis, Yi travels to another hot springs, this time much more remote from Keijō. Although his sojourn begins at the bucolic Yongch'ŏn Hot Springs, where he is scheduled to spend three weeks, he can endure only one. The other two are spent in the nearby town of Sŏngch'ŏn, located in present-day North Korea, where his friend is working for the colonial government. He is quite productive while there, and continues his relatively new focus on essays, sending back the renowned "*Sanch'on yŏjŏng* (Lingering Impressions of a Mountain Village)" in installments to the daily newspaper *Chosŏn ilbo*.

Despite his continuing literary success, when he returns to Keijō, he has still spent only about one month of his life outside the colonial capital. He has never even seen Japan, to say nothing of Tokyo. Yi appears to have harbored some very natural colonial intellectual fantasies. Many of his teachers were Japanese, and employees of the imperial government. His Korean mentors such as

---

11. A comprehensive treatment of the various definitions and iterations of "flâneur" is well beyond the scope of the present study. Its use here follows the simple yet relatively comprehensive definition put forth by Edmund White: "The flâneur is a loiterer, a stroller who ambles through the city without apparent purpose but is secretly attuned to the city, its history and secrets." See Edmund White, The Flâneur: *A Stroll Through the Paradoxes of Paris* (New York: Bloomsbury), 2001.

Chŏng Chiyong and friends like Kim Kirim had studied in Tokyo, and waxed poetic not only about their academic achievements in the capital but also their adventures in its streets, department stores, and cafes. Yi's first published essay opens with a dear friend's return from Tokyo, how the metropole had changed him, and the ensuing betrayal of their affection. He appears to have suffered from what might be called a "Keijō inferiority complex," but one that he was determined to remedy. With uncharacteristic decisiveness, in 1935 he ends a tempestuous three-year relationship with Kŭmhong. The following year he marries Pyŏn Tongnim. Finally, in October of 1936, leaving Keijō for only the third time in his life, his health in serious decline, Yi travels to Tokyo. While in Tokyo, he continues to write in both Korean and Japanese. He is arrested in mid-February of 1937 on the generic but oft-employed charge of being a *futei senjin*.[12] Although transferred out of prison in mid-March due to his poor health, he is not actually released. Rather, he is remanded to the Tokyo Imperial University Hospital, where he dies on April 17.

Despite Yi's high level of literary activity while in Tokyo, much of his writing was focused elsewhere. The essay "*Kwŏnt'ae* (Ennui)," for example, deals not with Yi's present location but rather revisits the two weeks Yi spent in Sŏngch'ŏn and originally recorded in "*Sanch'on yŏjŏng*." Yi leaves only a single work—the eponymous essay "Tokyo"—that is entirely devoted to recording certain of his impressions and evaluations of the heart of the Japanese colonial empire.

"Tokyo" on Tokyo

Yi Sang arrived in Tokyo with an admixture of trepidation and expectation. He also possessed a well-founded confidence in his abilities. Yes, he was a colonial subject, but he had competed

---

12. The term *futei senjin* (不逞鮮人) can be variously translated as "rebellious Korean," "unruly Korean," or "malcontent Korean." It is a deliberately vague term, which allowed authorities in both Japan and Korea to use it when no specific legal offense could be cited.

with and bested not only those numerous Koreans who had
returned from Tokyo but also Japanese students, architects,
and artists in Keijō. Finally, and equally important for the essay
"Tokyo," he was a practiced and confident flâneur. He had cut
his literary teeth writing both fictional and essayistic accounts
of his wanderings about Keijō. In 1934 he published *Sanch'aek ŭi
kaŭl*, only his second essay, in which he presents and comments
upon several different "landscapes" in and around downtown
Keijō.[13] Keijō by 1936 has become in certain ways a facsimile
of Tokyo. Yi will spend much of the essay "Tokyo" engaged
in *"Ginbura,"* or idly strolling the Ginza, but he has already
done something quite similar with his *"Honbura"* in Keijō.[14]
And in both places he is no mere "idler";[15] he always brings the
discerning eye of a trained architect and a born artist—many
used and use the word "genius"—to bear upon the landscapes
and people of the cities he assays. In "Tokyo" he "ambles
through the city without apparent purpose but is secretly
attuned to the city, its history and secrets."

The essay "Tokyo" begins in media res with the following
sentence: "The 'Marunouchi Building'—more commonly referred
to as Marubiru—I had envisioned was a magnificent affair, at least
four times larger than this 'Marubiru.'" Aside from the slight jar
provided by their abruptness, the opening lines establish some

---

13. Much of his prose fiction is also intensely autobiographical. While not as
transparent a lens onto the peninsula's capital as his essays, works such as "*Nalgae*
(Wings)" have a first-person narrator whose own flâneurial tendencies take readers
to and through Keijō's brothels, train stations, and department stores.

14. For a discussion of *Honbura* and of its intimate relationship to *Ginbura*,
see Yi Kyŏnghun, "*Ginja ŭi ch'uŏk: singminji munhak kwa sijang* (The memories
of Ginza: colonial literature and market)" in *Han'guk hyŏndae munhak ŭi yŏn'gu*,
No. 39, 2009.10, 309-344. A revised and supplemented version in English was
presented by Yi at the 2011 Annual Meeting of the Association for Asian Studies.

15. There is an uncanny correspondence between the literal meaning and the
various resonances of the word "flâneur" and the Sino-Korean term *hanin* (閑
人), which Yi uses to describe himself in "*Sanch'aek ŭi kaŭl.*" And although it will
have to await a separate treatment, many of Yi's observations in this early essay
mirror the sentiments put forth by Walter Benjamin in "The Work of Art in the
Age of Mechanical Reproduction." Yi was a voracious consumer of imported
works of and theories on art and literature, but he penned this piece a year before
Benjamin's.

important ground rules. First, Yi Sang is physically in downtown Tokyo, writing on site. In addition, he is among the cognoscenti. Unlike the casual tourist, he is well aware of the local term for this Tokyo landmark. Finally, and most importantly for setting the overall tenor of this essay, he is thoroughly unimpressed. While in Keijō, whether due to colonial propaganda, the exaggerations of fellow "Koreans," or his own fantasies regarding Tokyo, Yi had long harbored certain illusions regarding Tokyo and its iconic landmarks. He opens the essay "Tokyo" with an unequivocal pronouncement of his disillusionment. Deconstructing his initial sentence provides readers with the following: the actual "Marubiru" is not at all magnificent and only one quarter the size Yi had expected. Throughout his essayistic tour of Tokyo, he goes on to repeat, albeit in slightly altered forms, this process of re-discovery and de-valuation.

Nearly immediately following his opening remarks, Yi widens his gaze from the "Marubiru" itself out onto the surrounding area. He informs his readers that "(i)n this 'building' village known as 'Marunouchi,' there are no residents other than the 'building' itself." Yi is a flâneur; he desires to pace the streets and to observe the residents of Tokyo. But this part of the city is nearly desolate. "Automobiles have taken the place of dress shoes." Among the very few human beings he sights, the great majority "come and go with at least automobiles for footwear."

Yi, however, remains undaunted. It takes him only five minutes of futile walking before he too has "no choice but sensibly to hail a 'taxi.'" While inside the taxi, circumnavigating the grounds of the Imperial Palace and headed for Shinjuku, Yi "researched the topic of the 20th century." As he skirts the palace moat, still quite near Marunouchi, "countless automobiles clamor to perpetuate the 20th century." Yi, however, does not succumb. He is determined to experience for himself the places and people of Tokyo about which he has heard and read so much, and fantasized about for so long. Although he does concede that his "morality, reeking of the musty stench of the 19th century, cannot comprehend why there are so many automobiles," this is not a defect in his person. Rather, Tokyo itself is flawed. He confidently concludes that his morality "was, in the end, extremely dignified." He is among the select few, the "sacred philosophers looking askance at the *fin de siècle* and modern capitalism." He revels in the humanity represented by his "19th century morality." Tokyo, by contrast, is somewhat inhuman, mechanical; it " 'reeks of "gasoline!"'" and "the body odor of Tokyo's citizens shall come to resemble that of automobiles."

Yi arrives at his destination unannounced and with the following proclamation: "Shinjuku has a Shinjukuesque character."[16] He hardly appears excited or overwhelmed. What he does specifically comment upon is the precariousness of the place's affectation and inflated prices—"Extravagance like walking on thin ice." He drinks overpriced café au lait at "French Mansion," and spots signs written in the Roman alphabet, in all capitals. But he also knows, unlike the denizens of Shinjuku, that "ERUTERU" should properly be written "Werther," and that "HURANSU" is a mere Japanization of what should be "France." He sees through the illusion, leaving readers with the following before moving on: "Shinjuku—the chimerical prosperity of 3-*chome*—beyond it are wooden fences and unsold plots and signs saying don't urinate, and, also, of course, some houses." Shinjuku's opulence is artificial and fleeting. When Yi looks out beyond 3-*chome*, peers behind the veil, he sees not only a physical but also a cultural underdevelopment—the latter denoted by actual signs revealing the level of "the refinement of the people here." No better than or

---

16. Michael D. Shin, in his excellent translation of this essay, renders the sentence as follows: "Shinjuku has a character like its characters: New Lodging." Considering the overall context and Yi's selective usage of Chinese characters, this reading is not only valid but provocative. Shinjuku is the only area quite distant from his starting point at Marunouchi—and his lodgings in Kanda—that Yi visits in this essay. His comments also somewhat accentuate the new, and hence artificial, aspects of what little development he witnesses. See Yi Sang (Trans. Michael D. Shin), "Tokyo" in *Muae* (Seoul: Kaya, 1995), 96-101.

different from those in Keijō, "the people here" also have to be told not to urinate in public.[17]

Yi ends the first section of "Tokyo" with the above comments on Shinjuku; the second section begins with his first human interaction.[18] In rather typical fashion for Yi Sang, without any explanation of time elapsed or conveyance used, he simply appears back near downtown Tokyo. And he is now being guided to additional Tokyo landmarks by a Korean: "Mr. C first takes me, tired as if I could die, to the Tsukiji Little Theater." As with nearly everything he encounters in Tokyo, Yi's expectations are not met. "The theater is presently closed. This headquarters of Japan's New Theater Movement, plastered with all sorts of 'posters,' to my eyes resembled a poorly designed café." The theater's being closed, while perhaps disappointing, is not perfectly analogous to either the mediocrity of the "Marubiru" or the vacuity of Shinjuku. It does, however, quietly speak to a certain motif: the disconnect between expectation and reality in Tokyo. In this sense, Yi's pronouncement on the theater as a physical edifice proves extremely significant. Yi incorporates multiple identities. Yes, he is an imperial subject visiting the metropole from the periphery. But he is also an acclaimed artist and imperially trained and certified architect. As an artist he is interested in visiting the "headquarters of Japan's New Theater Movement," while as an architect he is both qualified and prepared to pass judgment upon the building itself. After all, he graduated at the top of his overwhelmingly Japanese class at an imperial institution of higher education, after which he was immediately hired by same imperial government to work as an architect. As both adept flâneur and adroit architect,

17. It is not difficult to imagine the sorts of supercilious comments on Korean hygiene and refinement (*kyoyang* 教養) Yi would have grown up hearing in Keijō from his Japanese teachers and peers. In addition, as mentioned above, his Korean mentors and friends also significantly contributed to his exaggerated expectations regarding Tokyo. In any case, Yi literally and figuratively reads the signs that undermine claims of superiority.

18. Although he observes a few people in Marunouchi and takes a taxi to Shinjuku, he makes no mention of any conversation or other interaction.

Yi flatly pronounces that this cultural icon "to my eyes resembled
a poorly designed café." The original Korean possesses a clarity
and force born of Yi's own confidence not only in his ability but
also in his prerogative to judge. It begins with a representation of
both Yi's physical body and critical faculties—"*nae nun-e nŭn*"—
which literally means "in my eyes" but also possesses the obvious
connotation of "in my estimation/in my judgment." From here it
makes an immediate and seamless transition to Yi's professional
expertise—*sŏlgye*, or architectural design. He then combines the
artist's eye with the architects training to return the following
verdict: it "resembled a poorly designed café."

Yi's second encounter with another person immediately
follows. He has now moved from sightseeing to the practical
matters of settling in Tokyo. "Quite contrary to Mr. C, who
claims 'Plays are more interesting than life,' Mr. H is among the
skeptics." It is the skeptical Mr. H who will assist Yi in finding
a room. But there is a palpable sense that Tokyo is a dishonest
place. "Mr. H's 'apartment' room costs 16 *yen* in the winter, 14
yen in the summer, and 15 *yen* in the spring and fall. Regarding
such calculations, fickle as a turtledove, his skepticism and
ridicule run deep and wide." Yi, with a somewhat uncharacteristic
pragmatism, apparently takes Mr. H's skepticism concerning
and ridicule of Tokyo business practices to heart. He tactfully if
cynically requests, faulting not his Tokyo landlord but his own
"rather serious forgetfulness, a room that did not display such a
talent for fluctuating according to season." And it is only at this
point, well into the essay, that Yi records his first and only actual
interaction with a Japanese person—a servant girl working at the
"apartment." She detects his sarcasm, and attempts a riposte. "(T)
he servant girl consoles me by saying that a yokel like me also
displayed considerable talent by coming to such a faraway place
all by himself." Yi, however, is not one to shy away from repartee.
"I in turn console her by remarking that the wart dangling from
her left nostril must certainly be a symbol of her good fortune,

after which I added that if I could clearly see Mt. Fuji just one time I would have no further desires." Thus ends the second section of the essay. The exchange between Yi and the servant girl also appears to end here, Yi's infamous wit taking the day.

The third section of the essay, however, maintains an atypical spatial and temporal continuity, which provides an opening for the girl to resume. "The following day, at 7 in the morning, there was an earthquake. I opened the window and looked down upon quivering Great Tokyo; all was covered in a yellow light." Yi is employing an architectural vantage point—one he earlier employed in his poems ("Crow's Eye View") and prose fiction ("Wings")—in order to bolster his flâneurial observations.[19] As if inspecting a blueprint, he gazes vertically down upon phenomena and cities in order to grasp more clearly the totality that might be obscured by minutiae while strolling at ground level. And from this privileged position, Yi can finally see all of "Great Tokyo." No longer allowing a single building or block to occupy or occlude his gaze, he looks down upon the entire quivering city, and proclaims it "yellow." Yellow could, of course, simply refer to the early morning light, or to the dusty haze stirred up by the quake. In the Korean language, however, it also connotes a hopelessness or lack of chance for future success.[20]

---

19. For a discussion of this technique in Yi Sang's writings, see Kwŏn Yŏngmin, "Yi Sang chonjip *pyŏnaen Sŏuldae Kungmunkwa Kwŏn Yŏngmin kyosu* (Seoul National University Professor Kwŏn Yŏngmin publishes *Complete Works of Yi Sang*)," *Publishing Journal*, http://www.publishingjournal.co.kr/wp/?p=1294 (accessed August 11, 2011).

20. The expression *Ssaksu ka norat'a* (싹수가 노랗다), literally means "The sprout is yellow." As an idiom, however, it is used to express an utter lack of hope for future success. And the first figurative meaning given by Naver's online Korean-English dictionary (is the following: "이틀을 굶고 나니 하늘이 노랬다." For which the following translation is provided: "Having gone without food for two days, the sky seemed to be blackening." So "yellow" becomes "black," in the sense of "dim," "foreboding," or "hopeless." See: http://endic.naver.com/krenEntry.nhn ?entryId=d53d62e9e68d4006aef551d9d42de263 (accessed August 11, 2011)

In addition, Yi stresses the extreme condition of the "yellow-ness" by extending the word in the original: "*no—rat'a* (노—랗다)," or something like "yeeeellow." Finally, although it is far beyond the scope of the present study and Yi Sang was certainly no nationalist Korean, it is not a great leap to see the connections between this scene and pronouncement and the events in the aftermath of the Great Kanto Earthquake over a decade earlier. In a word, Yi's preference for an individual over a Korean national identity does not automatically translate into an indifference to or

It is at this point that the "servant" girl, the sole Japanese person with whom Yi converses in the entire essay, perhaps remembering Yi's remarks from the previous evening, interjects. "The 'servant' girl urged me to look at Mt. Fuji . . . in the clear sky beyond the city." The girl attempts to regain her "Tokyo advantage," to return Yi to his peripheral status, by urging him to shift his gaze to majestic Mt. Fuji.[21] Tokyo may be quaking but Japan remains unshaken. After all, *Nothing is as symbolic of Japan as Mt. Fuji.* Standing at 3,776 meters, the mountain that straddles the prefectures of Yamanashi and Shizuoka is by far the tallest in the country, *visible even from Tokyo* . . . . At the heart of Fuji's influence is its spiritual power."[22] Her importuning also serves as an attempt to level Yi's vertical gaze. If she can recast his eyes to the horizon, she can also return the veil to Tokyo. Yi acquiesces. He then offers his first and final evaluation of Japan's national symbol: "Mt. Fuji, . . . in the clear sky beyond the city, pathetic as a toy cake, has exposed its half-bald head." Thus, his gaze is redirected, but he is not misdirected. The sky is clear only beyond Tokyo, which remains thoroughly "yellow," and Fuji, its purported "spiritual power" notwithstanding, is "pathetic." This perspicaciousness

---

ignorance of Japan's various transgressions.

21. One popular website, collating information from various other sites including Mt. Fuji's own website and from Japan-Guide, provides the following:
"*When one thinks of Japan, one of the first things one imagines is Mt. Fuji.* The highest mountain in Japan, it rises to 12,388 feet and is *visible from as far away as Tokyo on a clear day.* It is one of the most visited mountains and has long been depicted as a *symbol of Japan in both photographs and art,* including many traditional Japanese forms of art, such as ukiyo-e woodblock prints, popular in the Edo Period. Mt. Fuji has also featured in Hokusai's famous '36 Views of Mount Fuji.'"

. . .

"Mt. Fuji is often shrouded in clouds, even from as close as the five lakes, so it is always *a nice surprise when it is suddenly visible on a clear day* . . . . *On clear days, it can be seen from as far away as Tokyo* . . . . While there are other mountains nearby, from far away, Mt. Fuji looks as if it is rising alone out of a vast plain and it is easy to see why the mountain has been sacred to so many people for so long." (emphasis added)
See http://www.examiner.com/asia-travel-in-national/mt-fuji-symbol-of-japan (accessed August 11, 2011).

22. See http://www.hiraganatimes.com/hp/travel/discover/kiji262e.html (emphasis added) (accessed August 11, 2011).

regardless of angle—horizontal or vertical—is what allowed him to deconstruct Shinjuku from ground level. Now, from his elevated position, he can do the same for all of Tokyo, and, coopting Mt. Fuji as national symbol, all of Japan.

Yi's focus here and in many of his other essays, however, is not on Japan, Korea, or any other nation. Yi is a writer of the city and of cities. The second sentence of "Tokyo"—following the opening reassessment of "Marubiru"—reads as follows: "If I go to New York's 'Broadway,' I might suffer the same disillusionment." Not only does he omit any mention of the United States, he also specifies a precise and culturally central area of the city— "Broadway." In similar fashion, he begins the essay's fourth section with an abrupt return not only to Tokyo but to yet another specific and iconic district: the Ginza. Here, too, the reality of Tokyo falls far short of his expectations. His confidence waxing, he opens with the following unequivocal verdict: "The Ginza is a mere textbook on vanity." In contrast to the neighborhood of buildings and cars, however, people do walk here. In fact, they are compelled to do so: "If you don't walk here, it's as if you lose your right to vote." This is the *Ginbura* that Yi assumed he was recreating in Keijō's Honmachi. But at its origin, where it should be most pure, he realizes it is utter affectation: "When women buy new dress shoes, before riding in automobiles, they must first tread upon the Ginza's sidewalks." They do not stroll for pleasure and observation, as does the flâneur, but rather as a form of exhibitionism, after which they are perfectly happy to jump back into the automobiles that "have taken the place of dress shoes." Walking here—*Ginbura*—is yet another of Tokyo's facades. But, to Yi, the Ginza is a "textbook," and he reads it as such. Much akin to "the chimerical prosperity of 3-*chome*" in Shinjuku, *Ginbura* is beguiling and ephemeral, and ultimately reinforces Yi's judgment from the essay's second paragraph on the decreasing humanity of Tokyo's citizens.

Although Yi has not finished his explication of the Ginza—he will later make an evening return to conclude the essay—he does make some definitive comments before temporarily moving on. Continuing with the motif of Tokyo's various semblances, he gives us the following: "Being a mere skeleton in the service of the Ginza at night, the Ginza during the day is more than a little grotesque." By day all is visible. He can see clearly "(t)he tangled form of the poker-like iron bones that support the 'neon sign' wrapped around 'Salon Spring' . . . bedraggled as the 'permanent wave' of a barmaid who has been up all night." He makes no attempt to hide his disgust. In a sentence that both harkens back to the signs forbidding urination on the streets of Shinjuku and openly displays his disdain, Yi concludes: "But because the police headquarters has posted signs all around that read 'Do Not Spit on the Street,' I cannot spit." But Yi's derision is not confined only to the people now physically before him, nor is it directed only at the Japanese. The final sentence of the essay's fourth section reads as follows: "While casually relieving myself in an underground public toilet near Kyōbashi, I tried reciting the names of all those friends who had boasted so of having been to Tokyo." The picture he creates with this single sentence is both striking and unambiguous. Now that he has leveled much of Tokyo, penis in hand, he figuratively pisses upon those back in Korea who are partially responsible for his inflated expectations.

This catharsis completed, Yi heads off for another metropole icon: the department store. In the fifth section, again sans segue, Yi observes: "Mitsukoshi, Matsuzakaya, Itoya, Shirokiya, Matsuya—recently these seven-story houses do not sleep at night. But we cannot go inside them." And in the following paragraph, he provides the reason: "the fact that they are not seven stories but one." Of course, he also discusses how easy it is to get lost among "the mountainous piles of merchandise and the profusion of 'shop girls'," but the first and fundamental factor he offers again relates to the stores' facades—"seven stories"—versus their realities—"one." Where the "Marubiru" was one-fourth the size Yi had imagined, the department stores are one-seventh. The metropole is being increasingly leveled.

In the essay's sixth section and penultimate section, Yi returns to Ginza: "Night has fallen, and so mere 'Ginza,' without an article, appears." Definite article removed, Ginza is now re-cloaked in darkness, but Yi has already seen it revealed. Perhaps again commenting on the superficiality of the area, he writes: "Tea from 'Colombin,'[23] books from Kinokuniya, these are the refinement of the people here." Although its exact relation to the bookstore is somewhat ambiguous, Colombin represents yet another example of Tokyo landmark qua empty shell, mere simulacrum. The paintings on its ceiling have been rendered by a Japanese artist who has taken the name "Leonard," while its outer wall is adorned with "a miniature sized Eiffel tower."[24] Such a toy, so far from Paris, meshes quite well with the following: "A common definition of the simulacrum is a copy of a copy whose relation to the model has become so attenuated that it can no longer properly be said to be a copy. It stands on its own as a copy without a model."[25] As the

23. In the original this is written k'orombang (코롬방). "Colombin," meaning woodpigeon in French, is the name of a company that, like Kinokuniya, is still in operation today.

    Colombin founder, Kuniteru Kadokura, was appointed steward by the Ministry of Imperial household in 1915, receiving the honor of providing trend-setting ceremonial and everyday confectioneries and ice cream to the imperial household.

    Owing to this history, Colombin has been the one and only provider of western confectioneries to the Japanese imperial household until this day since 1924.

    . . .

    Colombin has from its start, sent out many Japanese patissiere to France, contributing to their education and the development of Japanese confectionery industry. Kadokura felt it his duty to introduce to Japan not only the food and culture of France but also that of Europe as a whole, and had found pleasure in providing products and services that create a rich, beautiful everyday life, and at the same time bringing sensation to our customers.

    The teashop that Colombin opened in 1931 in the town of Ginza had a ceiling decorated with six paintings by Japanese artist Leonard Foujita, with a miniature sized Eiffel tower attached to an outer wall of the building. The place also included a refrigerated glass display case and air-conditioning, which were both very rare at the time."

    See http://jp116524900.trustpass.alibaba.com/aboutus.html for a full description. (accessed August 12, 2011).

24. *Ibid.*

25. "Realer than Real: The Simulacrum According to Deleuze and Guattari" by Brian Massumi http://www.anu.edu.au/HRC/first_and_last/works/realer.htm. (accessed August 21, 2011). Although somewhat focused on late-20th century postmodernist film, the essay provides an interesting overview of certain major

essay draws to a close, Yi much more forcefully and unambiguously distances himself from "the people here" and from the superficiality and derivative quality of their "refinement." Yi harkens back to the extreme dignity he discovered, and subsequently employed to differentiate himself from the citizens of Tokyo, at the essay's outset while he "researched the topic of the 20th century" from inside a taxi. Now, from Ginza, he writes: "But, more dignified, I stop by 'Brazil' and drink a 'straight.'" It does not, however, have the desired stimulative effect: "They say that in 'Brazil' trains run using 'coffee' for fuel instead of coal, but no matter how much of this black coal I swallow no passion blazes up within me."

By the seventh and final section of the essay, Yi appears less despondent than resigned. He has read, comprehended, and leveled Tokyo. He has witnessed "simulation: the substitution of signs of the real for the real." Thus he writes: "At God's discretion, the stars too would shine in the Ginza sky after the 'ad balloon' has landed." The stars still exist, but they are "long forgotten" by "these descendents of 'Cain'" in Ginza. The stars are real, yet they are compelled by "(t)he citizens here, who have been educated to fear poison gas more than the flood of 'Noah,'" to come after the "signs of the real," the artificial "ad balloon." It is a perversion of a natural order that parallels the subversion of Yi's own expectations of the metropole. Thus Yi ends with his gaze and concerns still fixed on the heavens, electing to ignore Tokyo in the final lines of "Tokyo": "Oh moon, once companion to Li Po! Wouldn't it have been much nicer if you too had perished along with the 19th century?"

---

ideas concerning and definitions of simulacra: "The airless atmosphere has asphyxiated the referent, leaving us satellites in aimless orbit around an empty center. We breathe an ether of floating images that no longer bear a relation to any reality whatsoever. That, according to Baudrillard, is simulation: the substitution of signs of the real for the real. In hyperreality, signs no longer represent or refer to an external model. They stand for nothing but themselves, and refer only to other signs." . . . "Fredric Jameson cites the example of photorealism. The painting is a copy not of reality, but of a photograph, which is already a copy of the original."

Conclusion

Yi ends "Tokyo" abruptly and with a rhetorical question. He moves from the usurped stars and 20th century Ginza to the moon, a poet fabled to have died chasing it, and the 19th century. Li Po died for his art, but not before fully embodying and partially creating a universal language and culture. Yi had similar ambitions. Influenced by mentors like Chong Chiyong, Yi Sang went to Tokyo seeking a universalism as promised in literature and art by Taisho modernism, and in society by the colonial rhetoric of assimilation.[26] Both turned out to be parts of the façades and false promises of Tokyo. From his disappointment at the size of "Marubiru" and the chimerical prosperity of Shinjuku to the deceptive department stores and the Janus-faced Ginza, Yi found only disillusionment in Tokyo. Like Li Po's moon reflected in the water, these all mirror the false promises of modernity (and empire), and a concomitant nostalgic desire to return to a mythical past. For Yi, born in 1910, knew the 19th century no better than he knew Li Po— through books and romantic fantasies regarding a time and place where true universalism existed, where true genius was recognized, and where he might finally feel at home. But this is not a criticism. Yi Sang is an enigma; he contained multitudes. He was a true flâneur, "secretly attuned to the city, its history and secrets." He also made direct overtures to Oscar Wilde, who once wrote that "(o)ne's real life is often the life that one does not lead." That Yi was not physically present in the 19th century is immaterial. That he died in prison in Tokyo is tragic.[27] Finally, nothing about Yi Sang's life and work lends itself to facile encapsulation. His friend and colleague Kim Kirim, however, grasped a meaningful piece of the reality when,

---

26. For a thoroughgoing discussion of Japanese modernism, including its various omissions and contradictions, see Seiji M. Lippit, *Topographies of Japanese Modernism* (New York: Columbia University Press, 2002).

27. Although Yi technically died in a hospital, where he had been transferred due to his failing health, he was never released from prison.

in an essay that fittingly opens with an excerpt from W.B. Yeats "Sailing to Byzantium," he referred to Yi Sang as having been "in charge of a tragedy." Kim too glimpsed the various contradictory and enigmatic elements that comprised the man and artist when he lamented that Yi "contained in a single body" not merely Korea's "most excellent and final 'modernist,'" but also the one saddled with the "grave fate of overcoming 'modernism.'"[28]

---

28. Kim Kirim, "The Historical Position of Modernism (*Modŏnijŭm ŭi yŏksajŏk wich'i*) in Inmun p'yŏngnon (1939.10), reprinted in Kim Kirim, (ed. Yun Yŏt'ak), Kim Kirim *munhak pip'yŏng* [Kim Kirim's Literary Criticism] (Seoul: P'urŭn sasang, 2002), 287-294.

The original sentence reads: "가장 優秀한 最後의 「모더니스트」 李箱은 「모더니즘」 의 超克이라는 이 深刻한 運命으로 한 몸에 具現한 悲劇의 擔當者였다."

烏瞰圖이詩第四號 患者의容態에관한문제. ○ ○ ○ ○ ○ ○ ○ ○ ○ 1 3

診斷 0:1

26.10.1931

行發 社文彰社式株 | 日八月七 年一十和昭 | 箱李 幀裝 | 著 林起金 | 圖象氣 詩長

이상 1910. 09. 23 ~ 1937. 04. 17

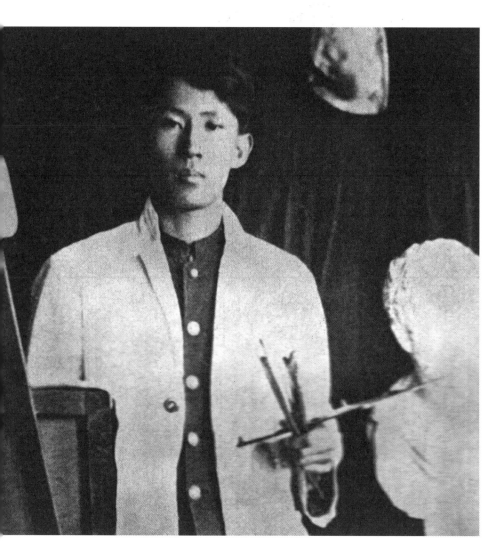

Tokyo[1]

by Yi Sang

The "Marunouchi Building"—more commonly referred to as Marubiru—I had envisioned was a magnificent affair, at least four times larger than this "Marubiru."[2] If I go to New York's "Broadway," I might suffer the same disillusionment. At any rate, 'This city reeks of "gasoline!"' is my first impression of Tokyo.

People like us whose lungs are unsound, first of all, are not qualified to live in this city. Whether closed or opened, my mouth is immediately permeated with the smell of "gasoline," so no matter what food I am eating I cannot avoid at least some taste of "gasoline." Therefore, the body odor of Tokyo's citizens shall come to resemble that of automobiles.

In this "building" village known as "Marunouchi," other than the "buildings" there are no residents. Automobiles have taken the place of dress shoes. Those people who do walk are sacred philosophers looking askance at the fin de siècle and modern capitalism—all others come and go with at least automobiles for footwear.

---

1. This essay was published posthumously in the May 1939 edition of the literary journal *Munjang*. For this translation I used the original as well as an annotated reprint contained in Kim Chuhyŏn, ed., *Chŭngbo chŏngbon Yi Sang munhak chŏnjip 3—sup'il kit'a* (The Complete Works of Yi Sang Vol. 3—Essays and Miscellaneous Writings) (Seoul: Somyŏng ch'ulp'an, 2009).

2. In order both to denote foreign words and to set off spoken language and written signs, the original text employs the following punctuation marks: 「 」. This translation will represent them using full quotation marks: ". . .".

But I absurdly paced this village for a full five minutes. After which I too had no choice but sensibly to hail a "taxi."

Inside the "taxi," I researched the topic of the 20th century. Outside the window, now beside the Imperial Palace moat, countless automobiles clamor to perpetuate the 20th century. Since my morality, reeking of the musty stench of the 19th century, cannot comprehend why there are so many automobiles, it was, in the end, extremely dignified.

Shinjuku has a Shinjukuesque character. Extravagance like walking on thin ice—at "French Mansion" we had a cup of "coffee" that had already been mixed with milk, and then, when each of us paid 10 *sen*, it somehow felt as if 5 *rin* were greater than 9 *sen* and 5 *rin*.[3]

"Werther"—the citizens of Tokyo write France as HURANSU. ERUTERU, as I remember it, is the name of the person who had the most delectable love affair in the world, so "Werther" is not the least bit pitiable.[4]

Shinjuku—the chimerical prosperity of 3-*chome*—beyond it are wooden fences and unsold plots and signs saying don't urinate, and, also, of course, some houses.

---

3. Hoping to preserve the enigmatic nature of much of Yi's writing, I have opted for a rather literal, rather than interpretive, translation. It appears here, however, that he is likely making a comment on the extravagant price of a café au lait (Later in the essay, Yi goes on at some length concerning the preciousness of a single sen.). In any case, it appears that the coffee cost a full 9 *sen* and 5 *rin*, thus making the meaning something akin to ". . . the 5 *rin* we got back somehow seemed greater than the 9 *sen* and 5 *rin* we had paid."

4. As in many of his essays, Yi Sang here plays with both language and script. "Werther" is written in Korean (「에루테루」), and set off with quotation marks, while both HURANSU and ERUTERU are written in the Roman alphabet, and in all capitals. Though Yi provides characteristically few clues, in context he appears to be walking flaneurially about Tokyo, now Shinjuku, making one suspect that these are signs posted outside places of business. In fact, the HURANSU may be from the café "French Mansion," mentioned just above, the Japanese name for which Yi writes in *han'gŭl* as *hŭransŭ yashikki* (흐란스야시끼) in the original. Interestingly, he opts for the Chinese characters *pullansŏ* (佛蘭西) to write France the "Korean" way, in contradistinction to the "Japanese" HURANSU and 흐란스.

340

Mr. C first takes me, tired as if I could die, to the Tsukiji Little Theater. The theater is presently closed. This headquarters of Japan's New Theater Movement, plastered with all sorts of "posters," to my eyes resembled a poorly designed café. But even though I suffered the regret of foregoing cheap movies, I did occasionally visit this small theater, placing me among the elite drama aficionados.

Quite contrary to Mr. C, who claims "Drama is more interesting than life," Mr. H is a skeptic. "Apartments"—Mr. H's room costs 16 *yen* in the winter, 14 *yen* in the summer, and 15 *yen* in the spring and fall. Regarding such calculations, fickle as a turtledove, his skepticism and scorn run deep and wide. I requested, citing my rather serious forgetfulness, a room that did not display such a talent for fluctuating according to season, to which the servant girl consoles me by saying that a yokel like me also displayed considerable talent by coming to such a faraway place all by himself. I in turn console her by remarking that the wart dangling from her left nostril must certainly be a symbol of her good fortune, after which I added that if I could clearly see Mt. Fuji just one time I would have no further desires.

The following day, at 7 in the morning, there was an earthquake. I opened the window and looked out over quivering Great Tokyo; all was covered in a yellow light. The "servant" girl[5] urged me to look at Mt. Fuji, which, in the clear sky beyond the city, pathetic as a toy cake, has exposed its half-bald head.

The Ginza is a mere textbook on vanity. If you don't walk here, it's as if you lose your right to vote. When women buy new dress shoes, before riding in automobiles, they must first tread upon the Ginza's sidewalks.

---

5. The first time Yi mentions the servant girl, *tchotchyuyang* (쪼쯔孃), he uses no quotation marks. In this second mention, however, he opts to separate the "Japanese" portion of the compound word using quotation marks (「쪼쯔」孃).

Being a mere skeleton in the service of the Ginza at night, the Ginza during the day is more than a little grotesque. The tangled form of the poker-like iron bones that support the "neon sign" wrapped around "Salon Spring" is bedraggled as the "permanent wave" of a barmaid who has been up all night. But because the police headquarters has posted signs all around that read "Do Not Spit on the Street," I cannot spit.

The Ginza 8-*chome*, according to my calculations, measures approximately two and a half feet! Why? Because I was able to run into the same "modern" young lady with dyed red frizzy hair two and a half times in 30 minutes. This young lady appears to have come out now in order to digest that part of the day in which young ladies appear most beautiful, while my insipid "promenade" is nothing more than a sort of rumination.

While casually relieving myself in an underground public toilet near Kyōbashi, I tried reciting the names of all those friends who had boasted so of having been to Tokyo.

Shiwasu—it must mean the 12th month of the lunar calendar. On every street corner of the Ginza, Salvation Army community pots are hung like artillery rifles. A single *sen*, with just a single *sen* I can buy enough gas to cook a pot of rice. I cannot toss so precious a single *sen* into this community pot. Not only do the words thank you enrich our lives less than one *sen* worth of gas but they can also occasionally even make a refreshing stroll unpleasant, and thus it is also no wonder that "boys" and "girls" look coldly upon these charity gourds. The young Salvation Army lass—since, save for a few pimples on her face, she overflowed with youthful charm, I wanted to say, "You could enlist after menopause and it still wouldn't be all that late," and thereby earnestly encourage her desertion.

Mitsukoshi, Matsuzakaya, Itoya, Shirokiya, Matsuya— recently these seven-story houses do not sleep at night. But we cannot go inside them.

342

Why? In addition to the fact that they are not seven stories but one, because of the mountainous piles of merchandise and the profusion of "shop girls," it is easy to get lost.

Specially priced items, markdown items, discount items—which shall I choose? In any case, these technical terms are not in any dictionary. Well then, there is nothing cheaper than specially priced, markdown, discount—items. As expected, since there are no "bargains" among items such as jewelry and furs, there are actually huge "slogans" posted everywhere that try to understand the psychology of the types of customers who despise bargains.[6]

Night has fallen, and so mere "Ginza," without an article, appears. Tea from "Colombin,"[7] books from Kinokuniya, these are the refinement of the people here. But, more dignified, I stop by "Brazil" and drink a "straight." The young ladies serving tea all wore clothes with the same autumn leaf design; regrettably, they looked to me like patterns of venereal disease. They say that in "Brazil" trains run using "coffee" for fuel instead of coal,

---

6. Here Yi uses quotation marks around the first appearance of the Korean word *nukkŏri* (「녹거리」), but omits them for the second appearance.

7. In the original this is written *k'orombang* (코롬방). "Colombin," meaning woodpigeon in French, is the name of a company that, like Kinokuniya, is still in operation today.

> Colombin founder, Kuniteru Kadokura, was appointed steward by the Ministry of Imperial household in 1915, receiving the honor of providing trend-setting ceremonial and everyday confectioneries and ice cream to the imperial household.
> Owing to this history, Colombin has been the one and only provider of western confectioneries to the Japanese imperial household until this day since 1924.
> . . .
> Colombin has from its start, sent out many Japanese patissiere to France, contributing to their education and the development of Japanese confectionery industry. Kadokura felt it his duty to introduce to Japan not only the food and culture of France but also that of Europe as a whole, and had found pleasure in providing products and services that create a rich, beautiful everyday life, and at the same time bringing sensation to our customers.
> The teashop that Colombin opened in 1931 in the town of Ginza had a ceiling decorated with six paintings by Japanese artist Leonard Foujita, with a miniature sized Eiffel tower attached to an outer wall of the building. The place also included a refrigerated glass display case and air-conditioning, which were both very rare at the time." (Emphasis added.) See http://jp116524900.trustpass.alibaba.com/aboutus.html for a full description.

but no matter how much of this black coal I swallow no passion blazes up within me.

At God's discretion, the stars too would shine in the Ginza sky after the "ad balloon" has landed, but these descendents of "Cain" have already long forgotten the stars. The citizens here, who have been educated to fear poison gas more than the flood of "Noah," are forthcoming regarding their use of the subway to return to homes within walking distance. Oh moon, once companion to Li Po![8] Wouldn't it have been much nicer if you too had perished along with the 19th century?

---

8. This line—*Yi T'aebaek–i nodǔn tal-a* (李太白이 노든달아)—is taken from the traditional Korean ballad *T'al t'aryǒng*.

파란 하늘 만지는 無我의 자유

345

ANOTHER
PERSPECTIVE ON
HYŎN TŎK

Children's Literature in Late Colonial Korea

by Dafna Zur

C hildren's literature[1] in Korea can be traced to the beginning
of the twentieth century. Ch'oe Namsŏn's magazine *Sonyŏn*
[Youth][2] was the first of its kind—it was intended for young
readers. The first volume of this magazine carried a poem that
Ch'oe dedicated to his imagined young readers, "From the Sea to
the Boy,"[3] a poem that is considered by some to be the defining

---

1. According to Nodelman, children's literature refers to texts that are
identified by various social authorities as being suitable for children, and as
literature that contains adult ideas about childhood that shape the literature
and provide it with its characteristic features. He notes that some of the shared
characteristics of children's literature include a description of "childhood
experiences written from a child's perspective"; a focus on "children or childlike
characters"; "A feeling of optimism and innocence"; and "a tendency toward
combining reality and fantasy". To this he adds, too, a simplicity of language,
limited manuscript length, a greater focus on action, showing rather than telling,
and the presence of what he calls a "hidden adult": a more complex and more
complete understanding of the world that remains unspoken and beyond the
simple surface. See Perry Nodelman, *The Hidden Adult: Defining Children's
Literature* (Baltimore: Johns Hopkins University Press, 2008), 189.

2. One of the indications of the rise in importance of the child in the
enlightenment period in Korea was the circulation of signifiers and the shifting
of their signified categories. The terms that define a young person—*sonyŏn*,
ch'ŏngnyŏn, *ŏrini*, and *adong*—were not new. Still, these terms acquired new
meanings: by the first decade of the twentieth century, *sonyŏn* and *ch'ŏngnyŏn*
became the subjects not only of two innovative magazines but also symbols
of Korea's modern youth. This magazine title is translated as "youth" in this
instance because the target readers were older than what the category of "child"
might indicate; the magazine was meant for independent readers capable of
reading a relatively dense mix script of *hangŭl* and Chinese characters with ease.

3. "海에게서 少年에게" Sonyŏn 1, 2-4.

AZALEA

Children's
Literature in
Late Colonial
Korea

by *Dafna Zur*

moment separating premodern and modern literature in Korea.[4] Ch'oe and others continued to publish magazines marketed for a young audience throughout the colonial period. Their numbers grew with the proliferation of print culture, and circulated with the growth of consumer culture and the gradual rise in literacy. But just as children's literature represents adult views of childhood and reflects what adults deem appropriate for children on their journey toward adulthood, colonial children's literature in Korea reflects the ideological shifts in politics and society that children were expected to adhere to. The socialization of children and their conformity to these changing ideologies was of critical importance for the transformation of children into modern citizens and loyal colonial subjects.

Given the intense militarization of the late 1930s and the strict censorship and control exercised by the colonial government in this period,[5] it is hardly surprising that children's magazines became sites for the reproduction and manipulation of hegemonic colonial discourse. What is particularly notable is that despite the tight control of censorship and accelerated assimilation policies, gentler voices also filtered through. So while the late colonial magazine *Sonyŏn* published between 1937-1940[6] was largely a channel for Japanese wartime propaganda, the magazine also featured prominent proletarian poets and fiction writers who, while stripped of their explicit leftist bite, still managed to comment on the evils of the colonial capitalist economy. They exuded a spirit of sympathy for children and the working class,

---

4. Peter Lee notes that "The 'new poetry' movement began with the publication of [Ch'oe's poem] . . . the poem's inventions include the copious use of punctuation marks (a convention borrowed from the West), stanzas of unequal length, a string of onomatopoeia in the first and seventh line of each stanza, and the dominant images of the sea and children, which had been little mentioned in classical Korean poetry." (See Peter Lee, *Modern Korean Literature: An Anthology* [Honolulu: University of Hawaii Press, 1990], xvi-xvii.) Ch'oe himself notes that his attempts at poetry were experiments with new poetry in Korea (*Sonyŏn* 1909.4, 2).

5. See Mark Caprio, *Japanese Assimilation Policies in Colonial Korea, 1910-1945* (Seattle: University of Washington Press, 2009).

6. The magazine was published by Yun Sŏkchung and the publishing house Cho'gwangsa, and is to be differentiated from Ch'oe Namsŏn's magazine from 1908-1911.

and expressed, though subtly, a resistance to authority that was a prominent feature of proletarian children's magazines like *Pyŏllara* and *Sinsonyŏn* of the early 1930s.

The most significant voice of contention in late colonial Korea is undoubtedly that of its most talented and inspiring (mostly children's) writer of the colonial period: Hyŏn Tŏk (1909-?). It was perhaps an unlikely venue for his work, but *Sonyŏn* published Hyŏn's short stories from August of 1937 until the cessation of the magazine in 1940. Yet despite his widely acknowledged talent, Hyŏn was doomed to anonymity in South Korea until recently, perhaps because of his short career, his relatively limited output, his defection to North Korea during the war, and the fact that he wrote for children. Hyŏn's works, which attest to a rich imagination, poetic expression, and a profound sense of identification with children, lack the usual overtones of patronizing judgment. His intimate and sincere voice reverberated even more strikingly in *Sonyŏn* because his stories often appeared sandwiched between essays praising the Hitler-Jugend and news from the front. He succeeded in being socially engaged while avoiding, for the most part, the traps of didacticism and judgmental condescension. He wrote with masterful subtlety and spoke from a place of deep affection and sincere sympathy for his child characters.

Hyŏn Tŏk was born in 1909 into a family that had once been quite prominent but had lost its riches due to his father's inferior management. He graduated from middle school and attended high school for only one year before his finances prevented him from continuing his studies. These events apparently brought him closer to the mission statement of the KAPF writers.[7] Hyŏn's debut took place with a short story that took first prize in a newspaper competition in 1927; he was seventeen at the time. His official appearance on the literary scene came several years later, in 1932.[8]

7. See Wŏn Chongch'an, *Hanguk kŭndae munhak ŭi chaejomyŏng* (Shedding new light on modern Korean literature) (Seoul: Somyŏng ch'ulp'an, 2005), 60-70.

8. It was apparently Hyŏn's friendship with writer Kim Yujŏng that changed Hyŏn's life and motivated him to become a writer (Wŏn, *Hanguk kŭndae*, 75-76).

AZALEA

Children's
Literature in
Late Colonial
Korea

by *Dafna Zur*

It was only in 1938, however, that Hyŏn entered the literary scene with full force with his adult novel *Namsaengi*, which was published serially by the *Chosŏn Ilbo*. During the span of his career in South Korea, Hyŏn wrote nine short stories, thirty-seven children's stories, ten young-adult novels, and two radio broadcast scripts.[9] Hyŏn's friendship with Kim Yujŏng (1908-1937) also brought him closer to the organization of the Kuinhoe,[10] where he became acquainted with An Hoenam[11] and other members. After liberation in 1945, he accepted a leadership position in the leftist literary organization, the *Chosŏn Munhakka Tongmaeng*, and moved to North Korea with his family during the Korean War. But he was not an active member of the KAPF, nor was he politically active.[12] He continued writing in North Korea until 1951, but was silent thereafter. Hyŏn was purged along with Han Sŏrya in 1962.[13]

Hyŏn's debut in Sonyŏn came in 1937, with "Hanŭl ŭn malkkŏtman" (Although the sky is clear . . . .).[14] This short story examines the psychological turmoil of a young boy, Mungi, who gets disoriented when the butcher accidentally gives the boy more change than he deserves. Mungi is distraught by this error and confused by the appearance of unexpected money in his hand, but his classmate Sumani devises a business scheme that will generate revenue on a regular basis. But when Mungi's uncle finds out

---

9. Wŏn, *Hanguk kŭndae*, 82.

10. The Kuinhoe, or Group of Nine, was created in August of 1933. It represented a form of proletarian counter-group to KAPF that differentiated itself by virtue of its lack of political affiliation. Members of this group included Chŏng Chiyong, Yi T'aejun, Pak T'aewŏn, Yi Sang and Kim Yujŏng. See Wŏn Chongch'an, "Kuinhoe munin tŭl ŭi adong munhak (Children's literature of the Group of Nine)," *Tonghwa wa pŏnyŏk* 11 (2006).

11. An Hoenam was particularly enthusiastic about Hyŏn's work, and greatly praised his novel *Namsaeng'i*. Hyŏn's work was also widely acknowledged by Im Hwa, Kim Namch'ŏn and Paek Ch'ŏl. Wŏn, *Hanguk kŭndae*, 79-82.

12. See Pak Yŏnggi, "Hyŏn Tŏk yŏn'gu: *Kyŏngch'ip*, *Namsaeng'i* rŭl chungsim ŭro (A study of the fiction of Hyŏn Tŏk)," *Hanguk adong munhak yŏngu* 12 (2006): 105-116.

13. See Yi Kyŏngjae, "Hyŏn Tŏk ŭi saengae was sosŏl yŏn'gu (The life and fiction of Hyŏn Tŏk)," *Kwanak ŏmun yŏn'gu* 29 (2004): 496.

14. *Sonyŏn* (1937.8) 10-21. The title is translated as "The Sky" in this volume of *Azalea*.

about the boy's mischief, Mungi becomes haunted; he struggles to assuage his guilt, but is unable to confess his crime.[15]

At first glance, the story appears to be a didactic one about taking responsibility and the consequences of lying. But the writer's skill layers the story in a way that communicates subtle details and provides insight into the boy's psychological and social world. Mungi may live in material comfort, but the house is not his own—his mother has died, and he has been abandoned by his father. It is money, in fact, which casts Mungi on a downward spiral; and his confusion is manipulated by his less fortunate friend Sumani. The material goods that he has purchased are the source of his growing paranoia and mental malaise.

The story is in essence a critique of material wealth and the corrupting power of consumerism. It is also a statement about children's disadvantages within this capitalist system. Hyŏn's poetic skill for the most part succeeds in masking the story's didactic messages by probing the mindset of the boy with scrutiny and deep sympathy. When Mungi goes on his first shopping spree, he purchases a ball; later, his guilt overwhelms and warps his sense of perception, so that "the darker night grew, the whiter and larger the ball felt." Later, an innocent Chŏmsuni gets blamed for his crime and is beaten; Mungi does not witness the beating, but her sobbing reverberates in his mind for hours. In his narration, Hyŏn succeeds in being critical and engaged, and yet he does not lose his sense of sympathy for the children's plight. Hyŏn's illustrator, Chŏng Hyŏnung,[16] contributes to Hyŏn's work with illustrations that

---

15. This psychological examination is reminiscent of the work of Dostoyevsky, who apparently exerted a great influence on Hyŏn's work. Wŏn, *Hanguk kŭndae*, 92.

16. Chŏng Hyŏnung was born in 1911 and studied at the Kawabata School in Japan in 1929. From 1937 he was an illustrator for the magazine *Sonyŏn*, and he also illustrated the works of Yi Kiyŏng, Ch'ae Mansik and Yi T'aejun. He went north after the Korean War and went on to enjoy a successful career as an artist. (See Cho Yŏngbok "Chŏng Hyŏnung: ch'ŏnnyŏn ŭi sigan ŭl toesallyŏnaen yŏksa hwaga [Chŏng Hyŏnung: a historical painter who brings a millennium back to life]" in *Wŏlbuk yesulga, orae ich'yŏjin kŭdŭl* (Seoul: Tolbegae, 2002) 107-134. Most of his illustrations in *Sonyŏn* tend to be very dark, such as the one above of Mungi and Sumani.

Azalea

Children's
Literature in
Late Colonial
Korea

by *Dafna Zur*

provide their own commentary on the text through contrasting inky shadows and bright light.

The story's didactic conclusion may disappoint; however, it is not typical of Hyŏn's work, which tends to be more open-ended, and leans toward showing rather than telling. Didacticism in Korean children's literature harks back to its very beginnings; in fact, the evolution of children's literature in general has been described as a transformation from "instruction to delight," to quote one commonly used classroom reader.[17] In a sense, the writer may have been reproducing a convention of the genre in order to position himself and his work clearly in the realm of children's literature; or perhaps he was responding to what he imagined his readers expected, which is an end to the boy's disquieting anxiety.

The Sino-Japanese War and the intensification of assimilation cultural policies effectively ended the period of leniency on publication in colonized Korea. For children's writers, this meant that the forum for discussing class-based issues or challenging the exploitation of children through a political lens was greatly limited. By the mid-1930s, both proletarian organizations such as the KAPF and the magazines that hosted their writing were no longer in print, and Sonyŏn took their place. Gone were the empowering messages conveyed by the proletarian writers. No longer was the child a righteous warrior who, seeing the exploitation and corruption around him, was ready to take a stand and correct his parents' mistakes. The child constructed by the many illustrations, essays, prose and poetry in Sonyŏn had reverted, for the most part, to the image of the child as natural and pure. The child was no longer to be protected so much as to be inculcated, as quickly as possible, into orderly colonial society. Its body was to be cleaned and disciplined; its mind informed about the sophistication of war and of the sacrifices of the soldiers at the front fighting for the sake of the Pan-Asian cause. Poetry showed children as inseparable

---

17. See Patricia Demers, *From Instruction to Delight: An Anthology of Children's Literature to 1850* (Don Mills: Oxford University Press, 2008).

from nature, and it is this natural quality that made them all the more pliable.[18] This magazine was not, however, without its fissures. As the work of Hyŏn Tŏk shows, there was room in the magazine for an authorial voice that could both envision and portray the complexity of the lives of children caught in the whirlwind of colonialism and war.

18. For a detailed overview of the transformations in children's literature, see Dafna Zur, "The construction of the child in Korean children's magazines, 1908-1950" (PhD diss., University of British Columbia, 2011).

The Sky[1]

by Hyŏn Tŏk

Translated by Dafna Zur

The ball, which he'd hidden behind the large wooden board in the inner gate, was gone. He reached out and felt for it, but the space was empty. Mungi's heart began to pound.

What if the kids in the neighborhood had gotten their hands on it?

On second thought, that might actually be for the best. Because if the ball had found its way into Aunty's hands, that would mean big, big trouble.

Mungi watered the flowers in the inner courtyard and tried to stay calm. All the while, his eyes darted searchingly to Aunty's face. She was in the kitchen making dinner. Their eyes met each time she walked in and out of the kitchen. He found nothing different about the way she looked at him. He started to feel better. *A street beggar or one of the neighborhood kids must have taken it. Otherwise she wouldn't be this calm*, he thought. He quickly returned to his room.

But when he opened his desk drawer, he made another shocking discovery. The binoculars, which he'd hidden so carefully deep inside the drawer, were gone. And that's not all. The inside of the drawer was a mess. Someone had been there.

---

1. *Sonyŏn* (1937.8)

Uncle will be home from the office any minute now. I'm doomed!

Mungi sat at his desk and tried to read. But his eyes were blurry and his heart was racing. There was no way he was going to be able to concentrate.

The whole thing started a few days earlier. He was given money by his aunt to go to the butcher's and buy a slab of meat for the evening meal. The local butcher's was always packed at that time of day. He waited forever for his turn. When it came, he presented the money. The fat owner took the money, placed it in the deep straw basket, sliced the meat carefully, weighed it, wrapped it in paper, and gave it to him. And then the change came: nine coins and several silver pennies . . . ?! Mungi was confused. When Aunty had given him the money, even when he had handed it over to the butcher, the boy was sure that what he had was a one-*wŏn* note. He looked suspiciously at the money, then at the butcher. But the butcher was busy slicing meat for the next customer. In his confusion he had been pushed to the back of the line. The more he thought about it, the less certain he was that Aunty had given him a one-*wŏn* note to begin with. And if she hadn't, then there wasn't anything amiss. The best thing to do was to check with her as soon as possible. On the way home he kept shaking his head and replaying the events in his mind. Was it his mistake? Or the butcher's?

He turned down an alley. There, a few paces away, was his buddy Sumani. Mungi hurried to catch up.

"When are you going home?" he asked Sumani, and threw one arm over his shoulder. "Want to hear something weird?"

"What?"

"I went to the butcher, right? And I thought I gave him a one-*wŏn* note but he gave me ten-*wŏn*'s worth of change."

"For real? Let's see."

Mungi opened the palm of his hand, and examined the money and the meat again. Sumani blinked. Then he spoke.

"I've got an idea."

"What?"

"First, give your aunt only the small coins."

"Then what?"

"If she doesn't say anything, come back and meet me. We've got work to do."

"Work? What kind of work?"

"Just show up, ok? It's a good kind of work."

Mungi did as he was told, and removed from his jacket pocket only the small change. Aunty took the money, counted it carefully twice, put the money in her pocket and turned around to wash the meat as if nothing was amiss. Just to make sure, he lingered for a while and watched her closely, and then he sneaked out. Sumani was waiting for him with a strange smile.

The "good kind of work" Sumani suggested was to walk up and down the street and buy all the stuff they had never been able to afford but had always dreamed of owning.

"We shouldn't use this money!" Mungi protested.

"Don't worry. Just do as I say." Sumani threw a confident arm over Mungi's shoulder and strutted forward. As for Mungi, well, the truth is that it wasn't like there weren't any toys that he'd always wanted to buy. Besides, he figured that he was just following orders, so it wasn't his fault, really. And Sumani, for his part, knew that it was Mungi, after all, who had produced this money; there was no way Sumani would be held responsible. The boys set off.

There was something about the walk through the deserted alleys that made their chests thump with fear. But as soon as they were out in the lit street, their foreboding turned to glee. The bright stores that lined both sides of the street were filled with things that could become their belongings, and these were calling sweetly to them. They bought a ball. They bought a pen. They bought binoculars. They bought a comic book. They watched a film. And they munched on all sorts of snacks as they went.

With what was left over now they had an exciting plan. They would buy a small film projector. Then they would put it to work, and charge the neighborhood kids one *chŏn* to watch what they made. That way they would create a constant flow of income. And they decided to start that very evening.

But now this plan was about to be thwarted. In the main bedroom, Uncle called for him from where he was having his supper. *Mungi-ya*, he called twice, three times, and his voice shook the windows of the boy's room. Mungi pretended not to hear and said nothing. After the fourth time, the sliding door of the main bedroom opened.

"Mungi, are you in here?"

His mind was drifting, but he couldn't pretend to be absent. He had no choice but to join Uncle and kneel respectfully across from him. Uncle continued with his meal. Under the table was the ball that the boy had hidden in the inner gate. Uncle spoke when the table was cleared.

"Have you been going to school every day?"

"Yes, sir."

Uncle rolled out the ball from under the table.

"What's this?"

"Sumani gave it to me, sir."

"This, too?" Uncle asked, reaching for the binoculars that he had placed under his folded legs.

"Yes, sir."

"Sound like this Sumani likes to waste his money. I bet this ball cost at least fifty *chŏn*. And these cost at least one *wŏn*." And then he added, "What do his parents do?"

Mungi sat quietly with his head lowered. Uncle drank a glass of rice-water and then pushed the low folding-table away.

"Sumani gave it to you, did he? I believe you. I'm sure you would never lie to me. But you should think twice about accepting such gifts." Uncle wasn't done. "Another thing: I heard that you've been eating out. Is Sumani paying for that, too?"

Mungi blushed furiously, his eyes still pointed at the ground. Uncle stared at him for a moment and then continued in a harsher tone.

"Your mother died young, and your father is hopeless; you're the only who can save your family's name. If you loiter with deceitful children and stray from the right path, just think about what that makes *you*, and also about what this says about me. I promised to support your studies as far as they'll take you and am doing my best to turn you into a proper young man. Be a man and do your part." Uncle then went on to list several examples of people who'd ruined their lives because of momentary lapses of judgment, and he ended his speech by accepting Mungi's oath to never, ever accept these kinds of gifts again. Mungi was dismissed.

The boy went back to his room. Now that he was alone, he blushed even more fiercely than he had in Uncle's presence. He had just stared right into the face of the one person that he had been trying so hard to avoid. And he knew that he, Mungi, in every cell of his body, had already strayed from the path that Uncle had mentioned. He knew, of course, that his insistence that Sumani made him do it, that he wasn't to blame, was a poor excuse from the start, a way of passing the burden of responsibility to someone else. Now he had lied to his uncle. And he'd spent money that was not to be spent. Mungi's mother had died when he was small, and his father was a vagabond who wandered aimlessly from countryside to city and back. It was Uncle who had raised Mungi. And Uncle was more concerned with his nephew's future than with his own, and wished the best for the boy. Why, only a few days ago Mungi had clenched his fists and had sworn that he would never, ever disappoint his uncle. This recollection made him cringe with shame. He picked up the ball and binoculars and stepped outside. Evening was settling on the streets. He turned into the alley. He was terrified that someone, anyone, might see the ball in his hands— the same ball with which he had played so blithely in the busy streets in broad daylight that very morning. The darker it got, the whiter the large ball grew, and Mungi became increasingly agitated about handling it. He turned a sharp corner and then turned again, avoiding eye contact. The binoculars in his bulging pockets were burning. When he came out of one of the alleys, he feigned carelessness and dropped the binoculars to the ground. Then he hurried and entered an alley across the way. He came to the stream. He placed the large ball at his feet, crouched, and waited until he was alone.

A bicycle passed by and then an old man, and in the brief intermission between the two Mungi hurled the ball into the flowing white water. Then he drew the leftover money from the inside of his jacket pocket. He was just about to toss that, too, but stopped himself at the last minute. His eyes followed the bobbing ball with great satisfaction before he turned to walk back.

He headed for the butcher's. He approached the store from the back alley, wrapped the remaining money in some paper, and flung the small package over the fence to the store's entrance.

His shoulders dropped, as if he'd just been relieved of hefty weights. His gut felt cleansed, and his affliction was now headed 10, 20 *li* downstream with the bobbing ball. Never again. Never again. Mungi swore a hundred times to never, ever take on such an affliction again. He walked home. But all this was still not enough to rid him completely of his affliction. An unexpected visitor awaited him at his doorstep.

"Where'vya been?" Sumani stepped out of the house's shadows to greet him. "I was looking for you," he said, throwing an arm over Mungi's shoulder and pointed him toward the main street. "Let's go."

Sumani wanted them to buy that projector they had talked about. They'd taken note of the projector and its price through the window of the toyshop across from the cinema. Sumani had double-checked again that morning.

"I hope no one's bought it!" Sumani started to walk faster. Mungi allowed himself to be guided until he stopped short, shook Sumani's arm off, and faced him.

"Forget it."

Sumani stared back. "Forget what? Forget the projector?"

360

"There's no money left."

"What?" Sumani's eyes rounded in surprise. He then flashed an insidious smile.

"I see what's going on. You're going to use that money all for yourself. C'mon now, don't be like that. Let's go."

"I'm serious. I just tossed the rest of it back over the butcher's fence. I threw out the binoculars and the ball, too." He turned his pockets inside out to prove it. Sumani snorted.

"You think you're the only one who can play games around here?" His voice dripped with sarcasm. "The butcher's, huh? That's a good story."

"It's not a story. It's *true*."

Mungi didn't know what else to say. He hung his head, and was on the verge of tears. "Uncle yelled at me. I'm not going to do stuff like this anymore."

"You still have a promise to me that you need to keep. If you don't want a part of it anymore, that's fine. Back out. Just give me the money." Sumani shoved an open palm under Mungi's chin.

"I already told you, I don't have it."

Sumani's hand was suddenly at Mungi's shirt collar. "So you're going to stick to your story, are ya?"

A neighbor passed by with a cough. Sumani jumped back. Mungi slunk away. "See you tomorrow! I can't *wait*," Sumani called after him.

The next morning, Mungi had turned onto the main street on his way to school when he saw that large white letters—*Kim Mungi is a you-know-what*—had been drawn with chalk on the wooden fence. The same words had been jotted across the door panes of the corner store. Mungi was startled. He quickly took off his hat and used it to erase his name. From across the street, Sumani watched with a twisted smile.

"You scared of something?" Sumani spoke under his breath as Mungi passed by. Sumani followed him and added in a smaller voice, "Go ahead. Use the money for yourself. I'm just warming up."

Mungi and Sumani, *Sonyŏn* (August 1937).

When he stood, unsuspecting, by the monkey bars, Sumani
snuck up behind and tripped him. Sumani pretended to be
practicing sprints and ran ahead only to break his speed at the last
minute and make Mungi crash into him. And when the two were
alone, Sumani said, "You think you can do whatever you like, don't
you? Well, guess what—so can I. You think I won't tell? You're
wrong." Then he counted on his fingers and told him, "This is
what's gonna happen if I tell. First—you're going to get kicked out
of school. Second—you're going to get kicked out of your house.

Once a thief, always a thief, you know, so you'll be dragged to the police station. I'm gonna tell."

After recess, it got worse. There, smack in the center of the blackboard, was *Kim Mungi is a you-know-what* printed in large letters. Then the teacher walked in. She didn't make much of it—she asked who the prankster was and erased it—but the time that elapsed from the moment he saw it until she came in felt like an eternity.

Sumani, however, was not done. When the school day was over, things got a lot worse. Sumani walked a few steps behind Mungi and chanted, "The boy in front of me is a you-know-what." Even worse, he scrambled the letters in 'thief' and chanted, "The boy in front of me is a fieth."

Mungi was almost home when Sumani caught up with him. "If you don't come up with the money right now, tomorrow's gonna be much worse. Tomorrow I'm going to spell it out: T-H-I-E-F."

Mungi ignored him and kept walking. He stepped through the front gate of his house. The house was silent except for Aunty's voice that came from the back wall. "Plant them here, and here," he heard her say; she was watering flowers and giving instructions to the errand girl who lived downstairs.

And there, in full view, was the safe where the family kept their valuables. Inside were a few notes and some loose change. And outside the gate was Sumani, waiting for Mungi to bring him money. Mungi embraced his affliction.

"See? You shoulda' listened the first time," he heard Sumani say as he flung the money at him almost like a slap to his face. He ran.

In his flight, Mungi ran past one intersection. Then another. Then he started to slow down. And he started to think.

OK, so I did 'kind of' take that money, but all I need to do is pay her back and it'll be as if nothing ever happened. I'll just eat less and be more careful with my school supplies and my clothes. It'll be just like paying her back.

He mulled over his plan again and again in an effort to gather enough courage to hold his head up high and go back home. Instead, however, he wandered the public park and streets for hours.

It was nighttime, and Mungi came home completely dejected. He sat on the front steps of his home. Aunty came out to greet him.

"Are you just coming from school?" And she added, "Did you happen to see the money that was in the safe?"

And before he could answer, she continued, "You just got here, how could you know? I tell you, that Chŏmsuni is a devious little wench. Earlier when I was watering the flowers in the back she said she was going home and guess what? She stole some money."

He listened in silence. He silently repeated, *Once I pay it back it'll be as if nothing ever happened.*

That night, the sobbing of a young girl could be heard from downstairs. It was Chŏmsuni, the errand girl. Aunty must have gone directly to talk to her, but since news travels fast the landlady must have gotten a whiff of the discussion. She beat the girl and chased her out. A group of children had gathered and were gossiping, but scattered one by one and nothing but the sound of sobbing remained. Mungi did not sleep a wink that night.

The next morning, he took only a few spoons of his breakfast rice. He wasn't sure this was the right way to go about repaying that money. But his appetite was gone. He went to school. The first class was ethics, and the topic of the day was, of all things, honesty. The teacher assumed his grave lecturing pose—hands joined behind his back, legs pacing back and forth across the classroom—and repeatedly expounded on the evils of lying and the virtues of truth-telling. His bespectacled eyes glimmered and settled on Mungi again and again. And each time they did, the boy felt as if an arrow had struck him right in the chest. He knew that the day's topic was intended only for him. The teacher, thought Mungi, could see straight into his soul.

He had no energy for the playground, either. He remained with his head lowered, deep in thought in the back of the empty classroom or by the willow tree. He paced the grounds, arms folded across his chest. Whenever someone tapped his shoulder, he shrank in surprise and fright.

The sky was its usual clear blue, but Mungi did not have the courage to look up. He did not think that someone with his load of guilt and shame deserved to look upon it. What Mungi yearned for most was to be able to once again play under the clear sky without a worry in the world. He longed for a heart with which he could once again gaze at the sky with pride, a heart with which he could face others with dignity.

The sun was setting. Mungi's backpack was slung over his shoulder, his head was bowed, and he passed back and forth in front of his teacher's house, unable to announce himself. After three attempts he made it to the front door. His teacher led him inside. At school he was strict, but now he smiled softly at Mungi. He had planned on throwing himself at his teacher's feet and confessing everything. But his teacher's gentle reception shut Mungi down completely. And then he heard a baby cry from the room across the way, and again he could say nothing. Then the wife came in, then a guest dropped by. Mungi left without being able to utter a word.

His heart was now a hundred, a thousand times heavier and darker. The burden had grown too heavy for Mungi's weak shoulders. His legs were headed for home but his heart was pointed in the opposite direction. He was scared of Aunty, Uncle, and Chŏmsuni most of all.

In his reverie he had arrived at the intersection. He heard a car horn and urgent cries to move away, first faintly and then, suddenly, right in his ear. He looked up in time to see a car headed straight for him. He sensed his body being lifted up, then down. Then he lost consciousness.

He had no idea how much time had passed. When his eyes opened, he was blinded by bright lights. The second time they opened, he slowly made out the outline of Uncle's face.

"Do you know who I am?" Uncle asked gravely. Mungi thought he must be dreaming and tried to smile, but then he remembered everything. He saw that he was lying on a hospital bed. Nothing hurt, but he couldn't move. Uncle looked upon him with distress.

"Uncle," he began, "I got what I deserved." Then he closed his eyes and told his uncle everything, slowly, from beginning to end, starting with the butcher giving him change, to the shopping splurge, to stealing money from the safe. He told Uncle all, and didn't hide a thing. And as he spoke, he felt his affliction leaving his body, one layer at a time, the darkness in his heart evaporating, and his heart brightening. And as his heart brightened, his body felt lighter. For tomorrow the sun will rise and the skies will be clear. And Mungi will be able to look upon them with dignity once again.

Choi Ho-Cheol

Flood Damage, 2004, Pen and digital painting on paper, 42.8 x 39.3 cm 172

Heated Street, 2005, Pen and digital painting on paper, 42.8 x 39.3 cm 180

Pipeline Construction, 1998, Pen and digital painting on paper, 31 x 36 cm 181

Ŭlchiro Circle Line, 2000, Pen, watercolor and gouache on paper, 220 x 87 cm 183

Bus Driver, 2005, Pen and digital painting on paper, 63.7 x 37 cm 184

Street, 2005, Pen and digital painting on paper, 39 x 54 cm 185

City Snow, 2005, Pen and digital painting on paper, 45 x 40 cm 187

Me, 2004, Pen and digital painting on paper, 42 x 59.5 cm 189

Heading Home after School, 2004, Pen and digital painting on paper, 39.5 x 36.1 cm 190

Opening a Soup Bar, 2004, Pen and digital painting on paper, 29.6 x 41.9 cm 192

Costume Exhibition, 2005, Pen and digital painting on paper, 33.5 x 48.3 cm 193

Discount Store, 2004, Pen and digital painting on paper, 42.8 x 39.3 cm 195

Restoration of Ch'ŏnggyech'ŏn, 2005, Pen and digital painting on paper, 39 x 54 cm 196

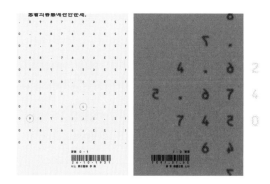

Ryu Myeong-Sik

AZALEA

*AZALEA generally adheres to the McCune-Reischauer system in transcribing Korean into English. However, many Korean contributors have not followed this convention, and we respect their way of writing their names in English.

Brother Anthony of Taizé was born in 1942 in England and completed his studies at the University of Oxford before becoming a member of the Community of Taizé (France) in 1969. Since 1980, he has been living in Korea and teaching at Sogang University, where he is now professor emeritus. Since 2010 he has also been chair-professor at Dankook University. He has published some thirty volumes of English translations of modern Korean literature, including works by Ko Un, Sŏ Chŏng-Ju, Ku Sang, and Ch'ŏn Sang-Pyŏng. For this he was awarded the Korean Order of Cultural Merit in 2008. He took Korean citizenship in 1994 and An Sonjae is his Korean name.

Darcy L. Brandel is an assistant professor of English at Marygrove College in Detroit, Michigan, where she organized the development of the first Women's Center on campus. Her fields of interest include literature by women, multi-ethnic literature, comparative women's studies, critical theory, aesthetic theory, creative writing, Buddhism, and translation. She has published work on Gertrude Stein, Grace Paley, and other experimental women writers, and along with Song Chae-Pyong, translations of Mun T'ae-jun's Buddhist poetry. She is currently working on her first manuscript of poetry.

Jamie Chang is a literary translator. Her projects include Kim Aeran's *Mouthwatering* and Ku Byung-mo's *Wizard Bakery*. Both projects were funded by a Korea Literature Translation

370

Institute (KLTI) grant. She also received the Korea Times MLT Commendation Prize in 2010.

Cheon Myeong-Kwan was born in Yingin, Kyŏnggido in 1964. He began writing fiction in 2003, publishing the story "Frank and I," included in this issue. He published three novels, *The Whale* (2004), *Senior Family* (2010), *My Uncle Bruce Lee* (2012) and a story collection, *Cheerful Maid Marisa* (2006).

Choi Ho-Cheol was born in Seoul in 1965 and studied painting at Hong'ik University. He has participated in numerous solo and group exhibitions, including at Kwanhun Gallery (1993), the National Modern Art Museum (1994, 2003), Angoulême International Comics Festival (2003), Seonam Museum (2000), Seoul City Museum (2005), and Rodin Gallery (2007). He published several dozen cartoon books, including *T'aeiri*, 5 vols, *Walking Picture*, and *Ŭlchiro Circle Line*. His works have been awarded many prizes, including the Grand Prize at the 2009 Bucheon International Cartoon Festival, and the Sinhan Cartoon Prize. He teaches at Chungkang College of Cultural Industries.

Eun-Gwi Chung is a poet-critic and translator. She received her Ph.D. from the Poetics Program, SUNY Buffalo, in 2005. Along with Myung-Mi Kim she is the recipient of a 2005 Daesan Foundation grant for the translation of Lee Seong-Bok's poetry collection *Ah! Mouthless Things*. Joining in the 2011 "Cordite 35: OZ-KO" project of *Cordite Poetry Review* in Australia, she selected and translated forty Korean poems with Brother Anthony of Taizé. Currently she is a professor at Inha University in Korea.

A native of South Korea, E. K. DuBois is currently in the Boston College English program, with a concentration in literature.

Nathan A. DuBois is a recent graduate of Boston College, specializing in economic development and national security. While the genre of their published works varies, this husband and wife team is dedicated mostly to the translation of children's literature. For an example of their other works, look for their translation of *The Hen that Left the Farm* later this year.

John M. Frankl is associate professor of Korean and comparative literature at Yonsei University's Underwood International College. He is the author of the Korean-language monograph *Han'guk munhak-e nat'anan oeguk-ŭi ŭimi* (Somyŏng, 2007), which explores representations of "the foreign" in Korean literature. He is currently working on a monograph that will include annotated translations of and commentary on Yi Sang's essays.

Hwang Byeong-Seung was born in Seoul in 1970. He debuted in 2003 by publishing five poems including "Primary Doctor h" in Para 21. He has published two poetry collections: *Sikoku, The Man Dressed as Woman* and *Track and the Star of the Field*.

Jeon Seung-hee is a literary scholar, critic, and translator. She is a member of the Editorial Board of Asia and a research associate at the Korea Institute, Harvard University. She received a Ph.D. in English Literature from Seoul National University and a Ph.D. in comparative literature from Harvard University. Her publications include "War Trauma, Memories, and Truths: Representations of the Korean War in Pak Wan-sŏ's Writings and in 'Still Present Pasts'" (*Critical Asian Studies* 42 [4], 2010) and co-translations of Bakhtin's Novel and the People's Culture and Jane Austen's *Pride and Prejudice*. She is the recipient of a 1988 Fulbright Research Grant, a 2005 Korea Foundation Post-doctoral Fellowship, a 2006 Association for Asian Studies Travel Grant, and a 2011 Daesan Foundation Translation Grant.

Jin Eun-young was born in Taejŏn in 1970 and received a B.A. and Ph.D. in Philosophy from Ehwa Womans University. She made her literary debut by publishing three poems in the spring 2000 issue of *Literature and Society*. Her publications include the poetry collections *Dictionary of Seven Words* (2003) and *We Everyday* (2008), and books on philosophy: *Deleuze and the Literature-Machine* (co-author, 2002), *Critique of Pure Reason Takes Reason to Court* (2004), *Nietzsche, the Philosophy of Eternal Return and Differences* (2007), and *Communist Manifesto* (co-author, 2007). She is the recipient of the 2011 Hyundae Munhak Award.

Kim Kyung-Ju was born in Kwangju in 1976. He studied philosophy at Sogang University. His poetry collections include *I Am a Season that Doesn't Exist in This World*, *The Strange Story*, and *Calming the Parallactic Eyes*. He was awarded the Today's Young Artist Award and the Kim Suyŏng Literature Award.

Kim Min-Jeong was born in Inchon in 1976, received a B.A. in creative writing from Chung'ang University and studied at the graduate school of the same university. She made her literary debut in 1999 by winning the Munye chung'ang Rookie Writer's Award. Her publications include *Flying Porcupine Maiden* (2005) and *She Began to Feel - for the First Time* (2009). She is the recipient of the 2007 Pak In-hwan Literary Award.

Sora Kim-Russell is a literary translator who lives in Seoul and teaches in the Graduate School of Translation and Interpretation at Ewha Womans University.

Krys Lee is the author of *Drifting House*, to be published by Viking/Penguin in February 2012. Her short stories and articles have been published or are forthcoming in The *Kenyon Review*, *Narrative Magazine*, *California Quarterly*, The *Guardian* and *Condé Nast*, UK. Her stories received special mentions in *Narrative Magazine*: 20 under 30 and the *Pushcart Prize Anthology 2012*. She divides her time between South Korea and the U.S. www.kryslee.com

Peter H. Lee is professor emeritus of Korean and comparative literature at the University of California, Los Angeles. He is the author and editor of some twenty books including *A History of Korean Literature* (Cambridge UP, 2003) and *Echoing Song: Contemporary Korean Women Poets* (White Pine Press, 2005). He was a fellow of the Alexander von Humboldt Foundation, the American Council of Learned Societies, the Bollingen Foundation, the Guggenheim Foundation, and the National Endowment for the Humanities.

Kevin O'Rourke (Columban Fathers) is professor emeritus, Kyung Hee University. He has published many volumes of Korean fiction and poetry in translation, including *Looking for the Cow* (Dedalus), *Our Twisted Hero* (Hyperion), *The Book of Korean Shijo* (Harvard), and *The Book of Korean Poetry: Songs of Shilla and Koryo* (University of Iowa Press).

Park Chansoon is a new writer with a background in translating English films into Korean. Her debut novel *Palhae Style Garden* (Moonji Publishing, 2009) was selected as Literature of Excellence by Arts Council Korea in 2010. Capturing the difficulties of marginalized people, *Palhae Style Garden* is highly acclaimed for its treatment of the aesthetics of youth and the insights of age. Her debut short story "The Karibong Lamb Kebab" was translated and won the New Translator Contest at KLTI.

Park Hyoung-Su was born in Ch'unch'ŏn, Kangwŏndo in 1972, and earned a Ph.D. in creative writing at Korea University. His writings include the novel *Nana at the Dawn* (2010), the story collections *Those You Have to Know before Raising Rabbits* (2003),

Midnight Fiction (2006), and *Handmade Fiction* (2011). He was awarded the Daesan Literary Prize in 2010. He teaches creative writing at Korea University.

Anne M. Rashid is an assistant professor of English at Carlow University in Pittsburgh, Pennsylvania. She and Chae-Pyong Song recently received the 40th Korean Literature Translation Award in Poetry Translation given by The *Korea Times*. She and Song have published translations in The *Korea Times*, *New Writing from Korea*, *The Kwangju News* and *Women's Studies Quarterly*.

Ryu Myeong-Sik was born in Pusan, Korea in 1951. He studied design and advertising at Hongik University and, in 1985, established Haingraph, a well-known printing company in Korea. Formerly president of the Visual Information Design Association of Korea, he is currently vice-chairman of the Korean Federation of Design Associations, Auditor of the Korean Society of Typography, and a professor at Hongik University's Graduate School of Industrial Arts.

Sin Yongmok was born in Kŏch'ang, South Kyŏngsang Province, in 1974. He studied modern literature as a graduate student in Korea University's Korean literature department. He made his literary debut when he won the 2000 Best New Writer Award from the quarterly *Writer's World* for five poems including "Inside the Glass Door of the Sŏngnae-dong Clothing Repairs." He has published two collections of poems: *We Have to Walk Through All That Wind* (Munji, 2004) and *The Wind's Millionth Set of Molars* (Changbi, 2007). He is a recipient of the Young Poet's Award.

Josie Sohn is a doctoral candidate in the Department of East Asian Languages and Cultures with a graduate minor in cinema studies at the University of Illinois at Urbana-Champaign. This essay is part of a dissertation project supported by a Fulbright IIE Fellowship and a Korea Foundation Graduate Student Fellowship.

Chae-Pyong Song is an associate professor of English at Marygrove College in Detroit, Michigan. His translations of Korean literature have appeared in *The Korea Times, New Writing from Korea, Kwangju News, Metamorphoses: Journal of Literary Translation, Women's Studies Quarterly,* and *Azalea: Journal of Korean Literature and Culture.* Recently, along with Anne Rashid, he won the 40th Korean Literature Translation Award for translating Kim Hye-soon's poems. His fields of interest include 20th-century English literature, postcolonial literature, translation studies, and globalization of culture.

Dafna Zur completed her Ph.D. at the University of British Columbia. Her translations have appeared in *Azalea* and the *Columbia Anthology of Modern Korean Literature,* and her published articles have appeared in *Acta Koreana,* and the *International Research on Children's Literature.* She is currently a faculty member in the Department of Korean Language and Literature at Keimyung University.